Filmmakers and Financing

Praise for *Filmmakers and Financing:*

"An excellent, insightful guide to attracting financing for indie films. Louise Levison takes a sane, balanced approach to research, comparables and projections, achieving honest outlooks in business plans that are accurate and convincing to equity investors. An important tool for filmmakers and producers seeking innovative financing models."

—Danny Glover, Actor/Director/Producer

"Thank you so much for all your help from the business plan to the emails and introductions. You have helped this film become what it is today."

—Rob Cowie, Producer, *The Blair Witch Project*

"How to raise funds for independent films was the best-kept secret in Hollywood until Levison's book was published."

—Rick Pamplin, Producer/Director, The Pamplin Film Company

"If you are an independent filmmaker trying to raise any private financing for your film, you absolutely must read, absorb, and understand the material and advice in Louise's book.... I tell all my clients to buy a copy, because they will continually use and refer back to it.... I do."

— Harris Tulchin, Entertainment Attorney/Producer and Co-Author:
The Independent Film Producer's Survival Guide

"Need money for a movie? Here's the road map every indie filmmaker needs to find it. It worked for me!"

—Paul Sirmons, Director/Producer, *The First of May* and
former Florida Film Commissioner

"If Louise Levison's *Filmmakers and Financing* were only about business plans it would be worth more than its cover price. In addition, Levison gives sage, savvy and clear introductions to every important aspect of film business—marketing, distribution, varieties of investors, financing options—it's all here, including a sample business plan. This book is a 'must have' for any filmmaker's bookshelf."

—Morrie Warshawski, Consultant and Author of *Shaking the Money Tree*

"A 'must have' educational and reference tool to help you conquer current industry practices regarding finance, production and distribution. Louise has consistently delivered a plethora of information that is easy for a beginning filmmaker to understand, while at the same time very useful to the entertainment veteran. NO filmmaker's library would be complete without it."

—J. David Williams, Distributor, *Shiloh* and *The Omega Code*

"Levison's book gives filmmakers an inspiring and coherent merger of plain English, film lingo, and traditional business-speak. It helped me create a straightforward and thorough business plan that ultimately raised $2 million for my new project."

—Stu Pollard, Producer/Director, *Keep Your Distance*

Filmmakers and Financing

Business Plans for Independents

Sixth Edition

Louise Levison

AMSTERDAM • BOSTON • HEIDELBERG • LONDON
NEW YORK • OXFORD • PARIS • SAN DIEGO
SAN FRANCISCO • SINGAPORE • SYDNEY • TOKYO

Focal Press is an imprint of Elsevier

ELSEVIER

Focal Press is an imprint of Elsevier
30 Corporate Drive, Suite 400, Burlington, MA 01803, USA
Linacre House, Jordan Hill, Oxford OX2 8DP, UK

Notices
Knowledge and best practice in this field are constantly changing. As new research and experience broaden our understanding, changes in research methods, professional practices, or medical treatment may become necessary.
Practitioners and researchers must always rely on their own experience and knowledge in evaluating and using any information, methods, compounds, or experiments described herein. In using such information or methods they should be mindful of their own safety and the safety of others, including parties for whom they have a professional responsibility. To the fullest extent of the law, neither the Publisher nor the authors, contributors, or editors assume any liability for any injury and/or damage to persons or property as a matter of product liability, negligence or otherwise, or from any use or operation of any methods, products, instructions, or ideas contained in the material herein.

Library of Congress Cataloging-in-Publication Data
Levison, Louise.
    Filmmakers and financing/Louise Levison. – 6th ed.
        p. cm.
    Includes bibliographical references and index.
    ISBN 978-0-240-81252-6 (pbk. : alk. paper)
1. Motion pictures—Production and direction. 2. Motion picture industry—Finance. I. Title.
    PN1995.9.P7L433 2010
    791.4302'320681–dc22

                                                                                    2009035250

British Library Cataloguing-in-Publication Data
A catalogue record for this book is available from the British Library.

ISBN: 978–0–240–81252–6

For information on all Focal Press publications
visit our website at www.elsevierdirect.com

09 10 11 12 13 5 4 3 2 1

Printed in the United States of America

Working together to grow
libraries in developing countries

www.elsevier.com | www.bookaid.org | www.sabre.org

ELSEVIER   BOOK AID
             International   Sabre Foundation

For Leonard the Wonder Cat,
who has left us but continues to inspire . . . .
For Buffy and Angel, who inspire me every day.

Contents

Introduction: Controlling Your Destiny   1

1
The Executive Summary   17

2
The Company   25

3
The Films   45

4
The Industry   59

5
The Markets   85

6
The Markets, Part II: New Media and Other Nontraditional Markets   115

Companion Site Contents

http://booksite.focalpress.com/companion/Levison
Register using the passcode: LVNFILM12526
(Note: Check the site for periodic updates)

The Company _____
        Goals Worksheet

The Films _____
        Sample Synopses
        Options

The Markets _____
        MPAA Ratings Definitions

Distribution _____
        Distribution Deal Points

Risk Factors _____
        Sample Risk Statement

Financial Plan _____
        Data Sources
        Financial Worksheet Instructions

Worksheets

Table 1
Table 2
Worksheet 1
Worksheet 1 answers
Worksheet 2
Worksheet 2 answers
Worksheet 3
Worksheet 3 answers a
Worksheet 3 answers b
Worksheet 4
Worksheet 4 answers
Worksheet spread

Short Film

Oscar eligible short film festivals

Foreword

Despite the near hero worship accorded successful independent film producers and studio executives, not one of them would be able to function without a strong backup team. The myth of the one-person band is just that—a myth. Without the talent and hard work of the lawyers, bankers, accountants, development personnel, and administrative staff—not to mention the literally hundreds of people involved in actually making the films—no independent producer could survive, much less succeed.

To marshal all the disparate talents involved in mounting a major film production, the most important element is a common vision of the ultimate end product. In the same way that directors need a storyboard to communicate their vision of what the film will look like, producers need their own version of a storyboard (that is, a business plan) to explain their objectives, hopes, aspirations, and, yes, even their dreams.

Gone are the days when a business plan was regarded as inappropriate for an artistic endeavor such as producing a film. These days, the risks are too large, the competition too intense, and the sophistication of investors too great to "leave the details until later." Completion guarantees, discounted cash flows, letters of credit, foreign sales contracts, domestic distribution deals, internal rates of return, gross deals, rolling breaks, third-party participants' security interest, bank discounting, residuals, cross-collateralization—all these terms, to name just a few, have become part of the regular vocabulary of today's independent producers. Without a detailed business plan to coordinate all these elements, it would be virtually impossible to produce a major film. So, dear independent producer, read on....

Jake Eberts

Jake Eberts has helped develop and finance films that have earned 64 Oscar nominations and received 27 Academy Awards. Among the films on which he has been Producer or Executive Producer are *Chariots of Fire, Gandhi, The Killing Fields, Driving Miss Daisy, Dances with Wolves, A River Runs Through It, The Legend of Bagger Vance, The Education of Little Tree, Chicken Run, James and the Giant Peach, Open Range, Journey to Mecca,* and *The Illusionist.*

Acknowledgments

To all the clients and students who have taught me as much as
    I have taught them.
To all the industry professionals who have generously given of their
    time in classes and seminars to share their knowledge.
To Jake Eberts for graciously contributing to this book.
To David Russell for sharing his expertise on short film distribution.
To Thierry Baujard for his contributions on European funding.
To Rick Pamplin for his ongoing encouragement and many contri-
    butions to the book.
To Michael Donaldson, Bill Whitacre, Michael Norman Salesman,
    Robert Seigel, Karen Corrigan, Dr. Linda Seger, and John
    Johnson, whose comments on and contributions to the text are
    greatly appreciated.
To Patrick Horton for his advice and always reminding me that the
    story comes first, whether in a script or a book.
To Suzy Prudden and Terrel Miller for helping me keep my mind
    and body in balance after spending hours at the computer.
To Tracy and the early morning crew at the Coffee Roaster for
    helping feed the mind as well as the body.
To Bill, Helen, Jeffrey, and Carl for their support and understanding.
To Faryl Saliman Reingold for her editorial contributions and com-
    ments and her tireless efforts to keep me on track.
To my editor, Elinor Actipis, and everyone at Focal Press for their
    patience and understanding.
And last, but not least, to the late Leonard the Wonder Cat, my
    inspiration for the cat tales.

Introduction

Controlling Your Destiny

A business plan always evolves.

ROB FRIEDMAN

Partner, Summit Entertainment

WHY SHOULD YOU BUY THIS BOOK?

King Ferdinand of Spain appointed a group of consultants to advise him on Christopher Columbus's enterprise for sailing to the Indies. This scholarly group of astronomers, mariners, and pilots pored over charts and graphs. They determined not only that the world was flat, but also that the ocean was too big to be conquered.

"Ergo," they said, "if you try to sail to the Indies, you will fail." But Columbus had done his homework and planned ahead. He replied, "I have researched my own charts and graphs, spoken to other sailors, and obtained years of technical experience that proves otherwise. I believe it can be done." Columbus was the prototypical entrepreneur. He examined his proposed business venture, made forecasts regarding pros and cons and plunder versus expenses, and then he decided to move ahead.

Neither Columbus nor any of his friends or enemies knew that he would run into the Americas on his journey. Nevertheless, he seized his opportunity and took appropriate action. By keeping abreast of the situation on his ships, and the changes in the outside environment, he was able to make an informed decision. When he landed in the wrong place, Columbus looked at the opportunity, measured it against his goals, and decided that he had discovered a better place than he had originally intended.

From the dawn of film—actually, from the dawn of time—there have been individuals who have wanted to do it their own way. People who are not content to live by the rules of others continually strike out on their own. Here we are in 2009. The world is in turmoil with terrorists and strange viruses, governments are changing, corporations are failing, and the number of independent filmmakers keeps growing.

A Constantly Changing Medium

My friend Jerry Quigg suggested calling this book *sex, films, and investing.* Good title. It is clear, informative, and to the point. All the elements for a book or a business plan are there. Your finest hour will come when an investor says, "What a sexy idea! It will make me money. How much do you want?" This book is sexy, too, in its own business-like way. It will bridge the gap for you between the passion of filmmaking and the day-to-day realities of creating a successful company.

As you read this, the motion picture business is changing right before your eyes. For four editions of this book, the big news in Chapter 4 on the industry was which company was buying Universal Pictures. That company has remained part of the NBC family since the third edition; however, the rest of the industry seems to be buying, selling, and making new alliances at a pace faster than ever before. Much of this is due to the continued growth and presence of the independent sector as well as the rapid application of new technologies to the film business. The "paradigm" (an in-vogue word meaning "pattern") shift that has been predicted for over 20 years is taking place, and its overall business effects are debated constantly. What hasn't changed is the audience. No matter how many products divide the finite viewing audience, theatrical motion pictures keep chugging down the track. Product is needed to fuel that engine, and you can be the one to provide it.

People go into independent filmmaking for many reasons. They are driven primarily by the subject matter, theme, or style of the pictures they want to make. I have talked to thousands of people who have told me what types of films they want to make. No two people have had the same vision, but they all share the same goal—to own their project and control it. Whether a filmmaker decides to make one film or many, it is up to him or her to understand how the business world functions. Of course, your goal may not be feature films at all. Instead, you may focus on other types of films—direct-to-DVD, television, cable, or even cell phone films. All of these are important, and all the principles stated in this book apply equally to them; however, their business models differ from that of film.

With new opportunities appearing for the independent film-maker, more and more people want their own companies. Books and articles have been written about the ins and outs of writing or finding the perfect script, how much it costs to make a film, finding the best location, and what camera to use. None of that information is in this book. The question before us is not how to make a film, but how to get the money.

You might argue, "But I'm making a film. This is different from other businesses." The details of any business may differ from industry to industry and from segment to segment, but the principles are the same. Movies involve lots of people, all of whom expect to get paid. Raising money involves intermediaries such as agents, finders, and lawyers, who expect to receive a fee for what they do. And do not forget the investor, who hopes to see a return on his investment. All films need certain standard ingredients to get going and stay alive. To get the show on the road, you need to put together a business plan.

It is true that independent films have been made and found success without a business plan. Many more films without one, however, have not been funded and never see the light of day. No plan can guarantee the thrill of victory, but not having a plan could bring you closer to the agony of defeat. When you read about all those productions setting up shop with a large influx of capital, which of these scenarios do you believe?

> *Scenario 1:* Louise, you've had such extraordinary success at Megalomaniac Studios that we would like to give you $100 million. Have fun and send us our share.
>
> *Scenario 2:* Louise, you've had such extraordinary success at Megalomaniac Studios that we would like to explore the possibility of having you head your own company with $5 million in seed capital. Why don't you get together with Victor Visionary and create a business plan? If we agree with your product analysis and the numbers look good, we're in business.

Trust me (a famous Hollywood term): Scenario 2 is far more likely. Wealthy people do not throw around big bucks on a whim. An investor may say, "Louise, you have a great idea." However, before that impulse becomes a reality, much thinking and analysis will be done. Someone will ask for—you guessed it—a business plan.

The purpose of this book is to show you how to make all that thinking and analyzing into a coherent story. It is more than just an outline, however. The standard business plan outline has not changed for over 100 years. Open any book on business planning and you will see the same types of headings: Executive Summary, Company, Product, Markets, Sales, Finance.

What do you do next? This book will help you take the next step to expound and polish your business plan within those guidelines. It specifies not only what you need to include, but also why and how. I will give you samples—both good and bad—for writing the individual sections of your business plan.

Movies as a Business

The biggest misconception about the movie business is that the *movie* is more important than the *business.* Many of us tend to think about filmmaking not as a business at all, but as an art form; in that case, it would be called *show art* instead of *show business.*

A movie is a form of art, but a very expensive one. Often the most difficult concept for filmmakers is looking at the movie as a commercial enterprise. The word *commercial* can be viewed in two very different ways. When it comes to artistic endeavors, many people give the word a negative connotation. The strict definition is "prepared for sale," but in many people's minds, the words "without regard to quality" are added to the end of that definition. Looking at the term in the broader sense, however, the filmmaker trades a seat at the film for someone else's dollar (or $4, $9, or $15, as the case may be). Whether this trade occurs at a multiplex mall theater or at a video store, the buyer expects to get value for the trade, and value is definitely in the eye of the beholder.

The Blair Witch Project, which earned $300 million worldwide and of which the business plan (yes, the filmmakers had one) called for raising $350,000, was always considered a commercial project. Audiences evidently liked it a lot; other filmmakers were more critical. But the filmmakers made the film they intended to make consistent with their vision and were successful in their effort. They were innovative not only in the filmmaking but also in their use of the Internet. The point is that they made a film that brought profit to themselves and their investors—the real meaning of the word *commercial*.

The definition of *independent film* depends on the speaker's agenda. Filmmakers often want to ascribe exclusionary creative definitions to the term. When you go into the market to raise money from private investors (both domestic and foreign), it doesn't matter if your film is a mini-budget production or a $75-million blockbuster. You are still finding your own financing. Sometimes filmmakers on panels declare that someone else's film is not independent by being "a genre" or "in a specific genre" (i.e., horror, comedy, family)—this drives me crazy. In the end, esoteric discussions don't really matter. We all have our own agendas. If you want to find financing for your film, however, I suggest embracing the broader definition of the term used in this book: An independent film is one made by those individuals or companies apart from the major studios that assume the majority of the financial risk for a production and control its exploitation in the majority of the world.

There are plenty of successful filmmakers who manage to find their own financing to do things their way—John Sayles, the Coen brothers, Jim Jarmusch, and Henry Jaglom, to name a few. They make films on whatever subjects please them. Their films may have a limited distribution, but the directors (who often are also the writers) have their own financing. They keep their budgets at levels comparable to the likely box office receipts for their film.

It seems to be a simple concept. If you produce a gizmo designed to lose money, you go out of business. Why would it be any different with a film? Many films lose money (ask the studios), but many films have success also. Film investors have a right to expect to earn back their money at least. Unfortunately, many auteur filmmakers find the concepts of creativity and attracting an audience mutually exclusive. If you suffer from this malady, try to reeducate yourself. Even relatives have their limits; they don't want to lose money either. You are using other people's money. Be respectful of it.

People Get the Money

A question frequently asked of me by students and clients is: "How much money have your business plans raised?" My answer is: "None. People raise money. Business plans are only a tool." Three of the best business plans I ever wrote are stored in drawers; they haven't raised any money. In addition, although you may have the most well-written and well-presented business plan ever done, to raise the money you have to

1. Be ready to go ahead with the film.
2. Understand the contents of the plan.
3. Look until you find the money.

To be ready to get your project off the ground, you have to be focused on your goal. If you are arguing with your partners, are not ready to make decisions, or are unwilling to look for money, the quality of your business plan is immaterial. The biggest consulting firms down to the smallest ones have plans stored on shelves gathering dust, because the client was not ready to be serious about taking on partners or making changes. Business plans do not find money by themselves.

Once you track down your "prey" and deliver this terrific plan, you have to explain what it is all about—how it represents you. A plan is only a guideline with strategies and forecasts. You have to demonstrate to others that you can carry out the steps described within. Unless you understand every step of the plan—rather than just handing over a document written by someone else—you will not be able to do this.

Finally, are you adept at handling business in a professional and impressive manner? When all is said and done, the company is only a reflection of your demeanor and presentation. After all the numbers have been added up, investors are still betting on people. If they are unsure or wary about you, no checks will be written.

All consultants have clients whom they would like to keep hidden. Sometimes it would be ideal if the entrepreneur and the investor never met. Some clients like to argue with investors and generally have a take-it-or-leave-it attitude. I once had a client who actually said to an investor, "I'm doing you a favor by giving you this opportunity. Take it or leave it." The investor left it.

How Does the Economic Climate Affect Financing?

As I will repeat continuously, this edition is being written in the middle of the 2009 recession. There is plenty of evidence that the people continue to go to the movies during periods of economic stress. It is an escape, a chance to let out emotions in a safe environment, and cheaper than vacations and other pursuits. However, it can be a very fluid situation.

Currently, the total box office is 12–14 percent above the same period in 2008. Likewise, the independent portion of that box office is about 10 percent for the same period. With a little research, you can find plenty of analyses on the subject of the recession to quote for your investors. If you are putting together a business plan in 2012, the entire economic picture may be different. A little research in the trades and major newspapers will give you plenty of analyses to quote for your investors.

Can Anybody Do This?

Developing a business plan involves the proverbial "10 percent inspiration and 90 percent perspiration." In other words, anybody can do it. Unfortunately, I have found that most people lose interest when faced with the amount of research and work that is required. If you want to make your own films, however, this is part of the price of admission.

To find financing for your films, you do not have to be part of the business world, have an M.B.A., or be an accounting genius. This book will help you bridge the gap between right-brain creative thinking and left-brain math stuff. All you need is the desire to be in control—a powerful motivation.

Hollywood Is Only an Attitude

"Hollywood" is not a specific place. This book does not restrict the term *filmmaker* to those toiling in Burbank, Century City, or other areas of the southern California movie scene. Moviemaking is a worldwide event. The person in Cincinnati, Ohio, with a camcorder who aspires to make a documentary or a feature film is as much a filmmaker as her counterpart in Brisbane, Australia. Watch the film festival rosters and you will quickly see that there is a lot of moviemaking going on outside of Los Angeles in places like Omaha, Boston, Orlando, Mexico City, Taipei, and Galway. My client Rick Pamplin, who owns Pamplin Film Company, lived and worked in Los Angeles for a number of years until reaching a different level of success in Orlando.

Other People's Money

For most entrepreneurs, the idea of boiling down a vision into a neatly contained business proposal is as foreign as the notion of taking a job. Nevertheless, the recipe for success in today's competitive business environment demands that we act as managers as well as artists. The most common blunder that entrepreneurs make is to assume that a business plan is a creative piece of fiction used to trick a bank officer into giving them money. Even worse is the assumption that creating a business plan is an interesting hobby for someone who has nothing else to do. The biggest mistake made by independent filmmakers is to see themselves not as businesspeople but as only artistes—creatures whose contact with the murky world of business is tangential to their filmmaking and unimportant. Nothing could be farther from the truth.

When a person has an original idea and develops it into a product, an entrepreneur is born—a person who has personal drive, creates an intimate vision, and is willing to take risks. Entrepreneurs want to make the decisions and be in charge of the show; they want to do what they want to do when they want to do it! I have never met an entrepreneur who was not convinced that he was right, who did not believe that the world couldn't live without her film, and who did not want to control his own destiny. Independent filmmakers are the best kinds of entrepreneurs, because they want to push the edge of the envelope and seek new horizons. They are major risk takers.

Film investors are the biggest risk takers of all, however. They bet their dollars on an idea and help it become a reality—a contribution not to be taken lightly. Too often filmmakers believe that investors should donate their money and then quietly go away. Of course, this attitude is not unique to filmmakers. Most entrepreneurs feel that their ideas have more value than the capital needed to make them a reality. Think again, or you won't see any cash.

Rick's Story

Independent filmmaker Rick Pamplin has had his own film company since 1994. After selling scripts and projects to studios and major independents in Hollywood, and after teaching screenwriting, low-budget producing, and directing for 9 years, Pamplin moved to Orlando. "It wasn't easy and most of my friends and family thought I was crazy. At the time I had a wife and small child and no income. But in my heart I knew I was an independent film-maker and believed in my talent and myself." Unfortunately, such struggles can play havoc on a family, and eventually the Pamplins divorced.

"My first project was with a partner. Although we had a script, raised development money and attached talent, we could never get the film off the ground. We then raised money for a comedy concert film, *Michael Winslow Live*, by asking everyone we knew and everyone they knew for money." The film was sold to the STARZ premium cable channels, Australian television and received American and European DVD deals. Their second project, *Hoover*, starring Academy Award–winning actor Ernest Borgnine, had a small theatrical opening and is now on DVD. A third project, *Magic 4 Morons*, was an award-winning instructional video, debuted on the Home Shopping Network, got a distribution deal, and reached several foreign markets.

Pamplin and Business Strategies then developed separate business plans for three feature films and set out to find production funding. "We had raised the money for our first three projects in a relatively short period. Raising money for independent films is a marathon, not a 100-yard dash, so you'd better be prepared for it. Luckily our business plans were solid, investors liked our packages, we signed Borgnine to a three-picture deal, which gave us credibility, and we have been able to raise development funds to sustain us during the lean years."

Each of the projects attracted talent, development money, and endless meetings. A New York company, a Tampa, Florida, home-builder, and a doctor all came to various stages of contracting for the financing, but the deals never closed. In June 2006, Pamplin and investor Harry Green signed deals for financing the three films. Unfortunately, a month later Harry, who also had also become a good friend, passed away unexpectedly. Following that, one of Green's employees said he had an uncle who might be interested in investing, a fundraiser from Palm Beach called, a South African source got involved, and so on and so on. "Over the years we have reduced the budgets, raised the budgets, changed casts and constantly updated the business plan," Pamplin said. Once again, as this book goes to press, the saga is unfinished. Pamplin has a crucial deal-signing meeting scheduled shortly after the book's manuscript is set for printing.

I asked Rick if we should keep his story, knowing that his intention from the beginning was to show filmmakers that, like any business, getting a film made is 20 percent inspiration and 80 percent perspiration. His response was, "We have made four movies, all of which are in worldwide distribution and have won awards. We are a successful indie company. I have survived doing script doctoring, consulting and living as a frugal film-maker. I just finished my first documentary feature, made a deal with a Los-Angeles-based distribution company and it has been released on DVD."

"I'm still in the game, making the movies I want, controlling my destiny, and living my dream. Was it a good decision? YES. Would I do it again? YES. Did I ever imagine it would be this hard? NO."

WHY BOTHER WITH A BUSINESS PLAN?

The business plan is the entrepreneur's single most valuable document and his or her best safeguard for success. The majority of businesses that fail usually have paid little attention to proper planning. In Jake Eberts's book *My Indecision Is Final: The Rise and Fall of Goldcrest Films,* he mentions several times that the company, which he founded, had no business plan. Although its first film, *Chariots of Fire,* won the Academy Award for Best Picture, the company (different from the one in operation today) did not succeed in the long run. Would Goldcrest have fared differently had the company had a business plan? No one can say for sure, but it is obvious from reading Eberts's book that this group of very talented people had widely divergent professional and personal agendas. They also had very different business styles.

Whether you are making one film or several, you have to identify who you are, where you are going, and how you are going to get there. The business plan allows you to plot this path. It gives you the opportunity to develop a clear picture of the growth and bottom-line prospects for your film company. It also enables you to make more effective decisions, and it helps everyone follow the leader. When you have a clear course laid out, you have guideposts to follow that will show you where you are vis-à-vis your goals. While you may find this secondary to raising money, it really is a priority for fulfilling that goal.

The ideal length and depth of a business plan vary. You have something to accomplish and a specific path you must travel to accomplish it. The steps that you take along that path are defined in your plan. Before beginning any business, you want to know the nature of your goals and objectives, the desired size of the company, the products and/or services it will sell, its customers and market niche, the amount of revenue likely to flow, and its sources. When you think of a business plan, your first thought may be how to impress the investor. Before you worry about the bank or the distribution company or the wealthy investor, however, you have to make a personal business plan. For all of those people—and for yourself—you have to come up with an agreeable course of action, and you have to stick to it. This book will help you do that.

Is This Book for Someone Making One Film?

In a word, "Yes." After five editions, people still call or email and ask me this question. Any movie proposal—whether for a single film or a company—that seeks to raise money from private investors needs a business plan. If you are doing a single film, the outline is exactly the same, except you have fewer numbers to project and there is no separate overhead. The results of one film will take you out three years, from the beginning of development to 80 percent of your revenues being returned. It is essential to remember that before going into business, you must find out for yourself whether business is your thing. One film is a business, and the producer (or executive producer) is the manager. You have the same responsibility to investors as if you were making four or five films. Reading this book will help you determine if a business is what you really want.

The Facts and Nothing but . . .

The structure of a business plan is standard, but the contents are not boilerplate. Each film has its own unique qualities. All plans must be substantive, promotional, and succinct, with a length generally about 20–25 pages for a one-film plan—that is, comprehensive but not too long. The business plan needs to contain enough information in a readable format that it excites, or at least impresses, potential investors. Perhaps even more important, however, is that the plan clearly represents you and your ideas. Copying someone else's plan is like copying someone's test paper in school. You may give the right answers to the wrong questions.

A few years ago, a friend of mine wrote a business plan that was very professional and cleverly laid out. He found that he had to keep it under lock and key because other producers kept making copies of it. What they failed to recognize was the specialized nature of his company. It was structured to fund development money, not produce films. The payback to the investors is quite different with development money. The "borrowers" of the product were so enamored of the text and graphics that they were blind to the obvious: The business plan promoted a type of company that they did not plan to run. How they ever managed to explain the relatively lower return to investors we will never know.

NEGOTIATION STANCES

The first strategy that I suggest in negotiating with an investor is to leave the negotiation deal points out of the business plan altogether. By doing so, you keep yourself open for the best deal. Notice that the financial examples in the sample business plan in Chapter 11 do not show a breakdown for the split with investors. They simply show the pretax dollars available for sharing. How the interested parties decide on equitable shares will depend on the number of parties involved, the types of entities involved, and proposals not foreseen by this plan. Even if you have a limited liability company (LLC) or limited partnership (L.P.) (or any other offering memorandum) that specifies shares, you may find an investor who wants to put in all the money. In this case, he will probably want to negotiate one on one with you and your attorney. Several of my clients have had this happen.

I advise my clients to hold their cards close to the vest and to let the other person go first. Even though you have determined your needs and expectations in advance, a situation may arise that you had not anticipated. For example, one group that I worked with assumed in advance that they were looking for an investor in the company as a whole. I convinced them to forego detailing this investment share in their business plan. In the beginning, equity investors for the whole amount were hard to find, but the filmmakers knew several people who would invest in individual films. This option was better for them in the end. They kept control of the company, as there were no new partners, and they found the resources for financing features on an individual basis.

The Investor Wants How Much?

It is always perplexing for creative people who have put their hearts and souls into a project to give away 50 percent or more to an investor. A common complaint is, "I'm doing all the work. Why should he get 50 percent?" Your decision has to be based on whether the amount of investment money is worth giving the investor that large a share of the profits. I cannot answer this question for you. Your priorities and goals are part of this decision. A standard business plan ploy that seldom gets funded is the 70/30 or 60/40 split in your favor. There may be someone out there willing to take it—never say never—but chances are that you will give your business plan to a variety of people, so reserve the bargaining for the individual. If potential investors seem unsophisticated, you can try it. If you are lucky, they will only laugh. If you are unlucky, they will laugh while leaving the room. At least, the thought is not written in stone in your Executive Summary.

Specialized Financial Instruments

If your company is a limited partnership, LLC, or other private placement, the amount of ownership is set ahead of time in the prospectus. Many entrepreneurs think that the business plan and the prospectus are one and the same.

The business plan is a marketing and sales tool. It has to be factual. There will be additional explanations about what to include and what to say (or not) in each chapter of this book. Of course, the financial projects are forecasting the future. However, they need to be based on the best data that can be obtained from the most credible sources available.

Your private placement (PPM), which is the most usual form of legal document used when raising money from equity investors for film, is a nonpublic (not sold on the stock exchange) document that is your legal agreement with investors. It is separate from the business plan. The PPM includes arrangements for selling, discounts and commissions to dealers, subscription agreements, how monies are to be distributed, and responsibilities and rights of company management and investors. You cannot write your own by pasting together wording from previous documents. I don't care what your financial circumstances are. An attorney familiar with the format and the film industry *must* write this document. Otherwise, you run the risk of unintentionally opening yourself to accusations of fraud and future lawsuits.

Even if you plan to use one of these business structures, I recommend keeping the business plan a freestanding document. The business plan is part of the total package, and being able to circulate the plan separately could come in handy. You never know what opportunities may come your way.

⟿ ABOUT THIS BOOK

Whether you use this book as a step-by-step guide for writing a plan or as a test of your own ability to be in business, it will help you meld creative thought with business fundamentals. It has been written in language that is accessible to those who are not skillful with business jargon. Understanding business is not that hard.

Whether you want to take the time to learn about business, or even want to be bothered with the noncreative aspects of film-making, is another question, one that you will have to answer for yourself. What if, after reading this book, you decide you would be better off selling your script to a studio or directing for one? Have you wasted your money? No. You will have saved money by reading this book first. It is better to find out now, rather than several months or thousands of dollars down the road, that running a business is not for you.

Business Plan Outline

This book is best described as a movie within a movie. To find financing for your projects, you will have to describe how your production or company will function. Accordingly, this book describes how the business works as well as instructing you on how to put the business plan together.

The book is arranged so that the numbered chapters follow the steps of the business plan. They appear in the order that the sections of your plan should follow:

1. Executive Summary
2. The Company
3. The Films
4. The Industry
5. The Markets
6. The Markets, Part II: The Nontraditional Film
7. Distribution
8. Risk Factors
9. Financing
10. The Financial Plan

Note that the subheadings in these chapters do not have to appear in the business plan. This outline has been the stuff of business plans from time immemorial. Finally, a sample business plan for a fictional company appears in Chapter 11.

In addition, I've added Chapter 12, which deals with the distribution of short films. Unfortunately, this business plan format cannot be used for raising money as there are no data to show potential investors. However, it is important for you to know what avenues are open for making back some of the money invested in a short film.

No matter how independent you are, when writing your business plan, do not fool with tradition. You should make it as easy as you can for potential investors to read your plan. They are used to seeing the information in a certain way, so humor them. It is in your best interest not to be an auteur with your business plan. As you devise your plan section by section, you will find yourself being repetitious; likewise, you will find the chapters of this book somewhat repetitious. Think of the plan as a series of building blocks.

Goals of This Book

My goal in writing this book is to give you, the independent filmmaker, an introduction to the world of business and to provide a format to help you present yourself and your projects in the best possible light. People want to know who *you* are and what you will do. Dreams are good; the nature of an entrepreneur is to be a dreamer. Your plan will bring the dream and the reality together.

There are many filmmakers with projects who are struggling to obtain equity (partnership) dollars. Being able to see your project from the investor's viewpoint and being able to present it to the financial community in a recognizable form will give you a useful edge on the competition.

Throughout the book, I emphasize that this is your plan. When I write a business plan, it is always the client's plan, and that person or group must understand it.

ADDITIONAL INFORMATION ON COMPANION WEB SITE

Focal Press has a companion web site for *Filmmakers and Financing*. It contains files with additional information (see the CD Contents at the front of the book) that can be downloaded to your computer. Don't go to the files until you have gone through the book. The most important set of files is the Financial Section, which contains explanations and worksheets of my method of forecasting. I have used *Len's Thrill*, one of the films in the Sample Business Plan in Chapter 11, for a step-by-step explanation. Other information included are sample synopses of well-known films, a list of sources for data information, and film festivals that meet the Academy of Motion Picture Arts and Sciences eligibility rules for short films. In addition, I will post updated information on the web site as economic, financing, and other significant factors change.

The Executive Summary

"Begin at the beginning," the King said, gravely, "and go till you come to the end; then stop."

LEWIS CARROLL
Alice's Adventures in Wonderland

READ THIS CHAPTER LAST!

This admonition is like saying, "Don't open this package until Christmas!" You are, right this minute, ignoring me and reading this chapter anyway. Fine, but when it comes to writing your business plan, write the Executive Summary last. Typically, investors will read the Executive Summary first; nevertheless, it is the section you want to write last. It is the hook that pulls readers into your net, and it must represent your future plans precisely.

The Executive Summary is the place where you tell readers what you're about to tell them. Am I confusing you? Remember that old advice about writing term papers: "Tell them what you're going to tell them; tell them; tell them what you told them"? You do the same thing in the Executive Summary. It is a condensed version of the rest of your proposal. This is not a term paper; this is your life.

The beginning of your business plan is the section about your film (or films, if you are starting a multifilm company). You give a brief overview of the people, the products, and your goals. In the rest of the sections—Company, Film(s), Industry, Markets, Distribution, Risk, and Financing—you provide more detail about how the company is going to function. The last section you write is the Executive Summary, which is just that: a summary. It presents a review of the plan for the reader.

WHY WRITE THE EXECUTIVE SUMMARY LAST?

Developing a business plan is a process of discovery. Until you actually put your business plan together, you cannot be sure what it will contain. As you will see in reading the rest of this book, much research, thought, and skill go into a proposal of this type. The total plan is the result of everything you learn from the process, and the Executive Summary is the culmination of that full effort.

The Executive Summary is written last for the same reason that you prepare a full budget before you do the top pages. You may have a problem with this comparison if you do the top pages of the budget first or if you do only the top pages. At best, filling in numbers on the top pages is a "guesstimate." Only when you actually work out the real 20 to 30 pages of the budget, based on the script breakdown, do you know the real costs.

Perhaps your guesstimate will end up being right on the mark. I don't think anyone has worked out the precise odds on that happening, but you might be more likely to win a lottery. A more probable scenario is that you will have backed yourself into a corner with original numbers that are too low. The real budget will turn out to be greater than your estimate by $500,000, $2 million, or even more. When that happens, your potential investors will be extremely unimpressed. If you are not sure how their money will be spent, ought they to trust you with it?

A business plan is the same situation magnified a thousand times. All the reasons outlined in the Introduction of this book for writing a business plan come into play. You may be setting parameters for yourself that are unrealistic and that lock you into a plan you cannot carry out. In putting together the proposal, your investigation of the market may cause you to fine-tune your direction. Learning more about distribution—and we all can—may invite a reworking of your film's release strategies.

Even when inventing a fictional company, as I did in Chapter 11, the Executive Summary must be written last. I did not know what I was going to say in the summary until the rest of the plan was written. Although I invented the company and the statistics for the sake of an example, my Industry, Markets (except for the cats), Distribution, and Financing sections are all real. I did not know which facts about all those elements would apply to my particular situation. Likewise, until I worked out the numbers and cash flows, I could not summarize the need for cash. The most difficult task for many entrepreneurs is resisting the impulse to write five quick pages and run it up the flagpole to see if anyone salutes. A business plan is not a script, and you cannot get away with handing in only a treatment. Your business plan must be well thought out, and you must present a complete package. Think of this as a rule. Other guidelines are suggestions that you would be wise to follow, but this is definitely a rule. Go through the process first. By the time you have carefully crafted your document and gone through all the steps outlined in this book, you will be able to proceed with as few hitches as possible.

This process has to be a cautious one, not a haphazard one. You want to be sure that your proposal makes business sense; you want to be able to meet any goals or verify any facts that you set forth. Passion does count. The film business is too hard and it takes too long to tackle projects if you do not have a passion for your story and for filmmaking. However, business facts are the glue that holds everything together in a tidy package.

Investors are the second reason that you write the Executive Summary only after you have carefully devised your business plan. Before you approach any money source, you want to be sure that your project is reasonable and rational. Potential investors did not accumulate their money by chance, and they are not likely to give you money on impulse. If you appear rash and impulsive, your 15 minutes of fame will run out before you know it. Treat potential investors as intelligent people, even if you are approaching the stockbroker's favorite group—widows and orphans. They'll have a business advisor who will read the proposal.

Often an investor will ask to see the Executive Summary first whether you are making one film or forming a company. In order to present him with the summary, you have to write the entire plan first, or there is nothing to summarize. Since a crucial part of the two or three pages is going to be a financial summary, how will you do that without running out all the data first? You would be making it up, which is not a good idea. The investor will be making initial assumptions based on those numbers. You don't want to be in the position later of saying, "Gee, we were a little off. Our budget is $5 million rather than $2 million, and the net profit is $3 million rather than $15 million." You will have lost an investor.

Besides, five will get you ten that if the investor likes what he sees in the Executive Summary, the next communication will be,

"Let me see the rest of the plan." That person means today—now. As I pointed out above, he assumes that there is a body of work supporting your summary; therefore, the summary and the complete proposal have to match. You do not want to have to tell potential investors that you will have the complete plan in a month. When equity investors ask for a business plan, you must have all the market explanations, facts, and figures at hand and in order.

STYLE OF THE EXECUTIVE SUMMARY

The image experts say that you have 30 seconds to make an impression, whether it is at a job interview, in a negotiation, or at your local party place on a Friday night. Your business plan has a similar amount of time. First impressions count; they will make the reader either want to read further or toss the proposal aside.

Cicero said that brevity is the charm of eloquence; this thought is a good one to keep in mind. In a few paragraphs, you must summarize the entire business plan to show the goals driving the business, the films, the essential market and distribution factors, and the major elements for the success of the project. Each of the chapters in the outline has its own summary. I know that it is hard to understand this repetition; students and clients ask about it all the time. That is why I keep coming back to it.

Earlier I said that the Executive Summary is the hook; you can also think of it as the bait that attracts the fish. You want the reader to be intrigued enough to read on. You need not try to rival John Grisham or Stephen King as a writer of thrillers or horror stories. You should not expect to keep readers on the edge of their seats. Simply provide the salient points in the Executive Summary: Less is more. If the Executive Summary of your plan is as long as this chapter, it is entirely too long. You can be long-winded later. All you want to do in the summary is give your readers the facts with as little embellishment as possible. Remember that this is a business proposal, not a script.

LAYING OUT THE EXECUTIVE SUMMARY

Follow your outline when writing the Executive Summary. Give the basic information of each section. Do not deviate from the path that you have already chosen. Anything you say here has to appear in more detail somewhere else in the proposal. Refer to the Executive Summary of the sample business plan in Chapter 11 while reviewing how to lay out your own summary.

Strategic Opportunity

Typically, the first of the sections of the Executive Summary is called "Strategic Opportunity."

The Company

The section describes the outstanding elements of your goals and plans. From this section, the reader finds out what your production company name is, what type of film or films you are making, and who you are.

A short introduction to your *production team* is included to give investors an idea of your team's experience and expertise. If you happen to be starting a company, you may want to call this the *management team*, as it will include executives who aren't involved in production per se. Indicate any notable attachments—director, producer, and/or actors—but save their bios to follow in the longer Company section. If you have a company plan in which each film has its own director and producers, you may want to include their bios with each film rather than in the Company section.

As we will discuss later, be sure to include only people who have given consent to be involved in your project in some written form. Do not include people who you would like to work with but who have never heard of you. Typically, you can include consultants, such as the business plan advisor or attorney, in the longer Company section; however, if you feel it is important to put them up front to add immediate credibility for your team, do so.

The Film(s)

In this section, give readers only the most important information about your proposed film or films. Normally, I include one or two lines that have some punch or are intriguing while still giving the investor the essence of the story. Look at some of the one-line plot summaries in *www.imdb.com*. For example, for *Juno*, they have written, "Faced with an unplanned pregnancy, an offbeat young woman makes an unusual decision regarding her unborn child." This sounds much more interesting than if they just said, "The film is a coming-of-age story about a pregnant teenager." Both are correct, but you want to pique your investors' interest. It also is likely that the fuller explanation will make your investors ask what the choice is. If they like it, fine. If they don't, it saves you time. They won't like it any more later, after they have read the complete synopsis.

The Industry

Before describing your specific segment of the marketplace, it is necessary to give an overview of the industry. Just a short paragraph to show the current shape and financial growth of the industry will do. Include such things as the U.S. box office, worldwide box office, total admissions, and size of the independent film market.

The Markets

In this section, you should give readers a feel for the markets for your films. Spell out target markets (genres, affinity groups, etc.), as well as typical age groups. In addition, include any self-marketing methods you intend to use, with explanations of their value.

Distribution

Simply saying "We will get distribution" is not enough. Don't laugh. I've seen this in plans.

If you have distribution attached, give names here. Don't be shy. However, do be circumspect, as with the body of the plan. Mention only real companies from which you have received actual written commitments. Phrases such as "We have interest from many companies to distribute our films" are public relations jargon.

If potential investors think that they will find such meaningless generalizations in the rest of the plan, they may not read on. If you are planning to self-distribute your film, mention it here. Hiding that fact until readers have worked their way through 20 pages or more of the business plan will not help you at all. State your reasons and describe in a few sentences your knowledge in the area of distribution.

Investment Opportunity and Financial Highlights

This section summarizes all the financial information in your plan. The first item to include is that all-important fact that hundreds of people leave out of their plans—how much money you want. Do not keep it a secret. The whole point of handing this plan to potential investors is to relieve them of a little of the green stuff. They know that; they just want to know how much.

Follow with a summary sentence indicating the worldwide box office and projected profit. Whether you are making one film or several over five to ten years, the details will be in your Financing section. Many of your investors will have business experience, whether or not it is in film. They are likely to look directly from the Executive Summary to the tables to see the details of revenues and expenses.

Notice that I continually use the words *projection, forecast,* and *estimate* throughout the financial sections. Always qualify any expressions of future gain with one of these three words. I also include a phrase saying that there is no guarantee. For example, "Using a moderate revenue projection and an assumption of general industry distribution costs, we project (but do not guarantee) ...."

WHAT DOESN'T BELONG HERE

If by chance you skipped the Introduction, go back and read the "Negotiation Stances" section. The business plan is a freestanding document. It should not include any investor negotiations or legal language relating to how money will be distributed. The business plan is a marketing document that is part of a total package; however, it is not the total package.

The Company

2

To open a business is easy; to keep it open is difficult.

CHINESE PROVERB

STARTING IS EASY

To start a business, all you have to do is choose a name and have a phone; ergo, you are in business. To be successful, though, a business involves much more. A company, according to the *American College Dictionary,* is "a number of people united for a joint action ... a band, party, or troop of people." The lone screenwriter is an island of self-absorption; the filmmaker is king—long live the king! When she becomes the producer of even one film, though, she is running a business.

Running a business embodies a totally different set of skills. It is a special kind of collaboration in which dictatorship does not work. For a business to run successfully, everyone must agree on its purpose, direction, and method of operation. This goal requires a lot of planning and communication.

I always like to recount my first seminar in which I started the day with a discourse on "Common Blunders in Business Planning." At the break, my assistant overheard someone say, "What is all this esoteric nonsense? We came here to find out where the investors are." To make my meaning clear, I started each full-day seminar by putting a list of companies on the board. I asked the seminar participants to tell me what these companies had in common. After attempts by several attendees, one observant person finally recognized that they all had declared Chapter 11 (bankruptcy with reorganization of the business) or Chapter 7 (bankruptcy with liquidation of the business) or shut the doors in some other way.

Now it is more appropriate to discuss specialty divisions that have become brands within a studio or the more complicated dissolutions of international conglomerates that caused their production or distribution divisions to become standalone companies with their own financing.

The first reaction from independent producers was that these companies were all big and that somehow their size contributed to their downfall. In reality, the reason companies—whether big or small—fail is the same in either case: lack of planning. Anyone can have bad luck. Part of planning, however, is looking at the future result of current decisions. In doing this, you can build in ways of dealing with bad luck and other problems. Granted, some crises are beyond your control. A bank failure or the bankruptcy of a distributor, for example, is such an outside event. But careful planning can help you anticipate even these external occurrences.

The business plan diagrams a path for you to follow. Along the way, there may be forks in the road and new paths to take; flexibility in adjusting to such changing conditions is the key. On the other hand, taking every highway and byway that you see might take you in circles. In that case, you will never get a project completed and in the theaters. A balance is needed, therefore, between flexibility and rigidity. Planning provides this balance.

KNOW YOURSELF FIRST

When asked what they want to do, many filmmakers (or entrepreneurs of any stripe) reply either "I want to make money" or "I want to make films." There is nothing intrinsically wrong with either answer, but there are more questions to be considered. For example, what is the nature of the films you will make? What are you willing to do for money? And, ultimately, who are you?

Before characterizing your company for yourself or anyone else, make sure that you really know yourself. For example, one filmmaker told me that she intended to live and work in Georgia; she would make her films there and seek all money there. For her, this goal was nonnegotiable. This position may seem rigid to some people, but you have to know the lines you are not willing to cross.

Goals 101

Having and keeping a clear vision is important; it is as easy or as hard as you want to make it. Ensuring that you understand what you are truly about is the first step. A full course in Goals 101 would be too long to include here, but we can quickly review the basic principles with a minimum of academic jargon.

Setting goals merely means clearly stating your main purpose. Objectives are often shorter-term accomplishments aimed at helping you meet your main goal. For example, writing this book was my ultimate goal; teaching university classes was a short-term objective to help me reach my goal. I felt that the best way to establish credibility for a book contract was by teaching at University of California at Los Angeles (UCLA). From the beginning, I knew that the pay would be low compared to consulting and other work; however, over the short term, the book was more important. Teaching at UCLA, then, became a greater priority than making lots of money.

The business and personal aspects of your life may mesh quite well, but any conflicts between the two need to be reconciled at the beginning. Otherwise, those conflicts may interfere with your success in one or both areas. Covert agendas are sometimes good to use with competitors, but fooling yourself is downright dangerous.

Formulating Your Goals

Formulating your goals may seem complicated, but it involves just two simple but essential steps:

1. Take a meeting with yourself at the start. (In Los Angeles and New York, everyone "does lunch.") Think about your plans, look at them, dream about them; then set out to test them against reality.
2. Write your plans down. Entrepreneurs love to declare that they can keep everything in their heads and do not have to write anything down. Big mistake! If your ideas are so clear, it will take you only a few minutes to commit them to paper. Anything you cannot explain clearly and concisely to yourself will not be clear to someone else. Writing down your goals allows you to see the target you are trying to hit. Then you can establish intermediate objectives or a realistic plan to accomplish these goals.

A word about money is in order. John D. Rockefeller said, "Mere money-making was never my goal"; other successful executives have made similar statements. Many talk shows have brought together groups of entrepreneurs to find out what motivates them. They almost always identify making the product, negotiating the deal, or some other activity as their main motivation; the money followed when they did the things they liked. Do something that you enjoy, that you are passionate about, and that you are good at; then the money, according to many popular books, will follow.

Whether or not you become rich, I cannot stress too often that filmmaking is not an easy business. Be sure that it is the filmmaking that draws you—not just the tinsel, glitter, and high-revenue prospects.

Personal Goals versus Business Goals

Finding fulfillment is an elusive goal. To start, you must list and prioritize your goals. Unless you know where you are heading, you will be severely hampered in making decisions as you walk down your path. People have both business and personal goals, so it is crucial to look at both categories.

First, take a look at your personal goals to make sure that you do not inadvertently overlook something you want. This question has been the hardest for students in my classes to answer. Often someone will say it is to move to Los Angeles to pursue film or hire a good director. Your personal goals have nothing to do with work per se; they are your private desires, your plans about your lifestyle, your dreams that will bring a feeling of satisfaction outside of work. Can you identify your personal goals? What is important to you? Is it family? Church? Riding horses in Montana? Consider the pursuits and activities that you find meaningful. Decide which are important enough to have time for outside of pursuing your business.

If the idea of personal objectives still perplexes you, take some time to think about it. Being passionate about films is one thing; having nothing else in your life is something else. Once you can identify your personal goals, continue on.

List your personal goals on a piece of paper, not in your head; writing in the margins of this book is permitted. Describe as many or as few goals as you want, as long as you have at least one. Here are some examples to help you get started:

1. Improve my standard of living.
2. Live in Albuquerque, New Mexico.
3. Play in poker tournaments (my list).
4. Work out with a fitness trainer on a regular basis.
5. Volunteer at a local food bank every two months.

Now identify your filmmaking (i.e., business) goals. Again, make a list, using the following examples as a guide:

1. Make inspirational films.
2. Form a company that will make action/adventure films with budgets under $10 million.
3. Win an Academy Award.
4. Create a distribution division in four years.
5. Make a feature documentary that will influence national health care.

On another piece of paper, list both the personal goals and the business goals side by side; then rank them in order, with "1" representing the most important to you. Only you can set these priorities; there is no right or wrong way to do it. Once you have made the two lists, compare them. What conflicts do you see? How can you reconcile them? Accomplish this task, and you will be ready to write the story of your business.

GETTING IT ALL TOGETHER

Putting together the story (or script) of your company is like making a pitch to a studio or writing a *TV Guide* logline, only longer. You want to convince an unknown someone of the following:

1. You know exactly what you are going to do.
2. You are creating a marketable product.
3. You have the ability to carry it off.

Essentially, you are presenting the basic "plot" of your company. The difference is that a script provides conflicts and resolutions as plot points. By completing the previous writing exercise, you should have resolved any conflicts. "Just the facts, ma'am," as Sergeant Joe Friday would say.

Remember what your teacher taught you in high school English: who, what, when, where, why, and how. These questions are your guidelines for formatting the Company section of your business plan. Before you go any farther, ponder these questions:

- Why are you making films?
- Who are you?
- What films or other projects will you make?
- When will you get this show on the road?
- Where are your markets?
- How are you going to accomplish everything?

Note that the standard order is changed a bit. The *why* needs to come at the beginning to set the scene for the rest of the story.

Why?—The Opening Pitch

Now that you have listed your personal and business goals, you can identify the underlying aim of your company, known in corporate circles as the "mission statement." This statement describes your film's or company's (remember that even if you are only making one film, you are a company) reasons for existence to you, your partners and managers, your employees, and, most of all, your money sources. It allows those marching forward with you to know whether you are all marching to the same drummer.

A major reason for failure is lack of agreement on where the management/production team is headed. A film is always a group project; there is far too much to accomplish for one person to do everything. It is important to ensure that company personnel do not go off in three or four different directions. Many companies that fail do so because of lack of focus; your company does not have to be one of them.

Do you have a specific philosophy? What do you want to do? Make the greatest films ever made? Make children's films? Make educational videos? Clearly define your philosophy for yourself and others. As long as people can identify with where you are heading, they will not get lost along the way.

When your philosophy or major goal is down on paper, stand aside and take an objective look. Does this sound doable to you? Would it sound reasonable if someone else presented it to you? Most of all, would you take money out of your own pocket for it?

By the way, in writing up this description, you are not required to incorporate all your goals for the world to see. Your personal goals are yours alone—unless they affect the production significantly. Suppose, for example, that you are active in animal rights organizations. For that reason, you are adamant that no animals ever appear in your films. Everyone working with you has the right to know about this dictum. It may affect scripts that have even innocuous animal scenes. Investors need to know about any major restrictions on your projects. Whether or not you put this in your business plan for investors, I will let you decide.

I am often approached by producers who have strong feelings about the source of investment money (how it was earned) or about certain countries to which they refuse to distribute their films. These countries always end up being major markets, so this credo strongly affects the company's potential revenue. Distributors do not like to give up lucrative markets, and investors do not like to give up potential profits. You have a right to your principles; if they affect future profits, however, you must tell your investors what they are.

This brings us to a brief discussion about honesty. What if you intend to make, say, environmental films, but fear that you will lose potential investors by being explicit? Should you keep your true plans to yourself? Should you claim to be making some other type of film, such as action/adventure? This question has come up in seminars and classes repeatedly. In one class, the following conversation took place:

STUDENT: If I tell them that I'm going to make environmental films, they won't give me the money.
L.L.: What are you going to tell them?
STUDENT: I won't tell them what kinds of films I plan to make.
L.L.: You have to tell them something. No one is going to buy a pig in a poke.
STUDENT: I'll tell them that I'm going to make action films. Those always sell well.
L.L.: Then you would be lying to your own investors.
STUDENT: So? The idea is to get the money, isn't it?
L.L.: If lying doesn't bother you, how about fraud? The best-case scenario is that they will take their money back. At the very worst, you can be liable for criminal penalties.
STUDENT (with shrug of his shoulders): So?

You may think that I invented this conversation to make a point. I wish that I had. Unfortunately, it is a true story. Is it surprising that, at the same time, the university offered an ethics course, and no one signed up for it? My job is not to lecture anyone, although it is tempting. Your moral values are your own. Suffice it to say that fraud is not a good offense to commit, and most investors do not respond well to it.

Who?

By this time, you ought to know who you are, both personally and professionally. Now you can use the mission statement to define your company. Start the Company section of your business plan with a short statement that introduces the company. Give its history, ownership structure, and details of origin. Include the following in the statement:

1. Type of company: LLC, L.P., corporation (type), and state and city origin
2. Names of principal owners (silent and/or active partners) and officers

A beginning statement might be something like this:

AAA Productions is a California limited-liability company formed for the development and production of Hispanic-themed films as well as the employment of Hispanic actors in primary roles. Over the next four years, the Company plans to produce three independently financed feature films with budgets between $2 million and $7 million. During recent years, the movie market has become more open to stories about ethnic groups. Films with Hispanic themes have led the way and proved that there is a market.

Not only has the writer said what films the company intends to make, but he has also identified a specific goal that is both professional and personal. The company's "principal purpose" describes its mission statement. It is closely tied to the personal beliefs and desires of members of the company.

What?

Mysteries do not work, except in scripts. The readers of your business plan want a straightforward summary of your intentions. Saying that you will make films without a discussion of content is not enough. What specifically do you plan to do? In the Company section of the business plan, include a short recap of your film(s). You will explain the individual projects in more detail later in the Film(s) section. You should summarize all the areas that your plan covers, such as the following:

1. Films
2. Budgets
3. Types of functions (development, production, distribution) in which you will be involved

Rationality must intercede here. What you want to do and what you are most likely to get done may be two different things. In one of the piles of business plans from outside sources at my office, for example, a group stated that it planned to make 10 to 12 feature films a year with average budgets between $8 and $15 million. This undertaking is laudable for a major studio, but it may be questionable for even a large independent production company because of the quantity of resources—both money and people—involved. For this brand-new company, it was a foolish goal. No one in the company had ever made a film before. Even if someone had, consider the effort. The films would require more than $100 million in production costs alone in the first year, not to say anything about finding the staff, cast, and crew to make them. Is this an investment that you would view as "reasonable" for your hard-earned money?

Of course, people beat the odds every day. If entrepreneurs believed in the word "impossible," there would be no progress in the world. Nevertheless, you should weigh the scope of your venture against the experience of the people involved in it. If no one in your company has ever made a film, the odds are against your getting money for high budgets and multiple films per year. Aiming to produce one low-budget film in the first year makes the odds of receiving funding a little better.

Experience producing or directing television programs, commercials, documentaries, music videos, and industrials is better than no experience at all; however, feature films are different in terms of time and budget. Being circumspect about the size of the feature budget in relation to your experience not only will impress investors but also will keep you from overextending your abilities.

With a one-film plan, you need only look ahead three years (one for production, two more for revenue return). If you are starting a multifilm company, however, you must consider where your company will be five years hence. Analyze everything you plan to be doing over that time. If you plan to go into book publishing in year four (I'm not recommending it), that goal needs to be part of your plan. Even plans to sell the company in five years must be mentioned. All of this is part of your projected bottom line. Although you may not know all the specifics, the size, scope, and type of your planned projects need to be stated.

Even if your company has been in business for a long time or if the principals have considerable experience, never assume that readers have an intimate knowledge of your business. If your genre is the Western, for example, you might write something like this: *We plan to produce Western films in which the Indians are the heroes.*

Treating the Indians as the heroes who they often were may attract a rich aficionado of American history to fund the film. The current status of Westerns is described in your Markets section (Chapter 4). Do not go into exhaustive detail. You will do that later. Remember that it is important in this document to keep the malarkey factor to a minimum. That does not mean that you cannot put in a little positive public relations, but leave your press clippings for the Appendix.

When?

In describing your project or company, you may have already stated how and when you began functioning as a company. You may have a great deal more to say, however. The majority of companies run by independent filmmakers are start-ups. If your company has only just begun, there may be a limited amount of information to provide. Be clear about the current situation, whatever it is. You may still be someone else's employee, for example.

But be sure that you really are in business or ready to launch. Go ahead and file forms that may be necessary for your type of company, have an address (even if it is your home or a post office box), and print business cards. To digress for a moment, I urge everyone to have a business card. I have found that writers or people with below-the-line jobs tend not to have one. Always have your name, a contact phone, and an email address available to give to anyone you meet. It is crucial once you have the desire to start your own company (and its name is filed in the correct way) to have a business card.

Starting Steps

You have already taken the first step of starting a business—translating the entrepreneur's vision into a concrete plan of action. Next comes the practical process of actually setting up shop. You must create all those minutiae that say to prospective investors, "This person knows what he is doing." Note the following checklist:

- Define the job descriptions of the production team.
- Determine the location and cost of offices.
- Have your stationery and business cards printed.
- Set up phones and a fax machine for easy communication.
- Arrange for professional guidance from an attorney and an accountant.
- Introduce yourself to your banker and set up a checking account.

A more important step is choosing your legal form of business. There is no one form that is best for everyone. When making this decision, consult with your attorney or accountant. The most common forms of business are the following:

1. A *sole proprietorship* is owned by one person. It is easy to initiate and faces little regulation. The individual owner has all the control but all the responsibility as well. It is the normal state of doing business for consultants and others who mostly work alone.
2. A *partnership* is a business with two or more co-owners. A *limited liability* (LLC) is a common form of partnership for independent filmmakers. It is an operating agreement that you register with your state. It is currently used for many film companies as the general operating agreement; however, it should not be confused with an Investor Offering, also called an LLC (see Chapter 9).

If the formation of your business is dependent on raising money, be clear about this. Just be sure that you will be willing and in the position to give full attention to the company upon receipt of the money. It is critical to show some preparation (your business plan is an example) before seeking investors.

Suppose you own a company that has had problems in the past. Don't be coy. Obviously, you need other people's money for some reason. Most investors will insist on full disclosure. They need to know the depth of the problems to overcome. If you have leftover equity owners from a previous incarnation or have imprudently spent money on cars, confess now. In the business plan, the sin of omission is as serious as the sin of commission.

You may find yourself in another situation. What if the company was in some other line of business before you bought it? The name is established, but the business has not yet functioned as an entertainment entity. On the other hand, you may have bought an operating film company that has been unsuccessful. Both circumstances add assets and credibility to your company. However, do not attempt to give the impression that the company was anything other than it actually was or that it has made more money than it actually has.

Do not be afraid to state the facts. If a company made garbage cans before you bought it, say so. Investors want to know what they are getting into. Besides, being candid has its own rewards. People with money tend to know other people with money. Even if one prospect is not interested, his friend may be. So do not be afraid to tell him something he may not like. Eventually, he will find out anyway, and you will lose not only an investor but also the chance for him to recommend you to someone else. It is a small world, and the investing community is even smaller. Once you start getting a negative rap, the word spreads quickly.

~ Where?

Potential investors want to know where you are going to sell your films. Although "worldwide" is a good thought, you should be more specific. If you are making your first independent film, it is not likely to have a $25-million budget. (If it does, please reconsider; your company is not Fox Searchlight yet.)

There are many different things to choose from when starting a film company. I strongly suggest sticking to films in the beginning. However, some people want to make television movies, cable movies, direct-to-DVD movies or even create their own distribution division. This may get complicated if you plan to produce more than one type of product and have different selling philosophies for each. Remember that the Company section is an introductory statement, not a thesis. A short summary, such as the following one, is all you need.

The company's objectives are to

1. Develop scripts with outside writers.
2. Produce theatrical films with budgets from $1 to $5 million.
3. Explore overseas co-production and co-financing potential for the company.
4. Create our own distribution division.

How?

Up to this point, you have essentially outlined everything your company proposes to accomplish. In the rest of the business plan, you will describe each step in detail. Chapter 3, "The Films," is a continuation of the *what*. It is an in-depth study of each of your projects. Chapters 4 through 10 describe the *how*. This is the central plot of your business plan. How do you fit into the industry? How will you identify your place in the market? How do distribution and financing work, and how will you pursue each one?

MANAGEMENT AND ORGANIZATION

Conclude the Company section of your business plan with a brief description of your production team and its key members. This means writing just a paragraph or two for each. Save the six- or seven-page résumés for the Appendix. How much of the organization you describe depends on the strength of the production team.

Maybe you'll be lucky and have a well-known former studio executive as part of your company. Perhaps your executives have business expertise in some industry other than film. Film track records are important, but business experience in other industries also counts. If no one in your company has ever made a film, find someone who has and sign that person up. If you have no one currently, describe the job position and make the commitment to have it filled by the time your financing arrives.

Following is an example of a company with some entertainment experience:

The primary strength of any company is its management team. XXX's two principals have extensive business and entertainment industry experience. Simply Marvelous is Executive Producer. Most recently, she has worked with MNY Co. in both acquisitions and production. Among the films that she was responsible for are Cat Cries at Sunset, Phantom of La Loggia, *and* Dreaded Consultants IV. *Marvelous will have overall responsibility for the company's operations and will serve as Executive Producer on all films.*

Freda Financial, Chief Financial Officer, brings to XXX varied business and entertainment experience, including five years' experience in motion picture finance with the Add 'Em Up accounting firm. Previously, Financial worked in corporate planning for the healthcare industry.

If you have a writer-director who has no feature film experience, you might write something like this:

Self Consumed will be writing and directing our first two films. Consumed has directed commercials for 15 years. In addition, he has done promotions for the Big Time cable system. Last year he directed the romantic comedy short film, Louise Loves. *It was well received at several film festivals and won the critics' award at the Mainline Film Festival. His fifth feature screenplay is in development at Crazed Consultant Films.*

Make these descriptions long enough to include the essential information, but the less important details should go elsewhere. For example, Mr. Consumed's commercials and the companies for whom he worked can be listed on a résumé in the Appendix. For the sake of your readers' sanity, however, do not create a ten-page listing of all of a director's commercials, even in the Appendix.

Catch-22 Experience

What do you do when no one in the company has any experience? Tread very carefully. My advice is to attach someone who does. Why would any investor believe that you can make a film with no previous experience and no help?

The amount of skill expected is related to the budget as well as the genre of the planned film. Suppose you have decided to make a $10-million film for your first venture. You have written a script and have partnered with people with financial or retail backgrounds, but no direct knowledge of or experience with film. Would you take $10 million out of your own pocket for this?

In certain circumstances, you can use the ploy of discussing below-the-line attachments of merit. Some clients of mine, for example, happened to have an Academy Award–nominated cinematographer or an Emmy-winning composer committed to their projects. It was to their benefit to include this type of experience in the production team descriptions.

Be careful how you do this, though. You want to avoid making the production of your films look like a committee effort. One wannabe producer came to me with a plan for a first movie, with himself as executive producer. He planned to start with a $20-million film and felt that running the computer system at a production company was appropriate film experience. His explanation read as follows:

> *So and So has 25 years' experience working with computer systems, 10 of them at X & X Production Company. So and So is the producer and has an experienced crew ready to work with him. These technicians have a combined experience of 105 years in the film business. If So and So has any questions, they will be able to help him.*

This is a dangerous trap. The expectation that your inexperience will be covered by other people working in various crew positions may backfire. The old saying, "A camel is a horse designed by a committee," is applicable here. The producer is the manager of the business and must make the final decisions; therefore, the person in this position must have knowledge on which to draw. Investors expect to see people in charge who have more than a vague idea of what they are doing. When describing their experience, some people elaborate on the truth to a fault. When applying for a job of any kind, it is frequently tempting to stretch your bio a bit, if not to make it up out of whole cloth. Think carefully before you do this. Filmmakers often put their most creative efforts into writing the management summaries.

Compare the following real biography to the "elaborated" version that follows:

> *Real biography:* Leonard Levison has worked as an assistant to the associate producer on *The Bell Rings*. Before that, Levison was a production associate on four films at Gotham Studios. He began his film career as gopher at the studio.

"Elaborated" business plan version: Leonard Levison produced
the film *The Bell Rings*. Prior to this project, he produced
four films at Gotham Studios. He began his film career as a
co-producer on various films.

"Exaggeration," you say? "Harmless public relations puffery,"
you add? This overstatement is similar to the inflated income some
people put down on a home loan application. You might assume
that this is just the way things are done, but this action can
come back to haunt you. A Los Angeles entertainment attorney told
me about a court case in which the fictional management biographies of the filmmakers were the investor's sole reason for suing.
He said that he "bet on people" and only read the management
portion of the Company section of the business plan.

Try to be objective about the film company that you are creating. It is less likely that an investor will give money to totally
inexperienced filmmakers than to a group with a track record. No
situation, as I have said, is impossible. The safer you can make the
downside (chance of losing money) for the investors, the likelier
it is that they will write you a check. No matter how emotionally
involved an individual investor might be in the project, there is
usually an objective, green-eyeshade type sitting nearby, trying to
make your plan fit her idea of a "reasonable" investment.

A Word about Partnerships

In forming a company to make either a single film or many, you may
want to take on one or more partners. The usual makeup is two or
three people who co-own a company and work full time in it. Each
one is personally liable for the others. It is quite common for good
friends to become partners. Because of the relationships involved,
however, many people doing business with friends often do not
take the same care that they would take with total strangers.

No matter what the affinity with one another, agreements
between people must be made and contracts signed. Over the years
I have had countless partners come to discuss the business plan
without first making their own agreement. In many cases, this has
resulted in the project not starting—or worse, being stopped once
they have paid—because the people involved had not made their
own formal agreement. Once they are faced with making a formal
agreement for the purposes of the plan, someone doesn't like the

original handshake agreement. Or people don't agree on the details of the original agreement for which there are no notes. Even if there are emails, nothing has been signed, and a change of mind over who will get what is not unusual. Make legal agreements first. Then proceed to books, hire employees, put together a prospectus, and all the other elements involved in making your films.

A good partnership requires the presence of two contradictory elements. First, you and your partners must be very much alike so that your goals and objectives mesh. On the other hand, you must be very unlike and complementary in terms of expertise. Often, one partner is more cautious and the other more adventurous. Whether to form a partnership can be a difficult decision. As in many other situations, the best step is to list on paper the advantages and disadvantages of a partnership and see how it works out.

The following are examples of such lists. First, the advantages of entering into a partnership:

1. I will have a measure of safety because it takes two to make any decision.
2. I will avoid the unremitting and lonely responsibility of doing everything by myself.
3. I will have a partner with skills that are different than my own.
4. I will have someone to share crises with.

Here are some reasons not to enter into a partnership:

1. My share of the profits will be a lot less.
2. I will not have total control.
3. I will have to share recognition at the Academy Awards.
4. My partner's poor judgment could hurt me and the film.

ASSESSING STRENGTHS AND WEAKNESSES

Casting an unbiased eye over your plans is always hard for entrepreneurs. A strong desire for everything to work often clouds your vision. Evaluating the strengths and weaknesses of your project(s) in the beginning, however, will save time, turmoil, and money later. You might be able to describe the strengths of your company as follows:

- Associates of the company possess unique skills or experience.
- We have special relationships with distributors or other professionals or companies in related fields.
- Unique aspects of this business that will help us are ….

Film production companies are often started with a combination of production and distribution personnel with varying levels of experience. Newer filmmakers team with experienced hands-on producers outside the company. Well-established companies often seek experienced personnel when going into new lines of endeavor. New Line Cinema, for example, grew into a major independent production and distribution company with low-budget, mass-market products, such as the *Nightmare on Elm Street* (1984) films and *Teenage Mutant Ninja Turtles*. Skip into the next century, and the company was instrumental in that fantastic $300-million trilogy known as *Lord of the Rings*.

On the reverse side of the ledger are your company's weaknesses. Be honest with yourself when identifying your company's failings. This exercise saves many companies from later failure. By converting the strength statements to negative statements, you can spot problems. Write them down on a piece of paper to review:

1. No one in this company possesses unique skills or experience.
2. Our films have no distinctive characteristics that set them apart from others in the marketplace.
3. We have no special relationships with distributors or other professionals in the entertainment industry.

Being good in one area of business does not guarantee success in another. For example, suppose an entrepreneur from one area of entertainment, such as commercials, decides to go into theatricals, an area in which he has no experience. Although he knows how to manage a profitable business, feature filmmaking has its own unique set of concerns. The business requires larger sums of money per project than do commercials and involves greater risks in terms of market.

In addition, running a company as opposed to being a studio producer or an independent working on one film at a time requires different skills. Successful executives often rush into new businesses without preparing properly. Used to calling all the shots, they may have trouble delegating authority or may hire lower-level development personnel rather than experienced producers in order to maintain control. The producer can counter these weaknesses by studying the new industry first and hiring seasoned film people. Running through this exercise will help you in two ways. First, you will locate the holes in the dike so that you can plug them before any leaks occur. Second, you can use it to assess how much confidence you or anyone else can have in your organization. In addition, pointing out the obvious to readers never hurts. You should not make readers work to see the good points. As to weaknesses, most investors are sophisticated executives and will see the problems themselves. If you do not mention how you will overcome the obstacles your company faces, the investor may question your ability to understand them. Being frank may help your cause rather than hurt it.

LESS IS MORE

The Company section of your business plan not only summarizes the essential facts about your company, but also is an introduction to the rest of the business plan. It should be short and to the point. Prospective investors want to know the basics, which will be described in exhaustive detail throughout the rest of your proposal. Many readers of this book's previous editions have told me that the phrase that was most important in writing their own plans was "less is more."

3

The Films

Why should people go out and pay money to see bad films, when they can stay at home and see bad television for free?

SAMUEL GOLDWYN

PROJECT SCOPE

Theatrical films are the backbone of most filmmakers' business plans. As the industry changes, however, the potential for artistic expression is growing far beyond the notion of a single theatrical. In recent years, many filmmakers have successfully specialized in documentaries, commercials, industrials, educationals, and info-mercials, as well as cable, video, and DVD productions. The focus of this chapter is traditional theatrical films. Chapter 6, "The Markets, Part II," discusses nontraditional films.

Whether one film or a company with multiple projects, all films in which your company will participate over the next five years should be addressed in the Film(s) section of the business plan. This chapter demonstrates how to describe them. It explains not only the amount of information that you need to include, but also what you should leave out.

How do you know what you will be doing five years from now? Undoubtedly, you know more about some films than others; some of you may not even have specific projects yet. You may have a script to shoot next year, but may not have a clue about the script for a film planned four years down the road.

Nor can you know what delays may occur along the way. It is less important to be psychic than to be as accurate as possible in terms of intentions and timing. If circumstances alter the original plan, everyone involved will reevaluate it.

The Right to Know

As your partner, the investor has a right to know what activities are contemplated in order to make an informed decision. Several years ago, a young man came to me with a proposal to create a highly specialized series of films. He planned to sell them in a narrowly segmented market. The plan contained much discussion about the future success of his company, but the only description of the projects was the word "films." He estimated that millions of people would go to see these unspecified films.

Being the curious type, I asked him what kinds of films he planned to make. His answer was, "Good ones." I pressed on, trying to elicit more information. After all, he guaranteed that millions would clamor to see these films. He replied, "I'm not going to tell anybody anything. They might steal the idea. Besides, it's no one's business; all they need to know is that it's a good investment."

Don't laugh too loudly. This story is only one of many, and this young man's attitude is not unusual. "Films," as you may have realized by now, is not a sufficient description. Putting yourself in the investor's shoes, how would this strike you? You would probably insist on knowing the content of these incredible films, who belonged to this guaranteed market, and how the films were going to pay back your investment.

There are certainly a couple of valid reasons why a filmmaker (or any other entrepreneur) might worry about revealing the details of a proposed project: (1) no identifiable plans exist, or (2) someone might steal the idea. Although theft of concept is not an unknown phenomenon, there is a difference between not telling the general public all about your plans and refusing to tell a potential money source. Prudent filmmakers refrain from describing script details in a loud voice at the local coffee shop or at a crowded party; they also resist the temptation to ask seven or eight friends to read their projects. However, the prudent do give the right people enough information to prove the advisability of the investment.

Success in any business revolves around the product. In film, where all forward motion to the goal is content-driven, the story is crucial. To sell your projects, remember the refrain, "Story, story, story."

Hype has a place also, but it must take a back seat in the context of this plan. The trick is to do some jazzy selling around a solid idea. All the public relations in the world will not save a bad film.

From Chapter 2, "The Company," you know that the first goal for the business plan is to identify your future course of action. The second is to show investors how profitable your business will be. There is no way to forecast your success without specific ideas to evaluate. Does this mean that you must have all your scripts, directors, and stars in tow? Not necessarily, but you do need to have a framework. At the very least, for example, you want to know that you are going to produce X budgets and Y genres over a Z-year period. You must provide enough information to estimate revenues and give the investor a chance to agree or disagree with your forecast.

The Facts and Nothing But

Think of the Film(s) section of the business plan as a story you are telling, with factual material as the priority. Fantasies may play an important part in scriptwriting, but using wish lists in this document can present a problem. Confusing the issue by citing a cast that has never heard of the project or books you do not own may give investors the wrong idea. Whether you create a false impression by accident or on purpose, the result is the same. Investors negotiate contracts based on the information you provide. In the end, if all is not as you indicated, promises can be broken and money withdrawn.

FILMS

When describing your film projects, the objective is to present a descriptive overview of all the critical particulars without going into excessive detail. You should disclose each film's assets (components that may add commercial value to the project) as well as any nonmonetary values that are important to the types of films you want to make.

Show and Tell

The trick is to tell enough to engage readers, but not so much that you risk losing them. As we go through the different elements of this section, we'll attempt to draw a line between sufficient content and excessive wordiness. Readers who must wade through pages of information that is hard to follow will just go to sleep.

Writers of scripts, books, and other literary pieces have a tendency when writing nonfiction to create a stream of consciousness that is hard to follow. Fiction requires emotional and subjective content that will draw readers into the fictional world. Business writing—and nonfiction of any kind—requires simplicity and directness. Dr. Linda Seger, noted author of books on screenwriting, says:

> *Screenwriting is about being indirect; proposal writing is about being direct. While the object of good fiction writing is to be subtle, hide exposition, and present many ideas indirectly, good proposal writing insures that the audience is getting the information clearly and consciously.*

This is the reason why some genius invented the Appendix. In the business plan, it contains details that may be outside the formula of simple and direct information. As you proceed through the following sections, you will get a clearer picture of what this means. There are no official rules as to how much information you ought to include in the Film(s) section of your business plan. You can do anything you want, but bring your common sense into play, and always try to be alert to the reader's point of view.

Scripts

Disclose enough material about each script so that readers understand its value. A short synopsis is the usual format. In a page, you can tell the essentials of the story and indicate the genre of the film.

A student once questioned whether or not to include the title of his script. He feared that someone would steal it, because it was innovative and catchy. Whether or not to reveal the film's title must be your decision. More often, writers fear that someone will pirate their ideas rather than their titles.

The first step to take to protect yourself from possible theft of your story is to copyright your project. Most writers register their scripts with the Writers Guild of America. An even better procedure is to file for registration with the Library of Congress in Washington, DC. Once you have done this, you can prove that your story existed as of a particular date, and you can feel free to give it to others. Keep in mind that registration does not prevent theft; it just helps you prove ownership in the event of theft. Unfortunately, you cannot copyright ideas themselves. Michael Donaldson, in his book *Clearance and Copyright*, says:

> Copyright law only protects "expression of an idea that is fixed in a tangible form." This means that written words are protectable; the ideas behind them aren't. You can't copy something that is just an idea in the air.

You also cannot copyright titles. An exception may be if you are working with a well-known series that has been trademarked, such as the *Harry Potter* books. However, there are other reasons your title can change. Distributors often reserve the right to change it, particularly, if they feel it will be confused with another film. If you go through the Motion Picture Association of America (MPAA) process, you may come into conflict with having your title approved. Please don't email me that you have seen multiple films with the same title. The point is that you want to check the situation for your own film—another good reason for working with a film attorney.

Title: Boys Who Wreak Havoc

> Four teenage boys decide to take over a small Wisconsin town. They kidnap the minister's daughter as a bargaining tool in their effort to make one of their members the mayor. Their attempt to control the population unites the townspeople, who, although previously selfish in their individual pursuits, come together to take back their town. The girl is saved without bloodshed, and peace reigns.

This paragraph does not tell enough about the story to give the reader a true idea of everything that is in the film; it would be better placed in the Executive Summary section. Several sample plot synopses have been included on Focal's companion web site for this book. Be sure to read them.

Briefly, you want to include the entire storyline within one page and include the ending of the film. You are not trying to get investors to go to the film. If they have money involved, they will go anyway. They need to have enough information so that they do not misconstrue the type of film you plan to make. If the girl is raped or there is a nude scene, be sure to mention it. Failing to mention a scene that affects the nature of the film because you think potential investors might not like it is a sin of omission. If, for example, you let your investor assume that you were making a PG-13–rated film although you know that it will be R-rated, your money source can object and demand his money back.

What if you do not have specific scripts? State this up front. Even without scripts in hand, you can define your projects in terms of size and genres. You may be looking for development money to obtain scripts. Concentrate on what you know about your project. You must tell investors at least the size of the films that you plan to make. One way to describe this situation is as follows:

> *We are planning to make three films with family themes over the next five years, ranging in size from $1 million to $10 million. The initial $50,000 will allow the Company to develop scripts and to option stories from other writers. Production is expected to begin by the end of the first year after funding.*

This scenario is not as tempting to investors as the first one, but it is doable. For investors, providing money for development is always a greater risk than providing money for well-planned projects. The danger for the investor is that the producer may never find the right project and begin production. Or an agreement made with the source of production money may further dilute the initial investor's position. However, if you have some experience and a credible team, try for the development money. On the other hand, rather than writing a full business plan, you may choose to have an attorney write a proposal for development money. It will specify how much money the investors will be paid when production money is raised and what points they will receive in the eventual production.

Suppose you know neither the subject of your films nor the size of their budgets. In one plan, the company stated: "The producers plan to make low-budget features with the formula that has proved most profitable both in theatrical and video releases .... scripts in this area are plentiful." Seems a little vague, doesn't it? Aren't you curious to know what these proven formulas are?

Typically, the information in a proposal of this type is not enough. The right mix of ingredients is always a balancing act, but you probably would have to be a known filmmaker with an impressive track record to get away with this proposal. Even for an experienced moviemaker, this pitch would be hard to sell. Most people want to see specifics to which they can attach a value, either monetary or personal. Anyone with a modicum of business sense understands that handing out money to someone with no real plans except "to make a film" would appear to be foolish.

No doubt you can find an exception to this rule somewhere. Perhaps you've heard about an eager young filmmaker who, with his toothy smile and youthful enthusiasm, convinced a jaded deal-maker to hand over money. Nothing is impossible, but the odds are against this happening. This scenario sounds too much like a script and not enough like real life.

At this point, you may also want to address the question of the potential audience for your flick. It does not hurt to add a qualifying sentence to your plot synopsis—for example, "Films about Wisconsin, such as *Walter from Wisconsin* and *Cheeseheads Reign Supreme,* have been popular lately. We plan to capitalize on this phenomenon." On the other hand, you may be shooting the film in Wisconsin and raising your money there. In that case, add "Director Buffy Angel was born and raised in Milwaukee, where the film will be shot." However, save the discussion of the distribution and financial ramifications of your films for later sections of the plan. If your readers follow custom, they will have read the Financing section before this one anyway. It is easiest for readers to follow your plan if you group all of the project descriptions together and do not digress with long discussions on other subjects.

ATTACHMENTS AND THEIR VALUE

In this balancing act, any person, place, or thing that adds value to the script is important. You want to give your project every chance to see the light of day, so recount any attachment with a perceptible value. Here are five examples of attachments: (1) options, (2) books, (3) stars, (4) director, and (5) dollars. Notice that your favorable opinion is not one of the choices.

Options

An option is a written agreement giving the producer exclusive rights to a project over some specific length of time. If the option is exclusive, it ensures that no one else can make the project while the producer holds the option. Obviously, if you are the writer, it is your project. However, if you are representing other writers' scripts as part of your package, you must declare the ownership status. Representing films as your own when they are not is clearly a no-no.

Not only the script itself, but also the subject may need an option. If you are dealing with true stories of living people (or deceased persons whose estates own the representation of their likeness and life), you may need to seek permission to do the story. Getting the option, or "rights," after the fact can be a costly process.

You do not want to be in the position of having a deal on the table for a film and having to go back to obtain the rights to it. After the fact, the subject can and often will deny having given verbal permission. If you have not done your homework, it is the subject's right to stop the production, which sometimes leads to an expensive payoff or a court injunction.

Books

A published book adds value to a film in several ways. The sales history adds clout to your project, the specialized market it represents provides a ready-made audience, and the book usually furnishes additional ways to hype the film. Unless it is your book and copyright, the first step is—you guessed it—an option. The cost of the option depends, again, on the person you are dealing with and the relative fame of the book. It would be useless to even try to give you prices. As soon as the ink is dry in this book, the market will have changed. In truth, a book option, like a script option, can cost anywhere from nothing to millions of dollars.

An author (or the representatives of an estate) may have a subjective reason for you to make the book into a film and be very generous in making an agreement with you. On the other hand, if money is the primary focus, the author will drive as hard a bargain as possible. This area is one of the few in which your sparkling manner can have a concrete impact. On occasion, deals have been done because the author liked the filmmaker and wanted to see the project get made. Passion for the project counts for a lot in negotiating with authors. One way to be sure that you cannot use the book, however, is to refrain from seeking the rights to it.

Options can be obtained for a reasonable price if the timing and people involved are right. For example, two producers bought the rights for a paperback mystery novel plus the author's next two books for a few thousand dollars. No one else had approached the author, and the books were not the type to make the bestseller lists. Nevertheless, the author had a large audience among mystery fans. With no competitive bidders, the producers were able to make a good deal.

Another producer optioned several books of women's stories. The books had a large following, but the subject was still "soft" at major studios. She couldn't get the deals that she wanted and the films deserved. Once *The Hours, Far from Heaven, My Big Fat Greek Wedding*, and *Real Women Have Curves* were released in the same year to critical acclaim and/or significant boxoffice results, however, studios and independent companies were falling all over themselves to make similar deals. It's all in the timing. A change in the attitude of the trendmakers (studio executives, agents, and distributors) increased the value of the producer's optioned books immediately.

Being able to read manuscripts before they are published gives you an advantage over other filmmakers. Agents have access to unpublished manuscripts all the time. If you happen to know about a book that is about to be published by an unknown author and you can strike a deal prior to publication, it may work to your advantage financially.

Real-Life Stories

As documentaries and films based on true stories have become more popular and successful at the box office, it is important to understand that all the options talked about above apply. Many times over the years, people have approached me to write a business plan for a film about a famous athlete or someone else in the news. When I have asked if they have an option on the story, the reply often has been, "He told me to go ahead." Not good enough. You must get the agreement in writing. It is best to have an attorney draw up the agreement but have something written that is signed by both of you. The same goes for stories about nonhumans. If you want to make a film about the horse that wins the Kentucky Derby, talk to the people involved and get their agreement. How many people have to give their permission to be portrayed in the film is best discussed with an attorney.

Stars and Other Fantasy People

Attaching star actors, star directors, and famous producers is the fantasy of many independent filmmakers. Having Brad Pitt or Tom Hanks in your $500,000 film might be a recurrent dream of yours, but, unfortunately, their salaries include several more zeros. Nevertheless, you can have attachments that add value to your project, as long as they are real. No wish lists.

With lower budgets, "bankable" stars (the actors whose names ensure a certain level of boxoffice revenue when the film opens) are probably not an option, but you still can have a name that interests an investor. The value of the name is often in the eye of the beholder. Foreign buyers may put value on names that are only a moderate attraction on a U.S. movie marquee.

Directors who command high salaries will also be out of the reach of very low-budget filmmakers. Emphasize your director's previous experience, but do not fabricate it. With higher budgets (over $5 million), the inexperience of the director may become a hindrance and possibly dangerous. You want the director to be able to handle the film and, especially, the actors. In addition, experienced actors are often unwilling to work with an unseasoned director, and investors become more nervous about spending their money.

Because the producer has the major responsibility for keeping the budget on track, previous experience with feature films is important. In independent filmmaking, the producer is often the only connection between investors and their money. Once the cash has gone into the film's bank account, investors must depend on the producer to protect its use. Not only does the producer watch the money, but also she has to have enough clout with the director to stop him from going over budget. Always keep in mind that this process is a balancing act of all the different elements.

Money

"Well," you say, "of course, money adds value." It seems redundant but really is not. Clearly, hard cash for development and production has a straightforward relationship to your project, but what about any partial funds attached to your project? For some reason, newer producers do not think to mention them as part of their project's description, but they should. If any money at all is attached to your project, announce it here. If you have paid money for any option, it should be described in the details of the option. Keep in mind that it always impresses investors that you have put your own money into securing an option.

You will discuss it at greater length in the Financing section. Remember that all attachments are of value to the film and belong in this section. You want to depict any ingredients of this mix that will positively influence someone to make your film. In addition to hard cash, you should mention any co-production agreements, below-the-line deals, negative pickups, or presales. But make sure you have your deals in writing before putting them in the business plan.

BUDGET

For prospective investors to evaluate your films completely, they need to know the size of the budget. Again, we have two types of films: those with complete scripts and those that are just a gleam in the producer's eye. When real scripts exist, real budgets should exist as well.

To save money, many filmmakers pass a tuning fork over their script and say, "One million dollars." Do not just make up a figure. Anyone who contemplates financing your film will take this number seriously. So should you.

Many independent films have been delayed because the money ran out during either principal photography or postproduction. The investors have said, "You told me $800,000, so that is all you are getting." Studios often have reserves for a certain amount of budget overruns; equity investors do not. This admonition also goes for digital movies. Include enough money for transferring to 35mm. (More about digital in Chapter 4, "The Industry.")

Some filmmakers develop only the two top sheets of the budget—this is just one step ahead of the tuning-fork method—and figure out the complete cost later. However, you should calculate the total cost now to save explanations later. Estimating the cost of the general categories (cast, location, wardrobe, and so on) can be very dangerous, no matter how experienced you are. Break down the script. Production managers, line producers, and unit production managers (UPMs) often work freelance. Be sure to hire one that has experience with budgeting independent films, however. Calculate the entire amount, and be careful to have enough money. It is always better to keep your budget forecast a little high rather than cutting it too close to the bone.

In describing your film, you should simply state the size of the budget along with its attachments. A paragraph or two on the entire project will be sufficient. Consider the following example:

> *This film has a $2-million budget, based on filming in Cincinnati. Susie Starstruck and Norman Goodlooking are set to star in the film. Ms. Starstruck has been featured in* The Gangbusters *and* Return of the Moths. *Mr. Goodlooking has appeared in several movies of the week. Herman Tyrant, the director, has made two low-budget films (*Be My Love *and* Girls Don't Sing*) and has previous experience in commercials. The film has partial financing of $100,000 for development from an equity investor.*

In this paragraph, the writer has explained the essentials. Here we learn the size of the budget, the location (much of the cost in this example is predicated on the film being shot in a right-to-work state), and the experience of the lead actors and director. One investor already has an equity position, but all the sales markets are available. Note that the writer has saved any discussion on the implications of adding another equity investor for the negotiation. All relevant information belongs in the Investor Offering (see Chapter 9), which is always written by an attorney, not the filmmaker.

Do not worry about repetition; it is part of the building-block formula. You give an overview of the film. Then, in the Distribution and Financing sections, you go into greater detail about pertinent elements.

What if you do not have a full script or any actors and you have little or no experience? Do not lose heart. You can still explain what you are planning to do. Look at this example:

> *The ABC Company plans to make four films over the next five years. The first two films will be low budget ($250,000 and $1 million), and will deal with coming-of-age themes. Both films are in the treatment stage, and the director, Fearless Author, will write the screenplays. Mr. Author wrote and directed four short films, two of which have won awards at film festivals. Mr. Experienced Producer, whose films include* Growing Up? *and* Life Is a Flower, *has given us a letter of intent agreeing to serve as Executive Producer. The third and fourth films will be in the $3- to $5-million range. Mr. New Producer will produce these films after serving as Co-Producer on the first two. Neither treatments nor scripts exist for the third and fourth films. They will be in development during the first two years.*

Common sense will tell you that this package has less substance than the first one. It may be harder to find financing, but not impossible. If you find yourself in a similar situation, all you can do is try to create as many advantages for yourself as possible. The worst approach you can take is to say, "We are nobody with no plans. We plan to find no one experienced in anything, but we want your money anyway." It's true that no one is going to be this truthful, but on many proposals, it is not difficult to read these words between the lines. You have to learn to make realistic compromises to reach your goals. And above all, don't lie.

Too Much Can Be Harmful

One of the biggest nightmares that financial folks have is to receive a ten-pound business plan that includes every piece of paper in the producer's desk. Your goal is to have people read your proposal; therefore, you want to give them enough information without making the plan too heavy to lift. Suppose you have a complete budget for each of your projects. Do not put them anywhere in this business plan. An interested party will ask for them soon enough, and you can have the dubious thrill of explaining every last nickel. If you have a strong desire to show detail, you can put the top sheets of the budgets in your Appendix for perusal at the reader's convenience.

The same goes for the biographies of the stars, director, producer, and anyone else involved with your projects. A few paragraphs describing each principal's background is sufficient. The three-page bios do not need to be in the body of the plan. If you feel strongly that someone will have a burning need for this information, the Appendix is the place for it.

Don't make potential investors guess about the applicable credits by including newspaper reviews in your business plan. Summarize the essentials. If you are bursting at the seams with your wonderful reviews, you know where they go—the Appendix.

As far as I am concerned, photocopies of any kind should be forbidden by law from appearing in business plans. When you are trying to separate investors from their money, a well-typed, neat page counts; it shows that you care enough to give them the very best.

One finished plan given to me a few years ago weighed in at two pounds. Thrown in with the appropriate and readable text were nine pages detailing every industrial and commercial film that the director made. Later sections included photocopies of numerous charts and articles from various publications. The investor was presumably supposed to wade through all this paper and reach a conclusion. Not wise. By filling your plan with extraneous paper, you might appear to be covering up an absence of fact, or you might give the impression that you do not understand the proposal yourself. Personal impressions are intangible, but they count. Always keep in mind that the human beings who read your treatise will have human failings. Once they are distracted or annoyed, their attention may be lost, and your package may be tossed in the "forget it" pile. Some rules are made to be broken, but the one about brevity and clarity is not.

START SMALL AND THINK BIG

Since the first edition of this book, Business Strategies has worked with filmmakers with all kinds of experience, from none to 40 years. Trying to have a start-up company with more than one film is difficult. Often clients want to do films, distribution, videogames, and music—all at the same time. My advice is to start small and expand as the company becomes successful. If it is your first film (or all your previous experience is short films), make one film. Then put together a plan for a company with several films. Once the company is successful with a few films, add a distribution division if you feel the need. I recommend adding an experienced distribution executive rather than all the expenses of a division.

Harvey and Bob Weinstein of the Weinstein Company (who many clients want to emulate) started Miramax in the 1960s as a small domestic distributor of videos. They produced their first feature film in 1986. Many successful years later, the company became the proverbial "800-pound gorilla" in the indie world. (See Chapter 4 for more on the brothers and their emergence from the Disney fold as the Weinstein Company.) The point is that they started small and grew to multiple films per year and assorted ancillary divisions through making profits over time.

For a new company, you need to have focus. A business plan is great, with the operative word being "plan."

4

The Industry

The cinema is an invention without a future.

LOUIS LUMIÈRE

Moving images had existed before. Shadows created by holding various types of objects (puppets, hands, carved models) before a light were seen on screens all over the world. This type of entertainment, which most likely originated in Asia with puppets, was also popular in Europe and the United States. Then in 1877, photographer Eadweard Muybridge helped former California Governor Leland Stanford settle a bet by using a series of cameras to capture consecutive images of a racehorse in motion. Little did he know.

William Friese-Greene obtained the first patent on a moving image camera in England in 1889. Next came Thomas Alva Edison with his kinetograph, in 1890, and shortly thereafter, the motion picture industry was born. Edison is widely credited with inventing the first camera that would photograph moving images in the 1890s. Even he did not have a monopoly on moving pictures for long. Since Edison didn't take out any patents in Europe, the door was open for the Lumière brothers to create the cinematograph, another early form of moving image camera, in Paris in the 1890s. Little theaters sprang up as soon as the technology to project moving pictures appeared. In 1903, Edison exhibited the first narrative film, *The Great Train Robbery*. Seeing this film presumably inspired Carl Laemmle to open a nickelodeon, and thus the founder of Universal Studios became one of the first "independents" in the film business. Edison and the equipment manufacturers banded together to control the patents that existed for photographing, developing, and printing movies. Laemmle decided to ignore them and go into independent production. After several long trials, Laemmle won the first movie industry antitrust suit and formed Independent Moving Pictures Company of America. He was one of several trailblazers who formed start-up companies that would eventually become major studios. As is true in many industries, the radical upstarts who brought change eventually became the conservative guardians of the status quo.

Looking at history is essential for putting your own company in perspective. Each industry has its own periods of growth, stagnation, and change. As this cycling occurs, companies move in and out of the system. Not much has changed since the early 1900s. Major studios are still trying to call the shots for the film industry, and thousands of small producers and directors are constantly swimming against the tide.

IDENTIFYING YOUR INDUSTRY SEGMENT

Industry analysis is important for two reasons. First, it tests your knowledge of how the system functions and operates. Second, it reassures potential partners and associates that you understand the environment within which the company must function. As noted above, no company works in a vacuum. Each is part of a broader collection of companies, large and small, that make the same or similar products, or deliver the same or similar services. The independent filmmaker (you) and the multinational conglomerate (most studios) operate in the same general ballpark.

Film production is somewhat different when looked at from the varied viewpoints of craftspeople, accountants, and producers. All of these people are part of the film industry, but they represent different aspects of it. Likewise, the sales specifications and methods for companies such as Panavision, which makes cameras, and Kodak, which makes film stock, are different not only from each other, but also from the act of production. Clearly, you are not going to make a movie without cameras, film, or video, but these companies represent manufacturing concerns. Their business operations function in a dissimilar manner, therefore, from filmmaking itself. When writing the Industry section of your business plan, narrow your discussion of motion pictures to the process of production of a film and focus on the continuum from box office to the ancillary (secondary) markets. Within this framework, you must also differentiate among various types of movies. Making the $300-million *Lord of the Rings* trilogy is not the same as producing the $150,000 digital video *Once*. A film that requires extensive computer-generated special effects is different from one with a character-driven plot. Each has specific production, marketing, and distribution challenges, and they have to be handled in different ways. Once you characterize the industry as a whole, you will discuss the area that applies specifically to your product.

In your discussion of the motion picture industry, remember that nontheatrical distribution—that is, DVD, free television/cable, pay-per-view, the Internet, and domestic and foreign television—are part of the secondary revenue system for films. Each one is an industry in itself. However, they all affect your business plan in terms of their potential as a revenue source.

Suppose you plan to start a company that will supply movies specifically for cable or the DVD market. Or you plan to mix these products with producing theatrical films. You will need to create separate industry descriptions for each type of film. Television has a different industry model from the DVD industry, which in turn differs from online. This book focuses on theatrically distributed films and how the ancillary and foreign revenue sources make up the total. The business models for other revenue sources when there is no theatrical release are discussed in Chapter 6, "The Markets, Part II."

A LITTLE KNOWLEDGE CAN BE DANGEROUS

You can only guess what misinformation and false assumptions about the film industry the readers of your business plan will have. Just the words *film* and *marketing* evoke all sorts of images. Your prospective investors might be financial wizards who have made a ton of money in other businesses, but they will probably be uneducated in the finer workings of film production, distribution, and marketing. One of the biggest problems with new film investors, for example, is that they may expect you to have a contract signed by the star or a distribution agreement. They do not know that money may have to be in escrow to sign the star or that the distribution deal will probably be better once you have a finished film, or, at least, are well into production. Therefore, it is necessary to take investors by the hand and explain the film business to them.

You must always assume that the investors have no previous knowledge of this industry. Things are changing and moving all the time, so you must take the time to be sure that everyone involved has the same facts. It is essential that your narrative show how the industry as a whole works, where you fit into that picture, and how the segment of independent film operates. Even entrepreneurs with film backgrounds may need some help. People within the film business may know how one segment works, but not another. As noted in Chapter 3, "The Films," it can be tricky moving from working for a studio or large production company to being an independent filmmaker. The studio is a protected environment. The precise job of a studio producer is quite simple: Make the film. Other specialists within the studio system concentrate on the marketing, distribution, and overall financial strategies. Therefore, a producer working with a studio movie does not necessarily have to be concerned with the business of the industry as a whole. Likewise, if you are a filmmaker in another country, your local industry may function somewhat differently. Foreign entertainment and movie executives may also be naive about the ins and outs of the American film industry.

The history of Universal Studios shows an interesting changing of ownership among foreign conglomerates. In 1990, Japanese conglomerate Matsushita Electric Industrial Co. bought MCA Inc., the parent company of Universal Pictures. After five years of turmoil and disappointing results, they sold MCA/Universal to Canada's Seagram in 1994, which sold it to French communications/water company Vivendi in 2000. In 2003, Vivendi sold Universal Pictures to General Electric. Some foreign companies have hired consultants to do in-depth analyses of certain U.S. films in order to understand what box office and distribution mean in this country. As you go through this chapter, think about what your prospective investor wants to know. When you write the Industry section of your business plan, answer the following questions:

- How does the film industry work?
- What is the future of the industry?
- What role will my film play in the industry?

The rest of this chapter compares studio and independent motion picture production. It also provides some general facts about production and exhibition.

MOTION PICTURE PRODUCTION AND THE STUDIOS

Originally, there were the "Big Six" studio dynasties: Warner Brothers (part of Time Warner, Inc.), Twentieth Century Fox (now owned by Rupert Murdoch), Paramount (now owned by Viacom), Universal (now NBC Universal), Metro-Goldwyn-Mayer, and Columbia Pictures (now Sony Pictures Entertainment). After the Big Six came the Walt Disney Company. Together, these studios are referred to as "the Majors." (Note: A good source for the early days of Hollywood is *The Moguls: Hollywood's Merchants of Myth* by Norman Zierold.) MGM was taken private in 2005 by a consortium composed of Sony Corporation of America, Providence Equity Partners, Texas Pacific Group, Comcast Corporation, and DLJ Merchant Banking Partners investors. After a year, the contract to distribute only Sony films ended and MGM started functioning as an independent distributor with a recent return to funding films. In most cases, the Majors own their own production facilities and have a worldwide distribution organization. With a large corporate hierarchy making production decisions and a large amount of corporate debt to service, the studios aim most of their films at mass audiences. Although the individual power of each has changed over the years, these studios still set the standard for the larger films.

Until the introduction and development of television for mass consumption in the 1950s, these few studios were responsible for the largest segment of entertainment available to the public. The advent of another major medium changed the face of the industry and lessened the studios' grip on the entertainment market. At the same time, a series of Supreme Court decisions forced the studios to disengage from open ownership of movie theaters. The appearance of video in the 1970s changed the balance once again. Digitally recorded movies, which will be the next big paradigm shift, are discussed at the end of this chapter.

How It Works

Today's motion picture industry is a constantly changing and multifaceted business that consists of two principal activities: production and distribution. Production, described in this section, involves the developing, financing, and making of motion pictures. Any overview of this complex process necessarily involves simplification. The following is a brief explanation of how the industry works.

The classic "studio" picture would typically cost more than $10 million in 1993. Or, conversely, seldom could you independently finance above that figure, unless you were a well-known international filmmaker like Ron Howard or Martin Scorsese. Now there isn't a real threshold, as independent companies such as DreamWorks and Summit Entertainment are capable of financing movies in the multimillions thanks to hedge funds and foreign investments. Still, many high-budget films need the backup a studio can give them. Occasionally, the studio will take a chance on a lower-budget film (from their perspective, $10 million) that may not have a broad appeal. However, the studio can spread that risk over 15 to 20 films. Currently, they prefer the "tentpole" films of which the budgets for a single film, like *The Chronicles of Narnia: Prince Caspian*, may top $200 million.

The typical independent investor, on the other hand, has to sink or swim with just one film. It is certainly true that independently financed films made by experienced producers with budgets of more than $10 million are being bankrolled by production companies with consortiums of foreign investors, but for one entity to take that kind of risk on a single film is not the rule. For a studio to recoup the investment on even a $10-million film requires at least a $25-million box office to cover both the budget and distribution costs.

There are four typical steps in the production of a motion picture: development, preproduction, production, and postproduction. During development and preproduction, a writer may be engaged to write a screenplay or a screenplay may be acquired and rewritten. Certain creative personnel, including a director and various technical personnel, are hired, shooting schedules and locations are planned, and other steps necessary to prepare the motion picture for principal photography are completed. At a studio, a film usually begins in one of two ways. The first method starts with a concept (story idea) from a studio executive, a known writer, or a producer who makes the well-known "30-second pitch." The concept goes into development, and the producers hire scriptwriters. Many executives prefer to work this way. In the second method, a script or book is presented to the studio by an agent or an attorney for the producer and is put into development. The script is polished and the budget determined. The nature of the deal made depends, of course, on the attachments that came with the concept or script. Note that the inception of development does not guarantee production, because the studio has many projects on the lot at one time.

A project may be changed significantly or even canceled during development. The next step in the process is preproduction. If talent was not obtained during development, commitments are sought during preproduction. The process is usually more intensive because the project has probably been "greenlighted" (given funding to start production). The craftspeople (the "below-the-line" personnel) are hired, and contracts are finalized and signed. Because of many lawsuits over the past 20 years over "handshake deals" that seem to indicate otherwise, producers need to strive to have all their contracts in place before filming begins.

Production commences when principal photography begins and generally continues for a period of not more than three months, although major cast members may not be used for the entire period. Once a film has reached this stage, the studio is unlikely to shut down the production. Even if the picture goes over budget, the studio will usually find a way to complete it.

In postproduction, the film is edited, which involves transferring the original filmed material to a digital media in order to work easily with the images. Additionally, a score is mixed with dialogue, and sound effects are synchronized into the final picture, and, in some cases, special effects are added. The expenses associated with this four-step process for creating and finishing a film are referred to as its "negative costs." A master is then manufactured for duplication of release prints for theatrical distribution and exhibition, but expenses for prints and advertising for the film are categorized as "P&A" and are not part of the negative costs of the production. Although postproduction can last from 6 to 9 months, continuing technological developments have changed the timeframe for arriving at a master print of the film.

Tracking the Studio Dollar

Revenues are derived from the exhibition of the film throughout the world in theaters and through various ancillary outlets. Studios have their own in-house marketing and distribution arms for the worldwide licensing of their products. Because all of the expenses of a film—development, preproduction, production, postproduction, and distribution—are controlled by one corporate body, the accounting is extremely complex.

Much has been written about the pros and cons of nurturing a film through the studio system. From the standpoint of a profit participant, studio accounting is often a curious process. One producer has likened the process of studio filmmaking to taking a cab to work, letting it go, and having it come back at night with the meter still running. On the other hand, the studios make a big investment. They provide the money to make the film, and they naturally seek to maximize their return.

If your film is marketed and distributed by a studio, how much of each ticket sale can you expect to receive? Table 4.1 provides a general overview of what happens when a finished film is sent to an exhibitor. The table traces the $10.00 that a viewer pays to see a film. On average, half of that money stays with the theater owner, and half is returned to the distribution arm of the studio. It is possible for studios to get a better deal, but a 50 percent share is most common. The split is based on box office revenue only; the exhibitor keeps all the revenue from popcorn, candy, and soft drinks.

For all intents and purposes, the distribution division of a studio is treated like a separate company in terms of its handling of your film. You are charged a distribution fee, generally 40 to 60 percent (we're using a 50 percent average), for the division's efforts in marketing the film. Because the studio controls the

TABLE 4.1

Tracking the Studio Dollar

Your Ticket	$10.00
Exhibitor Share (50%)	$5.00
Studio Share (50%)	$5.00
Studio Share (50%—see above)	$5.00
Minus distribution fee (50% of $5.00)	$2.50
	$2.50
Minus overhead fee (12% of $5.00)	$0.60
Amount left to apply toward film negative (38% of $5.00)— does not include interest charges	$1.90

Note: This example is based on average results. An individual film may differ in actual percentages.

project, it decides the amount of this fee. In Table 4.1, the sample distribution fee shown is 50 percent of the studio's share of the ticket sale, or $2.50, leaving 50 percent of the box office revenues still in the revenue stream. Next comes the hardest number to estimate: the film's share of the studio's overhead. "Overhead" is all of the studio's fixed costs—that is, the money the studio spends that is not directly chargeable to a particular film. The salaries for management, secretaries, commissary employees, maintenance staff, accountants, and all other employees who service the entire company are included in overhead. A percentage system (usually based on revenues) is used to determine a particular film's share of overhead expenses.

It should be noted that the studios did not make up this system; it is standard business practice. At all companies, the non-revenue-producing departments are "costed" against the revenue-producing departments, determining the profit line of individual divisions. A department's revenue is taken as a percentage of the total company revenue. That percentage is used to determine how much of the total overhead cost the individual department needs to absorb.

In Table 4.1, a fixed percentage is used to determine the overhead fee. Note that it is a percentage of the total rentals that come back to the studio. Thus, the 12 percent fee is taken from the $5.00, rather than from the amount left after the distribution fee has been subtracted. In other words, when it is useful, the distribution division is a separate company to which you are paying money. Using that logic, you should be charged 12 percent of $3.00, but, alas, it doesn't work that way.

Now you are down to a return of $2.40, or 48 percent of the original $5.00, to help pay off the negative cost. During production, the studio treats the money spent on the negative cost as a loan and charges you bank rates for the money (prime rate plus one to three percentage points). That interest is added to the negative cost of your film, creating an additional amount above your negative cost to be paid before a positive net profit is reached. We have yet to touch on the idea of stars and directors receiving gross points, which is a percentage of the studio's gross dollar (e.g., the $5.00 studio share of the total box office dollar in Table 4.1). Even if the points are paid on "first dollar," the reference is only to studio share. If it has several gross point participants, it is not unusual for a box office hit to show a net loss for the bottom line.

Studio Pros and Cons

When deciding whether to be independent or to make a film within the studio system, the filmmaker has serious options to weigh. The studio provides an arena for healthy budgets and offers plenty of staff to use as a resource during the entire process, from development through postproduction. Unless an extreme budget overrun occurs, the producer and director do not have to worry about running out of funds. In addition, the amount of product being produced at the studio gives the executives tremendous clout with agents and stars. The studio has a mass distribution system that is capable of putting a film on more than 4,000 screens for the opening weekend if the budget and theme warrant it. *The Dark Knight*, for example, opened on 4,366 screens, and *X-Men Origins: Wolverine* opened on 4,099 screens. Finally, the producer or director of a studio film need not know anything about business beyond the budget of the film. All the other business activities are conducted by experienced personnel at the studio.

On the other hand, the studio has total control over the filmmaking process. Should studio executives choose to exercise this option, they can fire and hire anyone they wish. Once the project enters the studio system, the studio may hire additional writers and the original screenwriters may not even see their names listed under that category on the screen. The Writers Guild can arbitrate and award a "story by" credit to the original writer, but the screenwriting credit may remain with the later writers. Generally, the studio gets final cut privileges as well. No matter who you are or how you are attached to a project, once the film gets to the studio, you can be negotiated to a lower position or off the project altogether. The studio is the investor, and it calls the shots. If you are a new producer, the probability is high that studio executives will want their own producer on the project. Those who want to understand more about the studio system should watch fictional treatments of it, such as Christopher Guest's film *The Big Picture*, Robert Altman's *The Player, The Last Shot*, or the "Aquaman" segments in HBO's series *Entourage*. I also suggest reading some insightful books on the subject from true insiders, such as William Goldman's *Adventures in the Screen Trade* and sequel *Which Lie Did I Tell?: More Adventures in the Screen Trade*, Dawn Steel's *They Can Kill You but They Can't Eat You*, and Lynda Obst's *Hello, He Lied*. The studios are filled with major and minor executives in place between the corporate office and film production. There are executive vice-presidents, senior vice-presidents, and plain old vice-presidents. Your picture can be greenlit by one executive, then go into turnaround with her replacement. The process of getting decisions made is a hazardous journey, and the maxim "No one gets in trouble by saying no" proves to be true more often than not.

MOTION PICTURE PRODUCTION AND THE INDEPENDENTS

What do we actually mean by the term *independent*? Defining "independent film" depends on whether you want to include or exclude. Filmmakers often want to ascribe exclusionary creative definitions to the term. When you go into the market to raise money from investors (both domestic and foreign), however, being inclusive is much more useful. If you can tell potential investors that the North American box office for independent films in 2008 was $3.5 billion, they are more likely to want a piece of the action. The traditional definition of independent is a film that finds its production financing outside of the U.S. studios and that is free of studio creative control. The filmmaker obtains the negative cost from other sources. This is the definition of independent film used in this book, regardless of who the distributor is. Likewise, the Independent Film and Television Alliance (IFTA) defines an independent film as one made or distributed by "those companies and individuals apart from the major studios that assume the majority of the financial risk for a production and control its exploitation in the majority of the world." In the end, esoteric discussions don't really matter. We all have our own agendas. If you want to find financing for your film, however, I suggest embracing the broadest definition of the term.

When four Best Picture Oscar nominations went to independent films in 1997, reporters suddenly decided that the distributor was the defining element of a film. Not so. A realignment of companies that began in 1993 has caused the structure of the industry to change over and over as audiences and technology have continually evolved. A surge in relatively "mega" profits from low-budget films encouraged the establishment of "independent" divisions at the studios. By acquiring or creating these divisions, the studios handled more films made by producers using financing from other sources. Disney, for example, purchased Miramax Films, maintaining it as an autonomous division. New Line Cinema (and its then specialty division, Fine Line Pictures) and Castle Rock (director Rob Reiner's company) became part of Turner Broadcasting along with Turner Pictures, which in turn was absorbed by Warner Bros. Universal and Polygram (80 percent owned by Philips N.V.) formed Gramercy Pictures, which was so successful that Polygram Filmed Entertainment (PFE) bought back Universal's share in 1995, only to be bought itself by Seagram-owned Universal. Eventually, Seagram sold October Films (one of the original indies), Gramercy Pictures, and remaining PFE assets to Barry Diller's new USA Networks, and those three names disappeared into history. Sony Pictures acquired Orion Classics, the only profitable segment of the original Orion Pictures, to form Sony Classics. Twentieth Century Fox formed Fox Searchlight. Metromedia, which owned Orion, bought the Samuel Goldwyn Company, and eventually was itself bought by MGM. Not to be left out of the specialty film biz, Paramount launched Paramount Classics in 1998 (reorganized as part of Paramount Vantage in 2006), and in 2003 Warner Bros. formed a specialty film division, Warner Independent Pictures.

In 2003, Good Machine, a longtime producer and distributor of independent films, became part of Universal as Focus Features. The company's partners split between going to Universal and staying independent as Good Machine International. Focus operated autonomously from Universal and was given a budget for production and development of movies by its parent company. Universal, in turn, used Focus as a source of revenue and to find new talent. In 2008, Focus was absorbed into the studio, and its executives took on studio titles. By the definition used in this book, then, the films produced by Focus are no longer considered independent, although the films that they acquire still are.

What is the payoff for all this recombining? Four Best Picture Oscar nominations went to independent films from 2003 through 2008, continuing the industry's demonstration of love for these pictures.

Then there is DreamWorks SKG. Formed in 1994 by Steven Spielberg, David Geffen, and Jeffrey Katzenberg, the company was variously called a studio, an independent, and—my personal favorite—an independent studio. In the last quarter of 2005, Paramount bought the DreamWorks live-action titles and their 60-title library plus worldwide rights to distribute the films from DreamWorks Animation (spun off as a separate company in 2004) for between $1.5 and $1.6 billion. Paramount then sold the library to third-party equity investors, retaining a minority interest and the right to buy it back at a future date. Spielberg could greenlight a film budgeted up to $90 million, which caused Business Strategies to count films solely financed by DreamWorks as independent. In October 2008, DreamWorks sought a divorce from Paramount, and is once again a standalone production company starting life anew with $550 million from investment partner Reliance Big Entertainment of India and a proposed additional $700 million from JP Morgan by December 2008. However, the subsequent economic downturn in 2008–2009 created problems in finalizing the total initial investment deals, but we have no doubt that DreamWorks will survive.

In-house specialty divisions provided their parent companies with many advantages. As part of an integrated company, specialty divisions have been able to give the studios the skill to acquire and distribute a different kind of film, while the studio is able to provide greater ancillary opportunities for the appropriate low- to moderate-budget films through their built-in distribution networks. Specialty labels have proven themselves assets in more literal ways as well. At one point, Time Warner planned to sell New Line for $1 billion (Turner paid $600 million for the company in 1993) to reduce the parent company's debt load. New Line's founder Robert Shaye and the other principals had always made their own production decisions, even as part of Turner Pictures. In the summer of 1997, New Line secured a nonrecourse (i.e., parent company is not held responsible) $400-million loan through a consortium of foreign banks to provide self-sufficient production financing for New Line Cinema. Making their own films meant that New Line kept much more of their revenue than they would have if they had been a division of Warner Bros. Everyone liked this situation until the release of *The Lord of the Rings: Fellowship of the Ring*, the first film of the trilogy, earned $1.1 billion worldwide, and all three films went on to earn $3.5 billion. In 2007, New Line was taken in-house and made merely a studio label by Warner Bros., which also swallowed up Bob Berney's Picturehouse and Warner Independent Pictures. Former New Line Cinema chiefs Robert Shaye and Michael Lynne formed Unique Features, a new independent company that plans to produce two to three titles a year. Paramount changed Paramount Vantage from a specialty division to merely a brand name. And Relativity Media bought genre division Rogue Pictures from Universal Pictures for $150 million. Looking at the label as not just a movie brand, Relativity partnered with the Hard Rock Hotel and Casino in Las Vegas to launch a clothing line that targets 15- to 25-year-olds with hoodies, T-shirts, and hats that will be featured in Rogue's films and a social networking site, *www. RogueLife.com*, to promote the label's films and products. The hotel also will rename its music venue the Rogue Joint and use it to host film premieres and screenings. As this edition is going to press, the only studio specialty divisions operating independently are Sony Classics and Working Title Films and, perhaps, Fox Searchlight.

If films remain independently funded, the prime definition of being an "independent" has been met, no matter which studio distributor's logo is tacked onto it. It is up to you, the reader, to track what has happened in the meantime.

How It Works

An independent film goes through the same production process as a studio film from development to postproduction. In this case, however, development and preproduction may involve only one or two people, and the entrepreneur, whether producer or director, maintains control over the final product. For the purposes of this discussion, we will assume that the entrepreneur at the helm of an independent film is the producer.

The independent producer is the manager of a small business enterprise. She must have business acumen for dealing with the investors, the money, and all the contracts involved during and after filming. The producer is totally responsible from inception to sale of the film; she must have enough savvy and charisma to win the confidence of the director, talent, agents, attorneys, distributors, and anyone else involved in the film's business dealings. There are a myriad of details the producer must concentrate on every day. Funding sources require regular financial reports, and production problems crop up on a daily basis, even with the best laid plans. Traditionally, the fortunes of independent filmmakers have cycled up and down from year to year. For the past few years, they have been consistently up. In the late 1980s, with the success of such films as *Dirty Dancing* (made for under $5 million, it earned more than $100 million worldwide) and *Look Who's Talking* (made for less than $10 million, it earned more than $200 million), the studios tried to distribute small films. With minimum releasing budgets of $5 million, however, they didn't have the experience or patience to let a small film find its market. Studios eventually lost interest in producing small films, and individual filmmakers and small independent companies took back their territory.

In the early 1990s, *The Crying Game* and *Four Weddings and a Funeral* began a new era for independent filmmakers and distributors. Many companies started with the success of a single film and its sequels. Carolco built its reputation with the *Rambo* films, and New Line achieved prominence and clout with the *Nightmare on Elm Street* series. Other companies have been built on the partnership of a single director and a producer, or of a group of production executives, who consistently create high-quality, money-making films. For example, Harvey and Bob Weinstein negotiated a divorce from the Walt Disney Company in 2005 and created the Weinstein Company, raising $490-million equity in only a few months.

Then there are the smaller independent producers, from the individual making a first film to small- or medium-size companies that produce multiple films each year. The smaller production companies usually raise money for one film at a time, although they may have many projects in different phases of development. Many independent companies are owned or controlled by the creative person, such as a writer-director or writer-producer, in combination with a financial partner or group. These independents usually make low-budget pictures in the $50,000 to $5-million range. *Facing the Giants* and *Once*—made for $100,000 and $150,000, respectively—are at the lower end of the range, often called "no-budget." When a film rises above the clouds, a small company is suddenly catapulted to star status. In 1999, *The Blair Witch Project* made Artisan Entertainment a distribution force to contend with, and in 2002, *My Big Fat Greek Wedding* was a hit for IFC Films (now owned by Rainbow Media) and gave Gold Circle Films higher status as a domestic independent producer and distributor. In 2008, Summit Entertainment, which heretofore had been a foreign sales company, earned more than $400 million with its first production, *Twilight*, making the company a major independent player.

Tracking the Independent Dollar

Before trying to look at the independent film industry as a separate segment, it is helpful to have a general view of how the money flows. This information is probably the single most important factor that you will need to describe to potential investors. Wherever you insert this information in your plan, make sure that investors understand the basic flow of dollars from the revenue sources to the producer.

Table 4.2 is a simplified example of where the money comes from and where it goes. The figures given are for a fictional film and do not reflect the results of any specific film. In this discussion, the distributor is at the top of the "producer food chain," as all revenues come back to the distribution company first. The distributor's expenses ("P&A," or prints and ads) and fees (percentage of all revenue plus miscellaneous fees) come before the "total revenue to producer/investor" line, which is the "net profit."

The boxoffice receipts for independent films are divided into exhibitor and distributor shares, just as they are for studio films (see Table 4.1). Here, the average split between distributor and exhibitor is 50/50. This is an average figure for the total, although on a weekly basis the split may differ. Generally, independent companies do

TABLE 4.2

Tracking the Independent Dollar (in millions)

REVENGE OF THE CRAZED CONSULTANT*	
Domestic Box Office Gross	10.0
Exhibitor Share of Box Office (50%)	5.0
Distributor Share of Box Office (50%)	5.0
REVENUE	
Domestic	
Theatrical Rentals (50% of total box office)	5.0
Home Video**	12.0
Television, Cable, and Other Domestic Ancillary	4.1
	21.1
Foreign	9.0
TOTAL DISTRIBUTOR GROSS REVENUE	30.1
LESS	
Budget	3.0
Prints and Advertising (P&A)	5.5
TOTAL COSTS	8.5
GROSS INCOME	21.6
Less Distributor's Fees (35% of Gross Revenue)	10.5
NET PRODUCER/INVESTOR INCOME BEFORE TAXES	11.1

*This is a fictional film.
**DVD, Blu-ray.

not have the same clout as the studios, and the exhibitor retains a greater portion of the receipts. In the example in Table 4.2, of the $10 million in total U.S. box office, the distributor receives $5 million in rentals. This $5 million from the U.S. theatrical rentals represents only a portion of the total revenues flowing back to the distributor. Other revenues are added to this sum as they flow in (generally over a period of two years), including domestic ancillaries (home video, television, etc.) and foreign (theatrical and ancillary). As you may already know, in 2007 the production of VHS tapes ended, although there was still minimal revenue from sales of tapes in 2008. Blu-ray was just beginning to make inroads when the economic collapse temporarily halted its progress.

Film production costs and distribution fees are paid out as money flows in. From the first revenues, the prints and ads (known as the "first money out") are paid off. In this example, it is assumed that the P&A cost is covered by the distributor. Then, generally, the negative cost of the film is paid back to the investor. In recent years, filmmakers have paid back from 110 to 120 percent of the budget to investors as an incentive. The distributor takes 35 percent or less of the worldwide revenue (35 percent is used in forecasting when no distribution deal exists) as his fee, and the producer and the investor divide the remaining money.

Pros and Cons

Independent filmmaking offers many advantages. The filmmaker has total control of the script and filming. It is usually the director's film to make and edit. Some filmmakers want to both direct and produce their movies; this can be like working two 36-hour shifts within one 24-hour period. It is probably advisable to have a director who directs and a separate producer who produces, as this provides a system of checks and balances during production that approximates many of the pluses of the studio system. Nevertheless, the filmmaker is able to make these decisions for himself. And if he wants to distribute as well, preserving his cut and using his marketing plan, that is another option—not necessarily a good one, as distribution is a specialty in itself, but still an option.

The disadvantages in independent filmmaking are the corollary opposites of the studio advantages. Because there is no cast of characters to fall back on for advice, the producer must have experience or must find someone who does. Either you will be the producer and run your production, or you will have to hire a producer. Before you hire anyone, you should understand how movies are made and how the financing works. Whether risking $50,000 or $50 million, an investor wants to feel that your company is capable of safeguarding his money. Someone must have the knowledge and the authority to make a final decision. Even if the money comes out of the producer's or the director's own pocket, it is essential to have the required technical and business knowledge before starting.

Money is hard to find. Budgets must be calculated as precisely as possible in the beginning, because independent investors may not have the same deep pockets as the studios. Even if you find your own Bill Pohlad (River Road Entertainment) or Jeff Skoll (Participant Productions) with significant dollars to invest, that person expects you to know the cost of the film. The breakdown of the script determines the budget. When you present a budget to an investor, you promise that this is a reasonable estimate of what it will cost to make what is on the page, and that you will stay within that budget. The investor agrees only on the specified amount of money. The producer has an obligation to the investor to make sure that the movie does not run over the budget.

PRODUCTION AND EXHIBITION FACTS AND FIGURES

The North American box office reached $9.8 billion in revenues in 2008, according to the Motion Picture Association of America (MPAA). Worldwide sales for independent films in 2008 were more than $8 billion. Included in this number is a North American box office for indies of $3.5 billion (as calculated by Business Strategies) and more than $2 billion in U.S. ancillary revenues. Aggregate international sales (i.e., countries outside of the United States, Canada, and Puerto Rico) for independent films are calculated by IFTA through a statistical survey of its members. While U.S. theatrical distribution is still the first choice for any feature-length film, international markets are gaining even greater strength than they had before.

Separating the gross dollars into studio and independent shares is another matter. While databases often include films distributed by specialty divisions of the studios as studio films, being acquired does not change the independent status of the film. In order to estimate the total for independent films, you have to add those from all the independent distributors plus films that have been acquired by the majors. As there is no database for "independent films acquired by studios," a precise figure is not possible.

Theatrical Exhibition

At the end of 2008, there were 40,194 theater screens (including drive-in screens) in the United States. This represents an increase of 7.5 percent screens in 2000 and an increase of 64 percent since 1991. A downturn in screens from 2001 through 2004 is attributed to the closing of rundown, out-of-date theaters that were competing with larger, state-of-the-art structures. Despite many ups and downs, such as the advent of the multichannel cable universe and the growth of the home video market, theatrical distribution has continued to prosper.

Film revenues from all other sources are driven by theatrical distribution. For pictures that skip the theatrical circuit and go directly into foreign markets, video, television, or another medium, revenues are not likely to be as high as those for films with a history of U.S. boxoffice revenues and promotion. The U.S. theatrical release of a film usually ends between three and six months. The average for both studio and independent films before going into DVD is four and a half months. While studio films begin with a "wide" opening on thousands of screens, independent films start more slowly and build. The rentals will decline toward the end of an independent film's run, but they may very well increase during the first few months. It is not unusual for a smaller film to gain theaters as it becomes more popular.

Despite some common opinions from distributors, the exhibitor's basic desire is to see people sitting in the theater seats. There has been a lot of discussion about the strong-arm tactics that the major studios supposedly use to keep screens reserved for their use. (This is sometimes referred to as *block booking*.) Exhibitors, however, have always maintained that they will show any film that they think their customers will pay to see. Depending on the location of the individual theater or the chain, local pressures or activities may play a part in the distributor's decision. Not all pictures are appropriate for all theaters. Recent events have shown that independent films with good "buzz" (prerelease notices by reviewers, festival acclaim, and good public relations) and favorable word-of-mouth from audiences will not only survive but also flourish. *The Visitor* is a good example. It started out in a small number of theaters and cities. As audiences liked the film and told their friends about it, the movie was given wider release in chain theaters in more cities. Of course, good publicity gimmicks help. People still ask me if 1999's *The Blair Witch Project* is a real story; I have even been accused of lying when I say that it is utterly fictional, a "mockumentary" no more real than *This Is Spinal Tap* or *Borat: Cultural Learnings of America for Make Benefit Glorious Nation of Kazakhstan*!

Future Trends

As this edition is being written in the second quarter of 2009, the United States is in a deep recession, as is much of the rest of the world, that began in 2008. It was generally caused by reckless financial practices among investment companies and banks. The former were major investors in film companies, both independent and studio, from 2006 through 2008. Although that investment source disappeared, the industry held onto the fact that film is traditionally recession resistant.

The New York Times, in an article titled "Suddenly, Hollywood Seems Like a Conservative Investment," said, "When it comes to Hollywood financing, the sky doesn't fall so much as it just changes color." In tracking the history of cash needs in the film business, the article noted that in the 1980s, the industry found individual investors through brokerage firms. In the 1990s, it was German tax credits. In the 2000s, money came from giant hedge funds. As the credit crunch has widened, however, the film industry in general, and the independent market in particular, has seemed a relatively safer place for individuals to keep their money than real estate, stock brokerages, and even banks. This doesn't mean that film is any less of a risk than it has always been; however, it isn't viewed as worse than any of the other choices.

In addition, history shows that when bad times hit, people go to the movies. They are an escape and a way to work out one's angst. Some moviegoers enjoy screaming and have their hearts race for the same reason they like horror and thriller films. It is a safe way to deal with their fear. Other moviegoers want to laugh and forget. Whether or not the current economy affects the types of movies made is doubtful. During the Great Depression and World War II, many of the popular films were about current events. From this vantage point, it may be unlikely that films about people being kicked out of their homes will score well. However, wars, nefarious political characters, and corporate espionage always have been fodder for filmmakers.

Overall, the exhibition business is doing well. Despite predictions of doom, from January through May 3, 2009, the North American box office was $3.2 billion, up 16.4 percent over the same period in 2008, according to *www.mediabynumbers.com*, and admissions were up 13.7 percent. The price of tickets was up approximately 2 percent. At this point, analysts are not fond of making future predictions. However, many feel it is reasonable to assume that 2009 will see the box office continue in its upward trend.

As you may be reading this book several years hence, be aware that the film industry is shifting at a greater rate than it ever did in past decades. Many different and competing analyses and projections appear in the news media. Despite fears that the audience will leave the theaters and stay at home, most experts believe that theatrical exhibition will always be the vehicle that drives the popularity of products played in homes and in other outlets. People have always enjoyed an evening out and are expected to continue to do so. Even though you can watch a movie on your personal computer or send that signal to your home television, theatrical exhibition is not likely to disappear during our lifetime and continues to flourish.

Digital Film

The film industry has been on the brink of a major technological revolution with digital filmmaking and screens. Convergence, however, is not another word for simplicity. The revolution is still waiting to take off, as it was in all previous editions of this book. There were 324 digital screens in the United States at the end of 2005, up from just 85 in 2004, according to *Screen Digest*. Worldwide, there were 849, up from 335 in 2004. By the end of 2008, however, the number had increased to 5,474. The count of digital screens outside of the United States in 2008 was 3,140 for a total of 8,614.

On June 5, 2000, Twentieth Century Fox became the first company to transmit a movie over the Internet from a Hollywood studio to a theater across the country. Well, to be more exact, it originated in Burbank, California, and went over a secure Internet-based network to an audience at the Supercomm trade show in Atlanta. (Trivia buffs, take note: The film was the animated space opera *Titan A.E.*)

As we roll rapidly through the ninth year of the 21st century, filmmakers keep calling me about the $30,000 digital film they are going to make that will look like a $10-million film and be distributed on 3,000 screens. Probably not likely on both counts. What is missing in those expectations? First, the filmmaker's expertise to put the production quality on the screen. That aside, there is not yet a significant business for low-budget digital films.

What is missing in the digital film business? The short answer is an agreement on the equipment. How much progress has been made since those convention goers saw *Titan A.E.*? Some movies have been digitally projected into select theaters. George Lucas put a digital *Star Wars: Episode I—The Phantom Menace* in five theaters. Disney's *Dinosaur* was also shown digitally. However, while at this point it is important, digital film is not yet a business. A report by SRI Consulting in 1998 stated that movies encoded as digital data files "either recorded on optical disc and physically shipped or broadcast via satellite will increasingly replace film prints as the preferred method for distributing movies to theaters by 2005." Of course, we know how shaky such predictions can be.

The conversion costs to "d-cinema" screens are considerable. The cost for each digital projector is $150,000, along with the more than $20,000 per screen required for the computer that stores and feeds the movies. Although 5,400 seems like a big number, it is only 13.5 percent of the total screens in the United States. In 2008, loans appeared available to bring the total of installed digital screens to 20,000. Then came the credit crunch. That money may be postponed but will eventually be worked out. In addition, there is a lack of standards between digital integrator companies (e.g., Cinedigm and Digital Cinema Implementation Partners) and disagreement about who is going to pay the costs. An ongoing hassle is over "virtual print fees" that money studios and large production companies would pay to theaters owners in order to buy the projectors, servers, and other equipment needed. Exhibitors argue that they shouldn't bear the full financial burden of converting conventional screens to digital. Recently, individual deals have been made, but there is not an industry-wide agreement.

For most independent filmmakers, it still will be a long haul. Despite the reported number of screens and the number of digital films sent to film festivals, we have yet to find a successful independent film that was distributed in digital format alone. Include money in your budget to upgrade your digital film to

35mm. Don't assume that the distributor wants to do it. Look at it from his viewpoint. If the distributor is planning on releasing 10 to 20 films a year, at $55,000 or more per film for a quality upgrade, he is likely to opt for a film that is already in 35mm format. "But," you say, "my film will be so exceptional, he will offer to put up the money." It is within the realm of possibility, but I wouldn't want the distribution of my film to rest on that contingency. Or you may say, "I'll wait until the distributor wants the film, and then I'll raise the money for the upgrade." Although this is not out of the question, don't just assume you will be able to raise the money. Those pesky investors again. Whether it is one investor or several in an offering, you have to go back to those people for the additional $50,000. Will they go for it? Maybe yes, maybe no. If they don't, then you may be stuck. If you raise the money from additional sources, you still have to get the agreement of the original investors. After all, you are changing the amount of money they will receive from your blockbuster film.

Then there is the question of quality. When technology experts from the studios are on festival or market panels, they always point out that audiences don't care how you make the film; they care how it looks. In a conversation shortly before the 2009 National Association of Broadcasters in Las Vegas, a Kodak rep told me that experienced filmmakers still prefer to shoot on 35mm, edit digitally, and then return the movie to 35mm for the final print. If you can really make your ultra-low-budget digital film have the look of a $5-million or $10-million film, go for it. But be honest with yourself.

3-D

This section would reasonably be titled "Everything old is new again." Readers over 60 will remember this technology's first incarnations in 1952 to 1954 with films like *House of Wax* (the first with stereoscopic sound) and *It Came from Outer Space*. It faded in the late 1950s but had a revival in the early 1980s when the large-format IMAX screens offered their early docs in three dimensional (3-D). Studios and other production companies discovered 3-D in the past four or five years as the "new format" that will revolutionize the film industry. As the industry has been through this before, we'll have to wait and see; however, here is the current state of the 3-D business.

Thanks to improvements in the technology, filmmakers believe that they can deliver a better product. Theater owners, once they get over initial costs, can charge more per ticket. DreamWorks Animation SKG says that it is releasing all its new films in 3-D. The company's comedy *Monsters vs. Aliens*, currently in distribution as this edition goes to press, earned $59.3 million in its opening weekend and has grossed over $340 million to date worldwide with an estimated budget of $175 million. On a more moderate budget of $20 million, Lionsgate released *My Bloody Valentine 3-D*, which has earned $71 million worldwide to date. One motivating factor is the belief that teens and twenty-somethings are staying home to play video games, and 3-D will bring them back to the theater. At the moment, much of the forward movement has been stalled for the same reason as the rest of the digital screens—the credit crunch. Digital projection systems are required for 3-D screenings. Currently, only about 2,000 of 40,000 screens in North America are 3-D ready. Since moviegoers have the same money problems, there also is the question of how many will be willing to pay an extra $2 to $5 for a 3-D film. Then another question recently became public: Who is going to pay for the glasses? Neither the distributors nor the exhibitors are prepared to take on the expense. The glasses cost 75 cents each; however, overall we are talking about millions of dollars.

WHAT DO YOU TELL INVESTORS?

All business plans should include a general explanation of the industry and how it works. No matter what your budget, investors need to know how both the studio and the independent sectors work. Your business plan should also assure investors that this is a healthy industry. You will find conflicting opinions; it is your choice what information to use. Whatever you tell the investor, be able to back it up with facts. As long as your rationale makes sense, your investor will feel secure that you know what you are talking about. That doesn't mean he will write the check but at least he will trust you.

Tables and Graphs

A picture may be worth a thousand words, but 20 pictures are not necessarily worth 20,000 words. The introduction of user-friendly computer software has brought a new look to business plans.

Unfortunately, many people have gone picture-crazy. They include tables and graphs where words might be better. Graphs made up about three-fourths of one company's business plan that I saw. The graphs were very well done and to a certain extent did tell a story. The proposal, put together by an experienced consultant, was gorgeous and impressive—for what it was. But what was it? Imagine watching a silent film without the subtitles. You know what action is taking place, and you even have some vague idea of the story, but you don't know exactly who the characters are, what the plot is, or whether the ending is a happy one. Similarly, including a lot of graphs for the sake of making your proposal "look nice" has a point of diminishing returns.

There are certainly benefits to using tables and graphs, but there are no absolute rules about their use. One key rule for writing screenplays, however, does apply. Ask yourself what relation your tables and graphs have to what investors need to know. For example, you could include a graph that shows the history of admissions per capita in the United States since 1950, but this might raise a red flag. Readers might suspect that you are trying to hide a lack of relevant research. You would only be fooling yourself. Investors looking for useful information will notice that it isn't there. You will raise another red flag if you include multiple tables and graphs that are not accompanied by explanations. Graphic representations are not supposed to be self-explanatory; they are used to make the explanation more easily understood. There are two possible results: (1) the reader will be confused, or (2) the reader will think that you are confused. You might well be asked to explain your data. Won't that be exciting?

5

The Markets

But the Devil whoops, as he whooped of old: It's clever but is it art?

RUDYARD KIPLING

You can view the 6.8 billion people in the world as potential moviegoers, but very few filmmakers have expected to sell tickets to all of them—that is, until *Jurassic Park* pushed the box office frontier farther than ever before in 1993. It earned more than $750 million worldwide. You didn't need to speak English or know anything about biology to enjoy this film. It had something for everyone who was old enough to watch it. Then, in 1998, *Titanic* racked up $1.7 billion worldwide. The three films of *The Lord of the Rings* trilogy, released between 2001 and 2003, all of which were financed independently, earned more than $3 billion worldwide.

What does this mean to you, the smaller independent? While studios are concentrating on very high budgets, there is no longer a ceiling for independents. This emphasis leaves a much larger part of the theatrical ballpark for the independent filmmaker making low- to medium-budget movies. And the home runs being hit in the past ten years have opened the game to many more players. In the mid-1990s, Steven Spielberg told *Premiere* magazine, "It's getting to the point where only two kinds of movies are being made—the tent-pole summer or Christmas movies or the sequels, and the audacious little...films. It's like there's an upper class, a poverty class, and no middle class." More of the film middle class has now arrived.

In previous editions of this book, I wrote about the financing of independent films by foreign companies and consortiums of investors and the growth in their numbers. With the change in the economic climate, many U.S. hedge and foreign country funds have failed; they will return, but we don't know when. In the short term, money is moving out of real estate and stocks into films. Many of these money sources may look for stars with a capital "A" as in "A-list." Realistically, though, your potential of having Tom Hanks star in your film is low. In fact, if you are a neophyte, it is probably a suicidal thought.

Whether your film's budget is $400,000 or $40 million and whether it has newbie actors or stars, you need to research the market for your film. The market comprises all those people who are going to buy tickets. In this chapter, we will be looking at the potential popularity of the themes and styles your films represent. To some extent, we also will look at marketing, but do not confuse these two concepts. Marketing involves selling your idea not only to the investor, but also to the distributor and audience. In this chapter, we will focus on selling to the investor through the business plan, but we will also touch on current forms of self-marketing; the distributor is dealt with in Chapter 7. To make terms somewhat more confusing, this book also refers to "the markets," such as the American Film Market and Cannes, the two largest international marketplaces where production and distribution deals are closed.

In the previous section of your business plan, the Industry section, you defined the industry as a whole and independent film as a segment of it. Now, in the Market section, you will build on that definition by further dividing your industry segment. Your segment may not be as global in size as "everyone," but it has its own value. You will also take the projects that you described in the earlier Film(s) section and use their components to pinpoint your market. This analysis gives you a base for later estimating those very important gross revenues.

MARKET SEGMENT

Your market segment, or niche, consists of the type of person out of the total movie going population who is likely to rush out to see your film the first weekend, as well as secondary target groups that will be interested. You need to identify, for yourself and those reading your proposal, the size and population characteristics of this segment. By devising a snapshot of your film's likely audience, you will be able to determine the film's ability, first, to survive and, second, to succeed. Who are the end users of your film—that is, the ticket buyers—and how many of them are there likely to be? Before you worry about marketing strategies and distribution channels, create a picture of the potential size of your market's population. How can you do this? Very carefully. But do not worry. It is easier than you think; it just takes work. You do not need to have inside information or to live in Los Angeles to do this. Research is your tool.

Having divided the industry into studio and independent, you now need to divide your segment into smaller pieces. In looking at this piece of the market, ask yourself these questions:

- How large a population segment is likely to see my film?
- What size budget is reasonable vis-à-vis the size of this segment?

Defining Your Segment

Filmmakers would like to appeal to everyone, and some mainstream films reach that goal. It is said that it is the big-budget tentpole films (a big-budget film that can "prop up" a studio's finances) that create the highest box office grosses. This is true to a certain extent; the more money you spend, the bigger the audience you will attract— and the bigger the audience you will *need* to attract. An independent film, for the most part, will attract moviegoers from one or two identifiable segments of the audience. To understand how to focus your investor's expectations (and your own), you will have to do a little research. You do not have to be a research expert, but investigation will help make you and your investor wiser and wealthier.

The profile of your target market in terms of audience might include the following:

- Popular film genres into which your film would fit— comedy, action, thriller, horror, drama, romance, etc.
- Underlying themes
- Affinity groups—ethnic, urban, religious, sports
- Age and sex groups
- Similar budget parameters

To Pigeonhole or Not to Pigeonhole

Your identification of the target audience for your film begins when you select the genre of the film. The term *genre* can be very confusing. Some people appear to use the term to refer to cheap and formulaic, as in "it is a genre film." One client of mine was upset that I was cheapening her films by using the term *genre*. For the business plans I write, it is used to refer to films that can be grouped together by plot, settings, and/or themes. Genre doesn't refer to how well you made the film or the amount of the budget. You could probably use the word *category*, but it doesn't have the same feel.

As a genre, horror films, for example, are generally movies that scare you for some reason and have lots of blood and gore. In the Internet Movie Database (*www.imdb.com*), there are almost 6,000 theatrical horror films listed in this decade alone, ranging from the no-budget *Open Water* to the higher-budgeted *One Missed Call*. These films have different premises (sci-fi creatures, blood and gore, childhood nightmares) and appeal to different audience segments. The over-40 group was more likely to be drawn to *The Sixth Sense* than anything with the word "bloodsucking" in the title, and therefore was the initial target audience for that film. *Saw* was definitely a grabber for the 12- to 24-year-olds, with the repeat attendance that is a hallmark of this audience segment resulting in the film's high box office. In the end, though, all of them are still horror films.

Genres can be big or small. Drama is considered the most pervasive genre but is inclusive of many films. The next most popular genre by number of films produced is usually comedy. Both of these genres include films that often carry descriptive adjectives, such as *family*, *romantic*, or *dark*, to further narrow the category. Then we have thriller and action/adventure, which are unique genres. Defining the genre of a particular film doesn't have to be difficult. In trying to be precise when describing a movie, the filmmaker may call it a drama/comedy/romance. This description covers all the bases. It fits *Rachel Getting Married*, which skewed to an older audience, and *The Sisterhood of the Traveling Pants 2*, which skewed younger.

There are also filmmakers who are linked with specific genres, and who have become their own genre. Saying a movie will be a Quentin Tarantino film, a Judd Aaptow film, a John Waters film, or a Michael Moore film creates a frame of reference for the particular experience moviegoers will have. You can even have a producer genre. For example, a Joel Silver film would immediately be envisioned as another *Die Hard, Matrix,* or *Lethal Weapon.* This does not mean that his films will not fit into other genres, such as comedy. However, if a filmmaker is so identified with a particular type of experience, the audience will pick the film based on that track record rather than anything else. If you feel that your style is akin to a particular director's niche, you can draw from that audience.

Why bother identifying the genre for your film? Many writers and directors believe that categorizing their films is not only meaningless, but also, in some cases, demeaning. There are always filmmakers who say, "My picture is different and can't be compared to any other films." This entrepreneurial attitude is the same in all industries. Nonetheless, all films can be compared, and you do have competition. By giving your investors these frames of reference, you are able to identify the groups of moviegoers to whom the film might appeal and explain the genesis of your projections. One of the challenges you face with your business plan is being understood. You must be certain that you convey your meaning correctly to investors. It is important, therefore, that you define your terms so that everyone is on the same page.

Art versus Specialty

For 22 years, I have participated in discussions on whether independent films are by definition *art films,* and, if they are, what an art film is. In one such discussion, one person claimed that Federico Fellini and art films were one and the same. Someone else said that they "explain human foibles in an intellectual way." Another suggested that the term had nothing to do with a film's subject. Various people still insist to me that *The Blair Witch Project* was a commercial film and, therefore, by definition, not art or specialty. The terms are not mutually exclusive.

In recent years, production and distribution companies have preferred the term *specialty* for their films rather than *art-house,* and with good reason. *Art* may bring to mind a very narrow image of a type of film. Many would assume the film to be an inaccessible film only for the intellectually intense. *Specialty,* on the other hand, is a broader term without these negative connotations. Until you define it, there may be no frame of reference for the investor. Creating a definitive description that everyone agrees with would be impossible. In writing your business plan, you have to find whatever phrases and film references best convey your meaning.

I have been involved with proposals for companies that the client intended to be like the Weinstein Company (a lot of people seem to think they are the Weinstein brothers), Lionsgate, or Sony Classics. What did we start with? We used those companies to define the genre. For example, you could write the following as your introduction:

> *We define the specialty market by the types of films acquired by Lionsgate Releasing and Sony Pictures Classics. Our films have a sensitivity of story and a delicate balance of characters that require unique handling. Therefore, our audience will be the same people who saw* Gods and Monsters, Monster's Ball, *and* Real Women Have Curves.

These pictures may have nothing in common in story or overall theme, but they are used to present a backdrop for the discussion; they give readers something to relate to. Of course, Lionsgate and Sony Classics do not have a lock on specialty films. Which companies you use for comparison depends on your feeling about their products and your reasons for making it.

An important aspect of specialty films is their distribution (and, consequently, revenue) potential. In recent years, the scope of specialty films has widened tremendously. Typically, a specialty film may open on 1 to 15 screens and expand to more screens as revenues become available. On the other hand, if the distributor has enough money and faith, a small independent film can play on many screens. *Little Miss Sunshine* opened on 7 screens domestically and played on 1,602 at its widest distribution. *Juno* opened on 7 screens, and due to its extraordinary success, was on 2,534 screens at its widest point of distribution.

Genre History

When describing the history of the Western genre, for example, you do not need to go back to Hopalong Cassidy or Gene Autry (ask your grandmother). For the most part, your primary reference period should be the past five to six years. Some genres, such as action/adventure or comedy, are always going strong. They are always popular in one form or another. This is not the case with other genres, however.

Take horror again, for example. This genre, once popular, languished in the ultra-low-budget, direct-to-video, and direct-to-foreign world until the release of *Scream* in 1996. (Note: The first DVD wasn't released until 1997, and the format didn't outstrip VHS releases until 2003.) Until *Scream*, the general wisdom was that horror films were not worth putting any money into; therefore, it was hard to get the investment community interested in the genre.

Timing is everything. Now production money is available everywhere, not only for the traditional scary film (*Hostel 1* and *2*, *Saw 1* through *5*, *Halloween*), but also for variations on the theme, such as the *Scary Movie* franchise (comedy/horror) and *The Blair Witch Project* (mockumentary). Suppose you wanted to make a horror film before any of the above films were released. How would you convince someone that your film would be successful? There are several techniques you could use:

1. *Emphasize other elements: The Haunting in Connecticut* is a paranormal/thriller/horror about a family who relocates for their son's health and begins to experience supernatural behavior in their new home, which turns out to be a former mortuary.
2. *Redefine the genre: Twilight* is a teenage Romeo and Juliet vampire story. Moving to a small town to live with her father, Bella meets the mysterious and beautiful Edward. The two fall unconditionally in love with each other. Even learning that he is a vampire does not deter her passion. How will they resolve this unnatural relationship?
3. *Override the horror genre altogether: The Sixth Sense* is a chilling mystery in which a child psychologist treats a disturbed young boy who thinks he sees ghosts. The film has a twist at the end that will bring interest from the potential audience in the same way as the "secret" in *The Crying Game*.
4. *Use the cycle theory: The Blair Witch Project* is a mockumentary/horror film. While neither of these genres has been financially successful in recent years, we believe that the filmmakers' fresh and original touches, such as the audience's uncertainty about whether the story is true or not, will create favorable word-of-mouth for the film and bring back these genres.

More about Cycles

The argument used in the last technique is not a spurious one. The popularity of a particular genre often rises and falls in cycles. For example, continuing our examination of horror films, this genre made up 24 percent of the product at the 1989 American Film Market, fell to less than 3 percent of the total in 1993 (interestingly, the genre fell out of favor in the book industry at the same time), and rose back to 6.3 percent by 2003. Statistics like these, by the way, can be part of your extended discussion.

A successful film often inspires a number of similar films that try to capitalize on the popularity of the original. *Film noir* is a term coined by French movie critics to describe American crime dramas in the 1940s. After a brief reappearance of the genre in 1962 with the original *Cape Fear*, the genre's real resurgence began in the 1990s with Martin Scorsese's *Cape Fear* remake in 1991 followed by, among others, *The Usual Suspects* in 1994. It encouraged a proliferation of updated film noirs (the darkly lit look of the 1940s films contributed to the term), such as *Fargo, Lost Highway, Devil in a Blue Dress, The Underneath, Exotica, L.A. Confidential* (which won two 1997 Oscars, for Best Supporting Actress and Adapted Screenplay, and was nominated for six more, including Best Picture), *The General's Daughter, The Bone Collector, Sin City, Street Kings,* and *The Dark Knight*. These films broadened the boundaries of the genre beyond the detective thriller to represent a way of looking at the world through a dark mirror reflecting the shadowy underside of life. (Note that, being purists about the term *film noir,* the Internet Movie Database lists all the post-1950 films in this category as "neo-noir.")

Considering the length of time from development to release, the market may be glutted with a particular type of film for two or three years. When this happens, the audience may reach a saturation point and simply stop going to see films of that genre for a while. Then someone comes along with a well-crafted film that makes money, and the cycle begins again.

Who Is Going to See This Film?

Do you know the age and sex of the person most likely to see your film? Market research properly belongs in the hands of the person doing the actual marketing (probably the distributor), but you can estimate the appeal of your potential market based on its age groups. For example, one animated film may be aimed primarily at children aged 12 and under. Another animated film, with a slightly more hip theme and a pop music soundtrack, may entertain children but also draw in teenagers and young adults. DreamWork's hits *Shrek* and *Shrek 2* were geared for the very young to the very old, while Tokuma's *Princess Mononoke* skewed to a teenage and older audience due to its content.

Teen films are targeted toward an affluent and sizable group. Think *Superbad, High School Musical 1* through *3*, and *How She Move*. Teenage movies are traditionally released at the beginning of the summer, when schools are out and kids have a lot of time to go to the theater. And they often go to the same movie more than once.

Studios are particularly eager to make films for the teen and young adult market—usually defined as people between the ages of 12 and 24. No longer the single largest audience block, they made up 28 percent of moviegoers in 2007, according to the MPAA's "U.S. Economic Review 2007," while filmgoers 40 and over made up 45 percent of the audience. The crossover group of the audiences (ages 25–29) made up 27 percent. These admissions measurements change from year to year; therefore, you will want to check the MPAA's web site (*www.mpaa.org*) for current information. Unfortunately, the National Association of Theater Owners (NATO), which collects these data for the MPAA, does not count anyone under 12; therefore, the previous percentages add to 100. Since family films, and especially animation, often have the largest audiences, such data would be very helpful in explaining that segment to investors. In its place, I use the revenues from comparative films.

Special Niche Groups

Certain groups of films initially appeal to a small segment of the population and then grow, often to the surprise of the filmmakers, to become crossover films. *Y tu mamá también* is an example of a film in Spanish that initially was targeted to an older, Hispanic/Latino audience and attracted a significant number of teenage Anglo filmgoers. The high cost structures of the studios inhibit their ability to exploit smaller, underdeveloped markets, but independent filmmakers have the ability to take chances. They can make a low-budget or even a "no-budget" film to play to a tiny initial market. If the film and its theme catch on, the audience grows, and the film crosses over to a larger portion of the public, introducing that genre to a new group. Subsequent films of that type then draw on the larger audience. When the first edition of this book was published, it appeared to be big news that African-American filmmakers could draw a wide audience. Throughout the rest of the 1990s, gay and lesbian films came to the fore, capped by the Oscar wins of 2005's *Brokeback Mountain* and *Capote*. At this vantage point in 2009, let's look at how some of the other target markets have developed.

Until 2000, the Walt Disney Company seemed to have a lock on family films. It was almost impossible for independents to break into that category. Now Hollywood seems to have discovered that not R-rated films but G- and PG-rated films are its next best thing. The industry makes its biggest profits from G- and PG-rated movies, according to many analysts' reports, and plans to fill the nation's screens in the next few years with even more princesses, monsters, talking animals, bright school kids, and scrappy ballplayers. The independent film *My Dog Skip* was part of the family film renaissance in 2000. This was followed by Dimension's *Spy Kids*, a breakout hit with a U.S. box office of $113 million that inspired a sequel and a flock of imitators. Feeding the burgeoning family film market through 2009 were such films as *Spy Kids 3*, *Akeelah and the Bee*, *Are We Done Yet?*, and *Monsters vs. Aliens*. John Fithian, President of NATO, said, "Family values are OK. Family values sell tickets."

What originally I categorized as "faith-based" films, I now identify as "inspirational" films. One of the popular film genres of the 21st century, inspirational films cover elements of good versus evil, redemption, and the eternal questions of who we are and why we are here. In the past few years, films such as *The Passion of the Christ*, *The Pianist*, the *Tyler Perry* films, *What the Bleep Do We Know?*, and even *March of the Penguins* have alerted production companies and distributors that there is a major market for inspirational films.

Now that this larger genre has been defined, faith-based films fit into it nicely as a subset, including the many films that are likely to appeal to the large Christian audience. For example, *Facing the Giants*, *End of the Spear*, *Fireproof*, and *Woman Thou Art Loosed* specifically espouse Christian values, even though they may contain some questionable elements. The tagline for *Facing the Giants*—"Never give up. Never back down. Never lose faith."—is a good example. With 150 million people of all ages going to church every week, the popularity of Christian-themed films is an important shift in movie entertainment. The extraordinary success of *The Passion of the Christ* and the more moderate successes of the other films identified above demonstrate the box office and retail clout of an audience previously ignored by mainstream filmmakers and marketers. What once was a video business supplied mostly by Christian booksellers has now become a part of the theatrical film experience. However, as Ted Baehr points out in his book *The Media-Wise Family*, in making a "good news" film, you still have to make a film with good entertainment value. Research indicates that the same percentage of Christian teenagers as non-Christian teenagers watch R-rated films, with the same frequency. There is no reason why you can't make a film that reaches a large segment of this audience. My admonition to my faith-inspired filmmaker clients is to make a film that has a subtle message and doesn't announce an agenda. Samuel Goldwyn has often been quoted as saying, "If you want to send a message, call Western Union" (ask your mother).

Inspirational films appeal both to people who are philosophically curious or generally spiritual in addition to people who adhere to specific religious and spiritual groups. As the filmmakers of the popular film *What the Bleep Do We Know?* stated on their web site, "There are a great number of mystical traditions and spiritual practices, many paths that lead people to wholeness and peace of mind." With this type of film, you may be describing different groupings of target audiences. For example, for one such film, I included yoga groups and "cultural creatives" in the target market. Or you may have a film that shows someone overcoming great odds that will inspire a few filmgoers to change their lives. Interestingly, *March of the Penguins* has been declared an inspirational documentary due to the great odds that the Emperor penguin has to overcome just to survive.

While some people prefer the term *Latino* and some prefer *Hispanic* (for example, a Latino client has suggested that I use the word *Hispanic* to describe the Hispanic/Latino market), films that appeal to this audience have been considered a "new market" for the past six years. Estimates are that there are 41 million U.S. Hispanics who are more frequent moviegoers than either Anglos or African Americans, going to movies an average of 12 times a year. Despite buying about 15 percent of all movie tickets, Hispanics are a relatively untapped group in terms of film marketing. A study by Global Insight predicts that, by 2012, Hispanics will account for about 18 percent of ticket purchases (equivalent to about $2.9 billion in sales) due to fast population growth. These moviegoers are concentrated in the trend-setting major markets that make or break Hollywood releases.

The success of Latin American imports is bringing more attention and investment to U.S. filmmakers who want to make films with Hispanic/Latino themes, but, at this point, it is still hard for these films to go beyond very limited distribution. Jack Foley, President of Distribution at Focus Features, told *The New York Times*, "The Latino market in the U.S. is not changing. Latinos most enjoy English-language Hollywood entertainment. They want escapism and entertainment, exactly as the majority of American moviegoers demand." Films like his company's Spanish-language feature *The Motorcycle Diaries* and Fox Searchlight's *La misma luna* (released in the United States as *Under the Same Moon*), as well as Lionsgate's *Amores Perros* and IFC's *Y tu mamá también*, worked in the limited independent specialty market and did well overall financially. Films from U.S. filmmakers, such as *Frida*, *Real Women Have Curves*, and *Tortilla Soup*, also have helped awaken what has been termed the "sleeping giant" of the Hispanic market. However, both the imports and the U.S.-made films have failed to attract the broad, multi-ethnic, Spanish-speaking population in the United States. Still, they have the attention of the power brokers—investors and distributors. That is what counts.

Production Cost

When writing a business plan, you need to find as many ways to support your argument as possible. A valid comparison for films concerns the amount of the production (negative) cost. In some cases, the cost is additional confirmation for your assertions; in other instances, it may be your only argument. There are as many configurations of a film's budget as there are producers. No two situations are ever alike. So we will review the most common cases and let you extrapolate from there.

Case 1: Similar films, similar budgets

Your films should be able to make equivalent or better revenues as films that share a genre or theme with yours and cost about what you're budgeting for your film. When preparing your proposal, the first step is to read every interview with the filmmakers that you can find. You will usually be able to find information on how they made their pictures work—creating a production budget, finding a distributor, and getting by on a low budget. The market is more open for a small film to be successful than it has ever been. The potential for having a breakout film increases with the release of each successful film.

Case 2: Similar films, higher budgets

If your film has a story or theme similar to that of others but will be made with a significantly higher budget, you can point out that better attachments are likely to help bring in more revenue. If you have a well-known director who will draw some attention, be sure to mention that it is another Arthur Artiste picture. For a film with a budget of up to $1 or $2 million, both the director and the stars can be unknown; the film will rely totally on its story and quality. For a larger film, story and quality will still matter, but name value will mean even more.

Case 3: Different films, moderate budgets

There may be a ceiling on the ability of niche films to grab the market. One strategy in this case is to start with moderate budgets that have mainstream potential. For this example, we will assume that you will start with a $5-million movie and move up to a much broader market. Always keep your genre in mind in addition to all the factors mentioned in Case 2.

There are many variations to putting together your comparative films and your explanations of the markets for your film. The point is that you should build on what exists. No matter what your niche market—and it may be a specialized one that has not really been explored yet—the same principles apply. Take the experience of similar films and use it to your advantage.

Even with these three cases, a discussion of the success of similarly budgeted films is in order. For example, I created a business plan for producers of a $7-million gay/lesbian romantic comedy a few years ago. Since there were no gay/lesbian films made within the $3- to $14-million budget range to use for comparison, I created tables of other romantic and comedy films.

Detailed tables showing the actual results of other films with similar budgets belong in the Financing section of your plan. Here, however, you can use the summary information to build a story. Gather comparative market information to prove the size and extent of the audience for your film.

What if you do not know the budgets of the films you are going to make? Your case will be much weaker, but you can still develop a rationale. Showing the results of films with various budgets will help. The other elements of your company, as described in Chapter 3, "The Films," can bring more credence to your proposal. If you have well-known directors or actors committed to your projects, you can use their previous films to describe a segment of the market.

What if you have someone else's budget for a $2-million film? Don't use it. Your film will have characteristics that don't match that budget and needs a knowledgeable person, such as your friendly production manager, line producer, or unit production manager (UPM), to create its budget. Make sure you are right before going to investors. At the end of the day, you have to work within this budget.

DOCUMENTARIES

In the last edition, documentaries were included in Chapter 6 with the "nontraditional" films. There are two types of documentaries: theatrical feature films and televison/cable movies. Theatricals belong in this chapter on markets along with the other feature films as they have proven to be a lasting niche in the independent film market.

Documentary films have entered the mainstream. The *Hollywood Reporter* recently commented that audiences are currently obsessed with documentaries. Throughout the 1990s and into the 21st century, documentary films grew in prominence and popularity on the theatrical screen. At the same time, films centered on political and social activism topics have grown in popularity with audiences. Part of the reason is the quality and diversity of the films. Documentaries ranging from the highly political *Fahrenheit 9/11* to the "artistic crime" (as *www.imdb.com* has characterized it) *Man on Wire* and the musical *Shine a Light* are among nonfiction films that have earned substantial sums at the box office. Audiences eager to see intellectually stimulating, well-crafted fare are being drawn to theaters showing documentaries, resulting in attendance figures that have increased the value of these films in the video/ DVD, cable, and foreign markets. In addition, a substantial portion of the television audience for documentaries—estimated by Nielsen Media Research at 85 percent of U.S. television households—appears unwilling to wait 6 to 12 months for a documentary to get to their home screens. Analysts also suggest that reality television has helped documentary films build their growing theatrical audience.

Markets

The target markets for documentaries are the same as those for fiction films, save one group. Documentary audiences themselves are the first target audience to list. There are enough films with high public awareness to give as examples. Then there is the substantial television audience for documentaries, as described above. In fact, that paragraph is my current description of the documentary audience as a target.

The rest of the market section is the same as that for fiction films. Every documentary has a subject, be it political, economic, inspirational, historic, sports related, etc. These market segments often can be quantified or at least described. Fiction films with the same genres or themes can be used as examples in the market section as well, although they can't be used as comparatives for forecasting.

Synopses

In Chapter 3, "The Films," I made a big point of telling the investor how the story ends. With documentaries, the filmmaker often doesn't know how the story ends. Often you are recording actual events. If it is an election, you won't know the results of the election when you approach investors. On the other hand, if in 2008 you traced what happened during the Florida recount in the 2000 presidential election, you and the investors will know the results.

Another example is raising money to look at health issues through a specific study. You may know what you wish the results to be; however, you won't know until after the study is over. The synopsis will include a description of why you are making the film, what the study will include, and what you hope the results will be. An example for the last lines of the synopsis might be:

> *The entire process will be captured on film. This visual record of the transformations that occur as a result of these basic The results of this experiment in* _____ *may directly and indirectly affect the over 100 million people living with supposedly incurable* _____.

Many documentaries are based on a large number of interviews. If you have already conducted some of the interviews, then list those people with their credentials. If you haven't already conducted the interviews, be careful how you mention people. I treat the contemplated list of interviews the same way that I treat listing stars in a film. You may want to talk to Queen Elizabeth in your film. Unless you have already gotten an affirmative response from her (or her social secretary), I wouldn't include her in the list. The interviewees give credibility to your potential film for the investor. Whether equity or grant money, it is not a good idea to get funded by making promises you can't keep.

Forecasting Has Some Differences

Until 2002, I didn't write any business plans for documentaries. The reason is simple: There weren't enough theatrical docs that had earned significant revenues worth talking about. The success of *Roger and Me* in 1989 began the reemergence of the nonfiction film as a credible theatrical release. After a few successful films in the intervening years, 1994's *Hoop Dreams* attracted a lot of attention by reaching U.S. box office receipts of $7.8 million on a budget of $800,000. The same year, *Crumb* reached a total of $3 million on a budget of $300,000. In 1997, a Best Documentary Oscar nominee, *Buena Vista Social Club*, made for $1.5 million and grossing $6.9 million, scored at the box office and with a best-selling soundtrack album.

Michael Moore's 2002 *Bowling for Columbine* raised the bar for documentaries by winning the Oscar for Best Feature Documentary and the Special 55th Anniversary Award at Cannes, and by earning $114.5 million worldwide. The same year, *Dogtown and the Z-Boys*, *The Kid Stays in the Picture*, *I'm Trying to Break Your Heart*, and *Standing in the Shadows of Motown* all made a splash at the box office. The success of these releases was not anything like *Columbine*, which had a political and social message, but was noticeable nevertheless.

In 2003, *Spellbound* seemed to confound the forecasters by drawing a significant audience, as did *Step into Liquid*, *The Fog of War*, and *My Architect*. The following year, 2004, Michael Moore surprisingly—and convincingly—bettered his own record with *Fahrenheit 9/11*, which was made for $6 million and earned more than $300 million worldwide. Distributors found more documentaries that they liked: *Riding Giants*, *The Corporation*, *Touching the Void*, and the little doc that could, *Super Size Me* (made for almost nothing and earning $35.2 million at the box office). In 2005, there was the popular *Mad Hot Ballroom*, *Enron: The Smartest Guys in Town*, and *Why We Fight*.

In 2006, the most successful was *An Inconvenient Truth* (made for a reported $1.5 million and earning $75.3 million worldwide), which won the Oscar for Best Documentary for director/cinematographer David Guggenheim and Best Original Song (Melissa Etheridge). Featuring a fledging actor, former Vice President Al Gore, undoubtedly added to the film's popularity. There also was Dave Chappelle's *Block Party*, which earned $11.5 million, plus a number of films that broke $1 million at the North American box office.

In 2007, the critics said that documentaries were "dead" as Michael Moore's *Sicko* was the most significant. Made for $9 million, it earned a respectable $53 million worldwide. For you and me (and our investors) that would be considered a success. Since his earlier films had gone so far over the top, however, the naysayers acted like Moore had failed. With all documentary filmmakers, however, the main ambition is to get the word out. Hopefully, the second one is to at least pay back their investors.

Some of these documentaries have worldwide distribution but many don't. A bigger problem is that we don't know the budgets for many. Reason number 1 given by many documentary filmmakers is that they have made the film over a long period of time and don't know the actual budget. It is true that many are made with a combination of cash from grantors and in-kind contributions, so it may be hard to know the real number. Or, reason number 2, they choose not to tell us. Therein lies the first problem of writing a business plan around a documentary film. However, it is far more doable now due to the number of films that have been released. There are other factors that make documentaries different from fiction films. First and foremost, there are fewer of them. Also significant is how widely their subject matters vary—comparing two documentaries to each other can still be a case of comparing apples and oranges. The method for forecasting differs slightly for these reasons. How it works is discussed in Chapter 10, "The Financial Plan."

Television Documentaries

Television documentaries are features and miniseries made specifically for television or cable network stations without the intention of showing them on movie screens. In June 2009, the Internet Movie Database listed more than 23,000 television documentary features and miniseries. Generally, they are financed directly by the broadcast/cable networks, although they may be acquired from private production companies under a variety of different deals.

Documentaries are not a staple of broadcast television, which relies on larger audiences than documentaries typically attract. PBS does finance some documentaries, normally at budgets less than $500,000. For them, it is the project that is important. While it is true that in recent years PBS has sent these films to film festivals and even put some into theatrical distribution, the PBS station responsible for funding a particular documentary normally controls all the rights and revenues. In addition, it is still a modest part of their yearly budget, so the funds available are limited.

A large number of cable and premium channels also finance documentaries, and they occasionally buy completed films. In a sense, however, this is the same as getting a license fee from the broadcast networks. The budgets can range from below $100,000 to $2 million, depending on the cabler. In addition, there was a large surge in the early years of the decade in digital channels across Europe, which has made the demand for docs of all genres greater. Currently, there is a greater focus on local films in most countries, which may hamper filmmakers from one country selling their documentary to local media in another country. Selling to any television, cable, or Internet outlet may bring very little payment. Covering the cost of making the documentary is often the best case.

Both theatrical and nontheatrical documentaries are financed by not-for-profit grants and other funding. Although some of the information that you would use in this book's business plan format would be useful in a grant application, you cannot write one business plan to send to all grantors. Each of these organizations has limited resources and specific subjects that it will fund. Of course, many will not fund films. You have to do your own research to find an organization whose goals match your subject. There are numerous books about raising grant money. For filmmakers, though, I always recommend Morrie Warshawski's books (see Chapter 9).

Often documentaries, or even fiction films, are made with a combination of equity funding and grant money. In that case, you will have to both have a "standard" business plan for the equity investors and make a separate grant application. However, there is no database to use in order to forecast the results of documentaries intended for nontheatrical release only.

MARKETING STRATEGY

Marketing strategy is usually defined as the techniques used to make the end user aware of a product. In film, you have more than one potential end user, more than one person who might queue up to the box office to buy a ticket. There is also an intermediate end user: the money person. The ticket buyer will not read your business plan. Instead, your marketing is aimed at those who might provide the financing to make those ticket purchases possible. First, we'll look at your own strategies for getting the film made. Then we'll look at some of the marketing tactics that distributors and producers may use for the film.

Experts often talk about the four Ps of marketing: product, price, place, and promotion. We have already touched on the first three in this section. In the Markets section of your business plan, you don't want to forget promotion. However, do not confuse what you will do and what the distributor will do.

Market Research

As cognizant as investors or distributors might be about the emergence of a particular market, they may not know its true scope. One step in promoting your projects is to obtain as much market research data as possible to bolster your contentions. Whether you are raising money for one film or a group of them, gathering data on the feasibility of your concept is important. Part of that information is contained in your description of the market segment. However, you can go a step farther and get real facts and figures. There are many formal and informal ways to gather information. Many of them are right in your own backyard. You can gain a lot of knowledge with a minimum of time and effort if you know how. Granted, some of these tricks of the trade are easier the closer you are to Hollywood or New York, but with the proliferation of events to which "Hollywoodites" travel and the proliferation of resources on the Internet, being from another city is not a good excuse for failing to do adequate research. Your task may be a little harder, but you can still accomplish it.

Reading—A Lost Art

The most difficult idea to get across to many filmmakers is that they need to become voracious readers. Many creative folks are too busy doing their own thing to take time out to read. Even seasoned professionals say, "But I don't have time." This is a big mistake. There is a lot of information available to you if you will take the time and trouble to find it.

The truth is that you cannot afford not to have time. The trade papers, primarily the *Hollywood Reporter* (*www.hollywoodreporter .com*), *Daily Variety* (*www.variety.com*), and the UK publication *Screen International* (*www.screendaily.com*), are the primary sources of information for people in the film business. Those who are serious about having a business or even participating in the industry will do themselves a favor by reading either the Web or print issue of at least one of the publications. The argument, "I can't afford it," has been taken away. *Variety* is now free on the Web, and the other two publications have a large amount of their sites free to the reader. Even if you log on and just read the first paragraph of stories, you will have enhanced your knowledge of the industry. In addition to reading one of the U.S. publications, I highly recommend *www .screendaily.com*. Even though there are some articles that require a subscription, there is still a large amount of free information. The web site's home page also has a section called "The Web Today," which has links to articles on web sites in the United Kingdom, United States, and other countries.

The trades have the news articles that tell you who is doing what with whom and how much it is going to cost. If you follow these sources carefully, you can pull out enough data to fill in the minimum financial information for any package. Nestled among the press releases and gossip are facts on the production costs of films and descriptions of how the producers found their financing. In addition, the trades also publish lists of films in production, preproduction, and development. From the production columns, you can learn what genres of films are being made and with what types of casts. Some of the preproduction material is real and some is fantasy, but it gives you a fair idea of what people want to produce. You can list your films in the development columns free of charge. Many filmmakers have gotten contacts with production companies and distributors that way. Placing announcements also gives private investors a chance to hear about you. Many people with the ability to finance films choose to remain incognito; otherwise, they would be deluged with unwanted phone calls or scripts. Some do read the trades, however, and it gives them the opportunity to contact producers whose stories interest them. Admittedly, this may be a long shot, but it does not cost you anything, and it gets your name out there. And if you see anything that looks just like your film, don't worry. You will make a better film! One interesting quirk about Hollywood, and this is probably true of other places as well, is that people have more respect for names they recognize than for those that are unfamiliar. They will not necessarily remember where they saw or heard your name, but familiarity results in returned phone calls. Therefore, any opportunity to get your name in print is helpful.

Another benefit of reading the trades is that you learn who the movers and shakers are. Take the case of Robert Rodriguez, writer/director of the reportedly $7,000 miracle film, *El Mariachi*. He did not know any agents or other film contacts in Los Angeles, but he saw the name of Robert Newman, an agent at ICM (one of the three largest talent agencies in the entertainment business), in the trade papers and sent him the film as a sample director's reel. Newman took it to Columbia Pictures. Rodriguez went on to make *Spy Kids 1* through 3 as well as *Sin City*, among others. Now people have to know his name!

Besides the industry publications, you can find a lot of information in regular monthly magazines that have no direct connection to the film industry. Let's look at just a small sampling of magazines. Interviews with producers or directors of independent films and articles with business statistics were published recently in such nonentertainment publications as *The New York Times*, *Vanity Fair*, *Time*, *Newsweek*, and *Forbes*. Local daily newspapers and *USA Today*, a national daily, also carry interviews in their entertainment and business sections. The proliferation of sites on the Internet has made this information far more accessible and, in many cases, free.

Networking

My first Sundance Film Festival was also my first entertainment industry event. Until then, I had worked in "real business," creating business plans and corporate strategies. Although I had mixed and mingled at meetings before, I had never tried to "work a town." I knew no one and had a general feeling of nausea as I got off the plane. On the shuttle to Park City, Utah, everyone was silent. Finally, I asked a gentleman sitting behind me if it was his first trip. He and his friend turned out to be film commissioners. We chatted the rest of the way. That night I went with them to the opening night gathering and met more people. The next day, I chatted with those people and learned a lot about how they had financed their films and other salient information. Had I not spoken to the first two people, I might never have met the rest. The concept of networking this way can be very scary, but you can do it. Being friendly is a way not only to gather information, but also to make yourself known to others.

Why do you want to network? Your best sources of information may come from attending seminars, college classes, luncheons, industry meetings, festivals, and markets. Besides listening to whatever public speaking occurs, you should go up and introduce yourself to the speakers and mix with the other people in the room. You don't have to be in Los Angeles or New York. Many states and cities have festivals and other meetings. Take advantage of whatever is in your area. Always check with your local film commissioner to learn about events in your area.

There is no better source of information for you than other independent filmmakers. Whenever you have a chance to meet filmmakers, grill them for advice and facts. People like to talk about their experiences and, especially, their successes. (If this were not the case, I would not be able to get well-known filmmakers to talk to my classes and seminars.) You will learn more from someone who has done what you are interested in doing than from all the books in the world.

The Internet and Libraries

This section was originally titled "Libraries and Computer Sources." Times have changed. Even I do most of my research on the Internet. Like reading, however, another lost art appears to be the ability to do research in a library. Libraries still contain information that can't be found—or at least can't be found for free—on the Internet.

When teaching a course, I have been stunned to find out that graduate students have never heard of the Business Periodicals Index and other common library reference tools. Rumor has it that they not only still exist but have books and database sources that would cost you money anywhere else. If you are a student, take advantage.

When writing a business plan, you must be concerned with more than just film grosses. You must be able to discuss the markets, the environment, ethnic groups, population figures, and societal trends—whatever is pertinent to your projects and to your ticket buyers. In addition, a business plan should contain specifics about other companies, industry mergers and acquisitions, new industries, and so on.

The first source for this information is all those articles and books you never read or even knew existed. Besides visiting bookstores, go to your local film school or university library. If you live near Los Angeles, or are visiting, you have the added advantage of the library at the Academy of Motion Picture Arts and Sciences.

Look up your subject in the Business Periodicals Index and other periodical guides in the library. Many libraries have systems that allow you to do a computerized search of subjects. Finally, do not forget your friendly librarians; they are there to help you. Through your computer, you can log onto the Internet and use online services to do library searches without leaving home. Good sources are the Internet Movie Database (*www.imdb.com*) and Box Office Mojo (*www.boxofficemojo.com*), both of which are free for basic information on cast and crew, synopses, and reviews. For worldwide data, however, I often recommend Filmtracker's Baseline (*www.blssi.com*), which sells data about individual films and has various levels of subscriptions available. It is a credible database with budgets, P&A, domestic DVD, television revenues, and VOD revenues, as well as foreign DVD, television revenues, and VOD revenues. Many of these data are hard to find anywhere else.

Promoting Yourself and Your Projects

We make our own opportunities, as every overnight success will tell you. By doing all that market research, you have prepared yourself for two things:

1. Quantifying your market segment
2. Approaching others with your project

At the beginning of this chapter, we talked about the market segment and how it is time to focus on marketing yourself and your project. As noted before, your goal is to find the money or links to the money. There are entire books that focus on this subject, so I am providing you with just the basic information.

Arm Yourself with Ammunition

As a good promoter, there are certain materials you can prepare before seeking out contacts. Business cards, sales sheets, press kits, and director's reels are among the promotional materials you might use. Some filmmakers have even made a 20-minute version of their film, often on videotape, for promotion. For first-time filmmakers with no other footage to show, putting a long treatment on film may be the way to go.

The materials just described serve to get you into meetings. Whether your aim is to sell a single film or to obtain financing for your company's group of films, the first step is to evoke interest. Making contacts is your objective, wherever you are. Earlier we talked about networking as a means of gathering information. Another purpose is to unearth those money sources, wherever they are.

People with like interests tend to congregate in the same places; therefore, entertainment-related gatherings are your most likely place for success.

FILM MARKETS

Knowing how to attend and network at film markets is critical. You do not want to be carrying around business plans, handing them to everyone who says, "I can get you a deal." That is why you bother with the materials described earlier. Those are the items you hand to people initially. Common sense will stand you in good stead in attending markets. There is no trick to meeting and greeting, no secret handshakes or passwords. (Just get out there and shake hands!) When you attend a market, remember that a distributor's goal in being there is not to meet you; it is to sell product. Here are guidelines for you to follow:

- *Be prepared*: Bring your short-term promotional materials, and bone up on who is who before you go. Let your fingers do some walking through the trades.

- *Be aware*: Distribution companies usually focus on certain types of films. Look at their posters and at the items listed in their market catalogs. Try to match your films to their inventory. After all, the distributor is your shortest route to those foreign buyers and presales.
- *Be inquisitive*: Ask questions of everyone you meet—in an office, in the lobby, on the street. Try to discover the person's qualifications before spilling your guts about your plans and projects, however.
- *Be considerate*: In introducing yourself to distributors, pick slack times. Very early in the day and at the end of the day are best. Whenever you reach a distributor's display room, notice if buyers are there. If they are, go back later.
- *Be succinct*: Keep the discussion short and sweet. Your objective is to get a meeting at a later time. You want your "prey" to feel relaxed and be attentive. Try for a meeting at the distributor's office.
- *Be dubious*: Lots of people are milling around screenings, hotel lobbies, and expo halls pretending to be something they are not. It may be a big rush for someone to tell you that they were the "real" investor behind *The Visitor* (when they had nothing to do with it) and are interested in financing your film for $2 million (when they have no money). Listen carefully, take cards, and try to verify the facts afterward. Do not give your scripts or proposals to anyone unless you can validate their credentials.

Advice from a Filmmaker

Joe Majestic formed Majestic World Entertainment in 2007 as a film, multimedia development and distribution company. Previous to that, in 2003 he co-founded the Ilya Salkind Company where he served as Vice President of Production. He was a contributing architect of the company's initial slate of film and television properties. In 2008, he partnered in Monterrey Pictures Entertainment. He left that company in 2009 to focus on film development and sales as President of Majestic. Having worked with Joe as a consultant since 2003, I asked him to lend his advice on both attending and being an exhibitor at the American Film Market. In addition, check the market's web site at *www.ifta-online.org/afm/* for its section "How to Work the AFM."

LL: How did you first start working the market?

Joe: I first attended the AFM with a visitor's badge. I suggest that filmmakers go ahead and get a badge, go around the film market, get all the materials, and network. It took me five years of having a badge full time as an attendee, because I didn't have a mentor or work with a distribution company. I had to learn by trial and error.

LL: Who are the companies that rent offices in the Loews during the market?

Joe: Any production or distribution company that wants to sell products to the more than 1,500 accredited buyers that come from countries around the world can obtain office space at the AFM.

LL: What are some of the activities you suggest for filmmakers attending for the first time?

Joe: People don't realize what a valuable tool the market is. Make a plan. I have seen many filmmakers waste their time by not scheduling their days. Do research. Get the attendee guide that comes with your badge. It tells you which companies are in each room. Then get the special AFM edition of *Variety* or the *Hollywood Reporter* that lists what each company is selling. Individual companies often have specific genres they sell, and you want to know who would be the most likely company to be interested in your film. You also can look them up on the Internet.

LL: How do you approach the distributors?

Joe: They are unlikely to speak to you on day 1 or 2 or on the last day when they are packing up. Spend the first couple of days gathering information. The middle to near the end is best, as the market tends to be slower. They will talk to you if you have a project and are seriously packaging it. Ask their advice. They will give it, because they need product.

LL: Can you just walk into an office?

Joe: Filmmakers think they can go in all the offices just because they have a badge. Technically, you should be invited. Remember that their main goal is to sell to buyers who will have appointments. Try to contact sellers in advance. If you have an appointment, the exhibitor can give you a guest pass to the office floors. You won't be allowed onto any of those floors without either a badge or pass. If you don't have an appointment in advance, ask the office assistant for one. That person will probably say, "Contact us after the market." Try to hold out for a meeting at the market. Be clear. Say that you are packaging your film project and give a specific genre ad budget. Don't get expansive with mixed genre descriptions. Ask them what talent they would like to see attached to the film.

If people look too busy, try for at least a brief introduction. If not, call them after the market. Say something like, "Congratulations on your great AFM. I went by your office several times, and you were too busy. I'd like to send you information on my film _____ budgeted at _____. I have found that it is better to call before sending an email and/or materials."

LL: Why are you meeting them?
Joe: You probably will be looking for a distributor to either help you do presales on a film to be made or to obtain a distribution guarantee to help you raise money from other sources.

LL: What made you decide to pay for office space?
Joe: My company, Majestic World Entertainment, had several projects to rep for sales. Having learned how the market works, it was time. I already had worked with Hector Grob of Monando Film Distribution, who has 25 years in film distribution going back to working with the Salkinds on the *Superman* movies. I met him while working with Ilya, and whenever he was in town during AFM, I spent time at the market with him.

It is important to work with someone who has experience in selling at international markets. If you are interested in being a sales representative, try to meet other sellers and buyers when you are initially at the market. Everyone has a badge. You can talk to people in elevators, on the terrace, at the pool, or at the bar in the lobby.

LL: What should I do if I need to hire someone with market experience?
Joe: The staff at AFM is extremely helpful. They will guide you through the details of obtaining and setting up an office and recommend people to work with you. You need a good assistant to set up meetings and work the phones.

LL: How many films do you need to have for sale?
Joe: You could have one film, although more is better. We were selling three horror films for our clients. General wisdom is that you should have no more than ten films.

LL: What materials should you have to give to buyers?
Joe: 1. Similar to the list above, the three most important pieces of information are cast, budget, and genre. Male actors are most important in obtaining foreign financing. Know what your actors are worth vis-à-vis your budget. Don't get an actor that was worth $250,000 last year and is now worth $25,000. As I said before, be specific about the genre. Don't say "sci-fi action drama." Just say, "action." There is also "contained action," which is a low-budget action film.
2. Promo teaser. You don't need a scene from the actual movie. Shoot a short 1½- to 2-min. section from the script. You need a visual for buyers, since it isn't a radio show. We had promos for all our films. Also, quality counts. You can have unknown actors and inexpensive surroundings, but the look of your 2 minutes has to be good. We did presales as a result of the whole package. In addition, we already had talent attached. That isn't a requirement, but attached talent gives your project more value.

LL: How do presales work?
Joe: Generally, the buyer gives you 20 percent down of the price they are paying for their specific territory and the rest on delivery of the film. You should have all the legal documents available for this transaction. Have them drawn up by an entertainment attorney familiar with distribution and markets. Don't write your own. Your attorney will probably be available for meetings also. Usually, an attorney with clients at the market will be there himself.

LL: Is it important to have someone in your office who speaks multiple languages?
Joe: No. It is nice, but the buyers will always have someone who speaks English. They are buying from you and want your product.

LL: I know that you previously went to Cannes. Is there additional advice for that market?
Joe: Cannes is very expensive. The offices are twice as much, and all other expenses are three to four times more expensive than going to

AFM. If a film project isn't completely packaged with a first-class promo, don't spend the money. Don't go there just to get experience.

LL: Assuming you have the project and promo, are there ways to save money?
Joe: American filmmakers can become members of the American Pavilion. You will have a headquarters and exhibition space, although you won't have an office. You will be able to go to the various Cannes offices and network. The Pavilion provides an array of business services, seminars, networking events, and parties. More networking is done at parties in Cannes than at AFM. For the parties given by major companies, you need to be invited, of course. The best parties are at the beginning of both markets. Other countries have pavilions also. They are all lined up together.

SELF-MARKETING

An important component for any film, especially the opening weekend of the film, is word-of-mouth. Without incurring additional costs, it is possible for a filmmaker to implement a marketing strategy that is complementary to that of the distributor. Or, in the absence of having a distributor, create word-of-mouth. You can get a "buzz" by contacting grassroots organizations with a process referred to as *viral marketing*. Many special-interest groups have email lists and will be happy to send out information on a film that attracts them. It is a strategy that encourages individuals to pass on an email or video marketing message to others, creating the potential for exponential growth in the message's exposure. The people on their lists then send the email on to other individuals and organizations, and the marketing message is spread exponentially. Don't forget to include your hometown newspapers in this activity. An important component for any film, especially the opening weekend of the film, is word-of-mouth.

With some films, it may also be appropriate to schedule free showings in a church, synagogue, or other spiritual gathering place. As many of you have read, this method was used to great effect by Mel Gibson with *The Passion of the Christ, Facing the Giants*, and *What the Bleep Do We Know?* This method doesn't only apply to religious or clearly spiritual films. Christian churches also embraced having screenings of *March of the Penguins*. By having such screenings, which often are free to the participants, you create word-of-mouth before a film opens on local screens.

Complementing this approach are the more purely social networks, which are a $1-billion industry projected to grow to $2.4 billion by 2012. MySpace (125 million unique users) and Facebook (200 million unique users) have become one of the focus sectors in media and entertainment. With their large communities, finding "friends" of similar film tastes in a social network is fairly easy. In addition, the success of Twitter and similar networks has encouraged a habit among members of sending short comments as soon as they leave the movie theater. As with any mainstream marketing, the strategy starts with the people at the top, the opinion-makers or "influencers," and their channel partners, and it extends through the ranks to the people who see films the first weekend. They then spread the word to everyone else. In 2009, Twitter has joined the social networking pact. It was an important way of sending out information during the 2008 presidential election and can work well with films, also. Fans get the opportunity to discover and impact the films of tomorrow, while getting insider access and VIP perks for their contributions. Be sure to research what is happening currently. In December 2008, the global Internet audience surpassed 1 billion people according to new figures released by comScore. The Asia-Pacific region accounted for the highest share at 41 percent, followed by Europe (28%), North America (18%), Latin America (7%), and the Middle East and Africa (5%). In terms of nations, China had the largest online audience with 179.7 million users, followed by the United States with 163.3 million.

No matter how big a site is and fast it has grown when I am writing this edition, it can fall out of favor with consumers just as fast. According to a Nielson spokesman, Jon Gibs, "Remember Friendster? Remember when MySpace was an unbeatable force? Neither Facebook nor Twitter is immune. Consumers have shown that they are willing to pick up their networks and move them to another platform, seemingly at a moment's notice."

Self-marketing is an area in which it is good to think outside the box. Explore what is best for your film. Remember, however, that anything you describe in your business plan is a type of promise to the investor. Do not say that you will do something for which you don't have the money or other resources.

6

The Markets, Part II: New Media and Other Nontraditional Markets

Prediction is very difficult, especially if it's about the future.

NILS BOHR

I couldn't decide what to call this chapter. Suggestions included Son of the Markets, Specialized Markets, When Your Film Is Different, One Size Does Not Fit All (my personal favorite), and A Special Film Deserves Special Handling (my assistant, Faryl's, favorite). Finally, I settled on the rather straightforward New Media and Other Nontraditional Markets.

In every online class, workshop, and by email I am asked about writing business plans for cell phones, downloading from web sites, large-format films, and direct-to-DVD. Every independent filmmaker should write a plan for himself, just as any other entrepreneur would do. However, I know that you creative types aren't going to go through this process, unless you are trying to raise money from someone else. And thereby is the conundrum. You can write about the industry, markets, and budget your costs, but how are you going to forecast revenues and figure distribution costs and net profits?

ART VERSUS PROFIT

Lately, this topic has been in heated discussions in Internet blogs, Facebook, and in trade paper articles. Such activity is often the result of any film festival or market, and the 2009 Los Angeles Film

Festival ended with another energizing keynote speech. In 2008, we had Mark Gill of the Film Department saying that the sky was falling. This year we had Jim Stern of Endgame saying to "respect the money" and "think market" when making a film. This caused a flurry of opinions on which was more important—one's artistic expression or money?

My view has always been that both are. If you are using your own money, you can do anything you want. On the other hand, if you are using someone else's money, it doesn't mean that you automatically have to forgo your artist intentions; you just have to make clear to your financial source what the chances are that they will every see a return on their money or profit. Then it can be their decision, which is more important.

Although I address this in other parts of the book, it is important to repeat here. We are about to review markets that either have fewer restraints on what you say and do (the Internet and direct-to-DVD) or are driven by a different artistic style and largely educational themes (large format). I could probably just repeat the chapter from three years ago. The most that would be missing is companies moving in and out of new media. Nevertheless, I am going to bring us up-to-date on where those markets are now, and what data exist and what don't. Then I will let you decide how you want to proceed.

THE INTERNET

> *This is going to be a very labor-intensive business, but we think that in 5 to 10 years it could be the most significant revenue source of all.*
>
> JOHN SLOSS
> *Founder, Cinetic Media, talking about*
> *film distribution over the Internet at Cannes 2008*

New Media (Internet, cell phone, and other wireless) rights have been the new focus of all discussion since the last edition of the book. More companies have become involved with Internet distribution. In 1999, CinemaNow was the first company offering secure digital distribution of a studio movie, 1997's *Heaven's Burning* with Russell Crowe. In 2006, Movielink and rival CinemaNow announced that they would offer permanent downloads of movies from several major studios day-and-date (on the same day as) with their

DVD release. Movielink, which started in 2002, was a partnership of MGM, Paramount, Sony, Twentieth Century Fox, Universal Studios, and Warner Bros. Meanwhile, Lionsgate, MGM, and Sony made their movies available for download-to-own through CinemaNow. Other companies began making films available on a nonexclusive basis to both systems. Finding that Movielink wasn't the cash cow it had been expected to be, the original partners finally sold the service to Blockbuster in August 2007. Blockbuster shut down the Movielink site in December 2008, in favor of downloading directly from the Blockbuster web site itself, which now also features movies from IFC.

Other players keep coming into the Internet market. There are both services through which you can download your films directly, and distributors who will make Internet deals. The argument is that distributing through theaters is very expensive compared to the vast audiences you can reach on a single day through the computer without making multiple prints. To get to a theater screen, you have gatekeepers. You usually have to go through distributors and convince bookers/exhibitors that they should both put your film on the screen.

Major DVD distributor Netflix has started streaming many of its films and Blockbuster is streaming from its own site. It is good for them. It reportedly costs Netflix 80 cents to send a DVD out and get it back. The company has a 12,000-title catalog available for unlimited streaming at $9 a month. However, they are selling films that were released in theaters.

With the Internet, theoretically anyone can download their film with a choice of several software systems. The technology not only is empowering, but allows you to send any film anywhere without a rating or, technically, censors to worry about. (There are ways to shut off technology as recent political events have demonstrated, but that isn't part of this discussion.)

So what's the problem? First, the movies being watched are primarily ones that have gone out theatrically. How is someone going to know that your film is available for download? You have to tell them. With social networks and email marketing, self-marketing keeps growing. Nevertheless, you still need some advertising push to alert people that your film is available. And how many of them are going to download? We don't know that. We don't really know except in macro numbers how many people are downloading all those theatrically released films.

Then there is the question of not only what people will pay, but how much will come back to the filmmakers. We know what different sites charge for a customer to download, but we aren't sure what the share is for the filmmaker. Many download sites are ad-supported. There is no common split the way that we can track with brick-and-mortar stores or Netflix.

Speaking of ads, there is YouTube, which made its debut in 2005. Created by three former PayPal employees, it allows users to upload and share videos. Google bought it in November 2006 for $1.65 billion, and they are still trying to make it profitable. The last time Google's financial statements broke out YouTube separately was in 2006, when it lost $276 million. According to a report by Credit Suisse in May 2009, their financial analyst estimates that the site would post an operating loss of $470 million on $240 million in revenue. While much of their site is dedicated to shorter videos, in November 2008, YouTube reached an agreement with MGM, Lionsgate Entertainment, and CBS that will allow the companies to post full-length films and television shows on the site, accompanied by advertisements. This creates competition for other sites, especially Hulu, which has films from Disney. However, the films being made by the studios are older, theatrically distributed films for which any additional income is welcome but not needed.

Short-Attention-Span Theater

Short-attention-span theater, or "video snacks," as *Video Business* has referred to it, is very popular. The small screen took a big step forward in 2005 when Google announced that it would download to cell phones. A first impression of downloading to cell phones and downloading from the Internet was that theater screens might become an anachronism. Of course, that incorrect impression has been dealt with already. The potential for selling entertainment products through mobile products is still a new frontier.

At the time of the last edition, the National Academy of Television Arts and Sciences Daytime Emmy Awards announced that they were going to cover this format for original content such as "video blogs, web programs event coverage, mobile phone serials and video-on-demand content." This step caused *The New York Times* to comment that the announcement gives new meaning to the line Gloria Swanson made famous in *Sunset Boulevard*: "I am big. It's the pictures that got small."

In 2006, the Yankee Group estimated that pure mobile entertainment—games, music, and video—accounted for about $500 million last year, less than 5 percent of the wireless carriers' data revenue. And the data revenue represented a small fraction of voice revenue. Although people are watching video on their phones in increasing numbers, another researcher, eMarketer, predicted that by 2009, fewer than 10 million subscribers would be willing to pay for premium services.

In the first quarter of 2009, 13.4 million Americans watched video on their mobile handsets for an average of 3.5 hours of content each month, according to Nielsen's quarterly "Three Screen Report." The company reports that mobile video viewer totals grew from 8.8 million in the first quarter of 2008 and 11.2 million in the last quarter. The most viewed categories were comedy and weather. Subscribers between the ages of 25 and 34 account for 34 percent of the mobile video viewing audience, followed by viewers ages 35 to 44 (20 percent) and teens ages 12 to 17 (18 percent). Men represent 59 percent.

Given the across-the-board economic problems, people are considering what expenses they really need. In June 2009, a new consumer study published by Strategy Analytics' Multiplay Market Dynamics service reported that 48 percent of Americans said they would drop their mobile data plan completely if circumstances dictated they must reduce household expenditures. Posed with the scenario "Imagine that, due to household budgetary constraints, you have to reduce home entertainment/communications services expenses," only 10 percent of respondents said they would halt their home broadband subscription, while 12 percent said they would eliminate digital television and 19 percent would sacrifice mobile voice services. "Given the extraordinary importance consumers place on home broadband, we fully expected broadband to have a high 'keep rate,'" the company said.

Under the same scenario, 17 percent of respondents told Strategy Analytics they would scale back to a lower mobile data tier, 33 percent said they would leave their service unchanged, and 2 percent said they would upgrade to a higher tier. At the same time, only 21 percent of broadband subscribers said they would scale back to a lower tier, and 2 percent would move to a higher tier. "These results suggest that, while American consumers consider home broadband service to be a vital utility, they see mobile data service as simply a 'nice to have,'" the report concluded.

At the same time, research firm SNL Kagan reported that U.S. mobile-video revenue will grow to about $350 million in 2009, up from $300 million in 2008, and will likely accelerate to a 25 percent annual growth rate over the next few years as more people buy Apple's iPhones, Palm's Pre, and updated versions of Research In Motion's BlackBerry. The most accessed programmers are ESPN, MobiTV, MTV Mobile, and CNN.

The business model for all of this activity has not changed much in the past three years. Not all companies will be able to download to all cell phones. If you are distributing a movie to theater screens, theoretically (and ignoring the clout that major distribution companies have with exhibitors) you can put the film on any screen, if you have the print money and a willing exhibitor. You aren't blocked by the fact that the exhibitor may be making his own films. At the very least, you can take similar films and see how many screens they played on, what revenue they grossed, etc. With cell phones, however, at this point the picture is different.

Certain cell phone providers have indicated that they want to have their own content. Some have agreements with Google, Yahoo!, and other content providers; others do not. In addition, there may continue to be limits on the amount of downloading an individual can do.

What Can You Tell Investors?

A distributor whom I know and respect very much told me that the thing I had left out of the last edition is that the digital wave is heading for the shore like a tsunami and that it is going to change the fundamentals of distribution. Clearly, things are changing. It is the timing that is the problem. If you are planning to distribute your own films directly through the Internet or any other new media technology, there simply is no sizeable money for Internet downloads for indie films. Most of the downloads are television and studio films. With or without a large number of downloads, there is no database to use for forecasting.

Then there are the anecdotal stories about how much money individuals have made selling their own films from their web sites. Clients have told me about money that has been made. Not large amounts of money. In terms of "no-budget" films under $50,000, they have sometimes been able to make back their costs. There are anecdotal reports from some filmmakers who say that they have made

$3 to $5 million by selling their films only over the Internet. It sounds impressive. However, these reports are subjective and very few.

All the above information is presented for your use. You should proceed as you think best. I agree with Director Michael Apted and President of the Director's Guild of America, who said, "All the talk is the Internet and all the deals we did for the future. In a sense, that's sort of fog. The real money and the real deal are in traditional media."

LARGE-FORMAT FILMS

Large-format films are made by several companies, among which are the IMAX Corporation, studios, and independent producers. Since the industry started in 1970 at EXPO '70 in Osaka, Japan, when IMAX Corporation of Canada introduced "the IMAX® Experience" at the Fuji Pavilion, the films tend to be referred to by that manufacturer's name. In 2008, the total number of IMAX and other giant-screen theaters increased by 53, from 412 to 465, the largest absolute increase in the 40-year history of the industry.

Until 1997, these theaters were located in museums, science centers, and other educational institutions, as well as a few zoos. In 1997, IMAX introduced a smaller, less-expensive projection system that was the catalyst for commercial 35mm theater owners and operators to integrate their theaters into multiplexes. Traditionally, the films were 30 to 50 minutes long, mostly documentaries. By 2000, the institutional theaters still comprised 70 percent of the market.

The first independent producers of these films were Greg MacGillivray and the late Jim Freeman. They began with surfing films in 1973. The cameras they used weighed 80 pounds, but they paid IMAX to make a camera with better specifications. Since that time, the MacGillivray Freeman Company has led the independent way with 20 productions. Among the other independent producers are nWave Pictures, 3D Entertainment, National Geographic Cinema Venture, and 3ality Digital Entertainment.

Formats

In 2002, IMAX introduced a process to convert 35mm film to 15/70 (15 perforations/70mm process), which is their standard. Known as DMR, for digital remastering, the process started a new wave of converting longer feature films to be shown on the larger screens. Since the film frame for large format is ten times the size of 35mm film, the films have better clarity and sound when projected on multistory screens. Although they either coincide with the 35mm version or are booked later, the DMR version of a film tends to remain in the theater longer. On the other hand, their average booking length is 77 days compared to films made specifically for the giant screen, which remain 211 days. These figures, from LF Examiner, are by year. An individual large-format film can appear on screens off and on for several years. *T-Rex*, which was originally released in October 1998, was making irregular appearances on *Variety*'s box office list in June 2009. There is ongoing controversy about whether or not fiction features belong on a giant screen. However, that is for you to decide. Suffice it to say that the economies of scale are vastly different.

Another controversy erupted when IMAX introduced a new digital screen to multiplex theaters in 2009. Since 2004, the size of the IMAX screens has been 76 × 98 feet (23 × 30 meters) while the new screens are 28 × 58 feet (8.5 × 18 meters). The newer systems cost $1.5 million to get up and running compared to $5 million for an "original" IMAX. The company's multiplex agreements allow the removal of the lower portion of seating in stadium-seat venues, creating the perception of greater screen size and viewing immersion. Presumably, the remastering of 35mm films boosts image resolution and brightness. Then there is the question if you can call them "giant screens." An IMAX representative insisted that "It's isn't a particular width and height of the screen. It's about the geometry." In the end, the audience will decide. They won't care about how much it cost to make the film, equip the theater, or remaster the film. They will care how it looks to them, and whether or not they should have been charged $5 more for a film that isn't on a six-story screen.

Finances

That brings us to the bottom line for these films. Since I have been covering the industry for *The Film Entrepreneur*, there have been few real data to obtain. As of December 2005, the *LF Examiner* discontinued box office information. Editor/publisher James Hyder said on the publication's web site:

Readers are advised not to assume that the box office information on LF films provided here (or in other publications or Web sites) is complete or representative of the entire LF film market. In the conventional film industry, an independent agency collects and tabulates box office data directly from theaters for all films in release. Box office data for LF films are not reported the same way. Some LF distributors choose to provide data for their films to trade publications, but the practice is not universal, nor are the data independently audited or verified. In general, distributors that choose to report do so for the perceived marketing value. Therefore, films reporting their box office numbers are typically stronger than average. Films doing poorly generally cannot afford or prefer not to report. However, this does not mean that all films that do not report are poor performers. Some would undoubtedly place in the top half of these lists. But their distributors have chosen not to report because they believe weekly box office numbers are not a very useful measure of the LF industry's performance. We agree.

That being said, *Variety* does print box office dollars. There are filmmakers who want to be a part of this industry, and it is the only reference they have to revenue. The problem comes on the cost side—not only the budgets, but also how distributors of giant-screen films calculate their fees. Even if the commercial theater owners work the same fee arrangement between themselves and the distributor, what is the deal with the institutions? In addition, in ten years of covering this part of the film industry, I have never found a written analysis of the split between the distributor and the producer. Anecdotally, various distributors have told me that the split is the opposite of what we would assume for an independent film—65 percent to the distributor and 35 percent to the producer. This makes it a little difficult to write a business plan for equity investors.

After attending the annual conference of the Large Format Cinema Association (in 2006 it merged with the Giant Screen Theater Association to form the Giant Screen Cinema Association), I have found that independent producers generally are funding films as they would other documentaries—with grants, corporate donations, and funds from specific groups that may have a social or business interest in the subject of the film. The ongoing independent producers, MacGillivray Freeman, nWave, and others, have made profits from earlier films and, in some cases, distribute their own films. This lack of financial knowledge also makes it difficult to approach equity investors with a business plan. Information does change over time, however. As with other subjects, it's important to do your own research.

DIRECT-TO-DVD

With the relatively flat sales of DVD and Blu-ray, premiere releasing of direct-to-DVD (and potentially direct-to-Blu-ray) has become more and more of a market for studios and independent distributors. Many indie filmmakers still see this as a market for their product. To consider mentioning this business segment as a future goal is one thing; trying to raise money from equity investors can be a problem.

While very few data exist about direct-to-DVD, it is clear that a majority of the product is from studios and/or franchises of films previously released and popular in the theatrical marketplace. These films have a ready-made audience. Formerly a haven for very mini-budget horror and urban films, the direct-to-DVD business now is dominated by those franchises for popular feature films. With consumers being more careful about their spending, "What's new is old," said Karen McTier of Warner Bros. Consumer Products Division at the 2009 Licensing Expo. "What retailers want is proven successes. In this environment they can't take any chances."

Even before this economic crunch, many of the films, and the top grosses, in the DVD premier market were sequels, prequels, or films starring older action heroes like Steven Seagal and Jean Claude Van Damme. In a recent week, Rentrak's list of top-ten premiere releases included two studio sequels (*Dr. Dolittle*, *The Cell 2*), an indie sequel (*S. Darko: A Donnie Darko Tale*), and assorted studio and independent films with stars. Both studio and independent producer/distributors have announced plans for multiple direct-to-DVD films. For example, Dimension Films plans to release 18 direct-to-DVD titles in 2009 alone, including "sequels, prequels and remakes as well as TV spinoffs." What do all of these films have in common? There is name recognition, a ready-made audience, and a company with money to spend in additional advertising. In addition, the companies that focus on the direct-to-DVD business are spreading their risk over multiple films.

Nevertheless, many independent filmmakers plan on sending their films directly to this market. There are always anecdotal stories about how someone has made money distributing this way. Using viral marketing through the Internet to niche interest groups, such as wrestling clubs or subscription DVD clubs, can bring in revenue. What we often don't know is the relationship of that revenue to budget.

There is no real database available for direct-to-DVD, even for a fee. The Rentrak report available at *Video Business* that I have been quoting includes only those ten films and ranked by index, with the top title at 100 and all others listed as a percentage of the top title's rental revenue. Therein lies the biggest problem for including direct-to-DVD in a business plan. Although you can find people to quote on how profitable they can be, investors are likely to ask for projections. Occasionally, someone tells me that they have written a business plan for direct-to-video. When I ask what they used for data, the answer is, "You don't want to know."

I advise readers not to go down that road. The best way to start a direct-to-DVD business is to use your own money, make a mini-budget film, and test the profit-making waters. Only then do you want to write a business plan to raise money from equity investors.

7

Distribution

We don't think of ourselves as arthouses. We're street fighters for signature films.

DAVID LINDE

Former Co-President of Focus Features and Current Co-Chairman

UNIVERSAL PICTURES

Long before Carl Laemmle produced his first maverick film, middlemen existed (as did agents, attorneys, and litigation). These intermediaries bought low and sold high even then. Among the most maligned of all entrepreneurs, middlemen are still harshly criticized for doing their job.

Motion picture distributors are middlemen, and they are a curious lot. They are viewed either as people of tremendous skill, nourishing the growth of business, or as flimflam artists reaping obscene profits. Like politicians, distributors are sometimes seen as a necessary evil. They perform an important function, however, without which many businesses, and certainly filmmakers, would not thrive.

When writing your business plan, you will need to explain the distribution system. As with other elements of the plan, you should proceed on the assumption that your reader does not know how the system works. Wrong assumptions on either side could block the progress of your films and your company.

This chapter looks at distribution strategies in general, glances briefly at studio distribution, and examines independent distribution in some depth.

WHAT IS A DISTRIBUTOR?

History does not tell us when the term *distributor* began to be used. If you look through any other business plan book, chances are you will not see a category for distribution. Examine the table of contents and browse through the index; distributors are not there. All industries have wholesalers, but their role is more narrowly defined than in the film world. Elsewhere, wholesalers are customers for the manufacturer. They buy inventory product at discount prices, add a price markup, and resell at the higher price. In this sense, these intermediaries are considered just another one of the channels for getting the product to the market. They are not involved in making artistic decisions about the product, changing the name for better marketing, or obtaining premanufacturing financing.

Distributors have tremendous power, and in independent film, their impact is magnified. Studios normally have committees and different levels of people making a decision. In an independent distribution company, one person, with no one to answer to, may determine the entire course of your film. The distributor has the ability to influence script changes, casting decisions, final edits, and marketing strategies; in addition, distributors often are intimately involved in the financing of the film.

They have this power by virtue of the distribution agreement. The specifics of the distribution deal and the timing of all money disbursements depend on the agreement that is finally negotiated. As a new filmmaker, you have no leverage for changing this agreement. Even an experienced filmmaker seldom can exact any substantive changes in the standard contract. One can debate fee rates or credits. In the end, however, even though each deal is different, the basic contents stay the same.

Before the audience can buy a movie ticket or rent a DVD, the movie has to get off the producer's desk and into the movie theaters. This method of circulation is called *distribution*. Simply put, it is the business of selling the film to various media, such as theatrical, cable, DVD, pay-per-view, television, and nontheatrical (army bases, airplanes, ships at sea, and so on). But it is not simply done. The distributor must be a salesperson, an entrepreneur, a skillful negotiator, and a raconteur, and must have a sixth sense about matching the buyer with the product.

The "rights" of a film stem from the ownership of the copyright, which endows the legal use of the film to the copyright holder.

Having secured a formal copyright, the producer contractually licenses, or rents, the film to a distributor for a specific length of time. The producer can relinquish all control of the film by shifting the entire copyright to the distributor in perpetuity, or she can license a specific right, such as domestic, foreign, DVD, cable, television, satellite, PDA, or cell phone, to the distributor for a specific length of time. In return, the distributor collects the rental monies or ancillary fees and remits the producer's share.

The following is from a sample domestic distribution contract. Although it is boilerplate (the starting point for negotiations), the following section is not likely to change:

> *The "Rights" consist of the sole and exclusive right, license, and privilege under copyright (including all extended and renewal terms thereof) to distribute, exhibit, market, reissue, advertise, publicize, and otherwise exploit the Picture and the literary material upon which they are based, the picture, sound, music and all other physical elements thereof, and trailers in any and all media and by any and all means (whether now known or hereafter developed, discovered, invented, or created) throughout the Territory.*

Armed with the rights, distributors go about the business of relicensing the film to the various media. The U.S. theatrical box office is the backbone in the chain of revenues for any film. All ancillary results are driven by the domestic theatrical release. Some products are designed to skip that step and go directly to DVD or foreign markets, but the value of a film in any other media and territories is generally greater with a good theatrical release. Even a small theatrical release can increase the value to buyers of an otherwise unknown film.

STUDIO DISTRIBUTION

How It Works

The major studios (and the larger production companies) each have their own distribution divisions. They not only release their own films, but also occasionally acquire other films. All the marketing and other distribution decisions are made in-house. The distribution division sends out promotional and advertising materials, arranges screenings of films, and makes deals with domestic and foreign distributors. Because of their size and the quantity of completed films each year, the studios naturally have a lot of clout in getting their films onto theater screens.

When it comes to foreign markets, studios have offices around the world, either singly or with other studios, to distribute their films in other countries. Often, a studio will partner with a local distributor, and the release will bear the names of both companies. The studio always retains the copyright, which it licenses to the foreign distributor for a specific length of time.

Based on the share formulas we saw in Chapter 4, "The Industry," the studio's distribution arm receives its share of the box office grosses from the exhibitor and passes them through the in-house accounting system. The studio charges distribution fees back against the film as if its distribution division were a separate company. These fees can range from 40 to 60 percent of the total film rentals. In addition, the studio takes the entire fixed cost of the distribution division (overhead) and applies a portion of it to each film. Overhead fees pay for running the division and cover expenses that are not covered by other fees. Before the accountants are done, the studio will also take a portion of the overhead from the production side of the studio and add it to the total cost of the film. A studio's total share of the revenue can end up being 65 percent or greater.

The formula in Table 4.1 in Chapter 4 shows a "net profit" model for a studio film. Each studio has a standard method in its contracts for determining revenues, expenses, and profits. These formulas are nearly impossible to change, even by influential filmmakers. Typically, the producer is paid a percentage of the net profits in addition to receiving a salary. With studio films, it is fair to say that the chances of the net profit being greater than zero are rarer than with independent films. The studios have more films to cross-collateralize (using the profits from one film to offset the losses from another) and more places to bury unreasonable costs, although many contracts now prohibit films from being cross-collateralized.

The Advantages

There are many advantages to studio distribution. The studio has the ability to put 3,000-plus prints of a film in circulation on the opening weekend. Its own channels of publicity and advertising are manifold. The studio has the financial resources to inundate television and the press with ads, and it has significant clout in getting placements for producers, directors, and actors on early-morning and late-night national interview television shows. For example, the Walt Disney Company owns its eponymous cable network (consisting of ESPN, ABC Family Channel, Disney Channel, Toon Disney, and SOAPNet), the ABC network (talk shows, such as *The View, Oprah,* and *Jimmy Kimmel*), as well as the ABC television stations. In addition, the studio is able to negotiate a deal with its own affiliate at a value on paper that is less than free market value.

As noted earlier, the studios have been able to monopolize the chain movie theaters in the past. Some have moved back into theater ownership. Be that as it may, with the success of independent films, exhibitors insist that they do not bow to studio pressure. They can only afford to have films in their houses that fill theater seats. If the audience does not come to see a particular film, the exhibitor must look for another that will be more popular. Consequently, more screens become available to independent films. As small films have received acclaim, they have gone into wider distribution (for example, expanding to 500 to 1,200 theaters) and gotten bookings in major chains that would not have played them previously.

INDEPENDENT DISTRIBUTION

The Players, They Are A-Changin'

In 1990, neither this author nor Bob Dylan, or even Harvey Weinstein for that matter, could have foreseen what would be going on now. Many would-be seers at that time thought the independents would disappear, even though the first edition of this book said that it wasn't true. The intervening years have shown a total change in which studios tried to emulate the success of independents with lower-budgeted films. The Majors acquired independent companies and made them into specialty divisions as the quickest way into the lower-budget market; recently, the majors have eliminated most of those divisions and returned to a policy of tent-pole films. Throughout this time, both experienced distribution executives and other individuals and corporate interests interested in getting into the game have continued to form new independent distribution companies. It seems clear from all this that independents will always represent a significant part of the distribution segment of the industry.

Too Many Films?

The idea that too many filmmakers are making too many bad films and have a 90 to 99 percent chance of failure has been around since I entered the business in 1988 and surely before. Whether or not the percentages are correct, there are many more films made than will ever see the light of day in a theater or make back their production costs. Will this information stop you from making a film? Probably not.

Even independent companies that were highly capitalized and making successful films in the 1990s have come and gone. Artisan Entertainment is a good example. At the same time that they were buying October Films in 1997, a consortium headed by investment firms Bain Capital and Richland, Gordon and Company bought Live Entertainment, which had one of the largest independent film libraries (2,000 titles) in the world, for $93 million. The new company became Artisan Entertainment. Then Boston-based Audax Group along with other investment companies bought a controlling share. Artisan slowly grew until 1999, when the success of *The Blair Witch Project* single-handedly moved the company into the front ranks of independent distribution. At that time, Bain was interested in purchasing Trimark Pictures (originally the motion picture arm of one-time video major Vidmark), but the sale did not happen. Meanwhile, an investor purchased Cinepix Film Properties and changed the name to Lionsgate Films. In 2000, Lionsgate bought Trimark Pictures for approximately $50 million. At least two of Artisan's investors wanted to cash out, and in a bidding war, Lionsgate bought the company. Did someone say independent distributors were dead? They did, but they were wrong.

Why do you care about all these financial machinations? First of all, you should know the history and personnel of the company with which you want to do business. How have they acted in the past? Are they likely to be dealmakers who are more interested in selling the company for a profit than being distributors for your film, or are they hands-on film lovers who are likely to be around for the long haul? Remember that the length of time that a company takes to negotiate a merger or buyout can hurt any film in its library. My favorite film from Sundance 2000, *Songcatcher*, was acquired by Trimark. By the time the Lionsgate/Trimark merger was complete, the film was in the library of the new company, which may not have had the same regard for its potential success as the original buyers. In addition, the film's resulting release in June 2001 may have been too late for the buzz press from its Sundance screenings to be meaningful.

This acquisition/merger mania only gives credence to the good health of the independent group as a whole. As mentioned in Chapter 4, "The Industry," most of the specialty divisions of the studios—Focus Features, Paramount Vantage (the former Paramount Classics is a division), Warner Independent Pictures Fox Searchlight—no longer could be considered as independent producers and distributors. Sony Classics remains the lone specialty division with autonomous control over its product. Warner Bros. absorbed Picturehouse and New Line with Picturehouse disappearing and New Line becoming merely a studio brand. THINKFilm, which had become a notable producer and distributor of documentaries and other films, became a victim, along with the U.K.'s Capitol Films, of their parent company's financial troubles, Pergasus Entertainment Group. Also gone are Fox/Walden Media, which was shuttered and absorbed into Twentieth Century Fox, long-time indie New Yorker Films, and Rogue, which was repurposed by Relativity Media.

Among some of the companies new to U.S. theatrical distribution are Anchor Bay, Peach Arch Entertainment, Oscilloscope Pictures, and Music Box Films. Bob Berney, former CEO of Picturehouse, debuted his new distribution company, Apparition, in partnership with and co-financed by Entrepreneur Bill Pohlad (River Road Entertainment) at Cannes 2009. They join independents, such as: First Look Studios, Gold Circle Films, IDP Distribution, Innovation Film Group, Senator Distribution U.S., Film Group, Magnolia Pictures (and its offshoot for genre films, Magnet Releasing), Palm Pictures, Zeitgeist Films, Roadside Attractions, Rocky Mountain Pictures, Yari Film Group Releasing (which often releases through other companies), Indican, and First Run. I always say that I should put the date (June 2009) on the list, as there will be companies being formed, purchased, or just giving up the ghost by the time you read this book. It is particularly important during the current economic challenges. The overall picture for the past 20 years has continued to be true. As one company merges, becomes a studio brand, or just disappears altogether, others quickly come in to fill the distribution void.

Do your own research to see who is doing what. Since the landscape is constantly changing in this dynamic industry, the independent filmmaker must function in a fluid environment. The small independent of today could be the Weinstein Company of tomorrow. It is also important to keep in mind that some companies specialize. For example, Eros Entertainment and Yash Raj Films specialize in distributing films from India in the United States. Strand Releasing and Regent Releasing specialize in the distribution of gay- and lesbian-themed films. Interestingly, in 2008 Regent also made a point of expanding into foreign-language films. According to Regent co-founder Stephen Jarchow, "Gay and lesbian people represent one third of the audience that goes to foreign movies. They are three times more likely to go and see a foreign-language film." He also pointed out that a small independent distributor considers a film that generates $2 million to $3 million at the box office to be a success.

Always look at how your potential distributor tends to distribute a film. The larger producer-distributors, such as Lionsgate or the Weinstein Company, have the ability to put a film on 1,000 screens. Of course, that doesn't mean they will. On the other hand, some of the smaller companies prefer to put a film on only one to three theatrical screens as a prelude to a DVD deal. On the other hand, some filmmakers have found that, after being picked up at a festival, their contract didn't require a theatrical release. It is always important to have an attorney carefully read your contract.

HOW IT WORKS

Watching an independent distributor bring a film to its audience is seeing a true master of multitasking at work. More than just a functionary for getting your picture out, the independent distributor can perform one or more additional roles, including participating in creative decisions and contributing to the film's financial resources. For most independent filmmakers, the independent distributor is the only game in town and deserves an extensive look.

Domestic versus Foreign

The domestic territory generally comprises just the United States, but it might also be considered to include Canada and, many times, Puerto Rico and other Caribbean islands. Many of the independent distributors consider the United States and Canada to be one

North American package and prefer not to have them separated beforehand. For one thing, the distributor may have output deals with Canada. If the opportunity for Canadian financing arises, therefore, producers must be careful. If the Canadian investors are going to take some or all of the Canadian territory for themselves, the producer might have a problem finding a distributor for the U.S. market.

Domestic rights refer not only to theatrical distribution but also to all other media, such as DVD, cable, and the Internet. A producer who secures an advance from one of these media for production financing makes the deal a little less attractive to the distributor, because the rights have been fractionalized, or split up. Any source of future revenue taken out of the potential money pie before a distributor is found makes an eventual distribution deal tougher for the producer to close. Most distributors make a substantial investment in print and advertising costs. Although they may recoup these amounts from the theatrical marketplace, it is not likely to cover their distribution fees. Therefore, they prefer that other revenue sources be available to them.

Being a domestic distributor usually means that a company does not sell foreign rights themselves. However, no rule says that a domestic distributor cannot venture into foreign waters. While distributors at the Sundance Festival used to pick up films for North American distribution only, they often now include all English-speaking territories. Or they pick up worldwide rights and sell off the other territories to subdistributors.

There also are U.S.-based distributors that specialize in foreign only. These companies deal with networks of subdistributors all around the world. It is sometimes confusing for producers to distinguish between a distributor and a foreign sales agent. If a distribution company is granted the rights to the film for the foreign markets, that company, whether it is 1 person or 20, is the distributor. The company may be referred to as a foreign sales agent also. There is no fundamental difference, just one of semantics. The *Hollywood Distributors Directory* is a good reference for both domestic and foreign distributors. Also, IFTA publishes an annual directory of their members.

Internet rights are a question. As was discussed in Chapter 6, "The Markets, Part II," how big this business will become is still unknown. What you have to know is that you do not want to license your film to anyone on the Internet before you have a contract with traditional domestic and international distributors. Whether or not they will do anything with those rights, the distributors want them available. As you will see in Chapter 12, "Short Film Distribution," this is particularly crucial for short films. Several companies, among them John Sloss's Digital Rights Management, have geared up in the past three years for managing those rights.

Generally, the producer retains ownership of the copyright and only grants someone a percentage of the receipts for obtaining distribution contracts for a particular territory and/or medium. A typical term for granted rights is seven years, although some distributors will want ten years.

A Deal Is a Deal

What is a typical deal? There is no such animal; no two deals are ever exactly the same. Distributors will take as much as they can get, and it is the producer's job to give away as little as possible. Do not under any circumstances enter into one of these agreements without the advice of an entertainment attorney experienced in film. Some distributors will try to get you to sign an agreement before their fees are specified or without any agreement for theatrical distribution. Their business is to be persuasive, and they are good at it. The attorney knows what needs to be in the agreement before you sign it. She can be equally persuasive.

The attorney's film experience is important. When I was first advising filmmakers, I would tell them to get an entertainment attorney. Sometimes they would find someone who worked in another area of entertainment but not film. Distribution deals in this business are different from other areas of the entertainment industry, however, and you want your attorney to be familiar with it. The other mistake that filmmakers often make is using their father's corporate attorney to negotiate their film contract. The filmmaker has to pay for the attorney's learning curve (lawyers charge by the hour) and ends up with a bad deal, or, worst case, no deal at all.

The distributor's fees vary from territory to territory or medium. This amount can be as low as 15 percent (for a "hired gun") or as high as 50 percent of the revenues from the film. Although most contracts treat domestic and foreign revenues separately, general wisdom says that the overall average for an indie distributor's fees is 35 percent or under. If the contract calls for more money than that, you probably don't want to sign. How much the distributor wants to take depends on the company's participation in the entire film package. The distributor may do the following:

- Get a finished picture
- Provide print and advertising (P&A) money
- Be rented
- Raise equity or presale financing
- Provide a minimum guarantee
- Pay an advance

There are no hard-and-fast rules. A lot depends on how much risk the distribution company is taking, whether or not it puts in production money, and how badly it wants the film. The amount of risk is primarily related to the amount of money the distribution company pays out of its pocket. The more upfront expenses it has to assume, the greater the percentage of incoming revenues it will seek. These percentages apply only to the revenues generated by the distributor's own deals; if that company is only making foreign sales for you, then it takes a percentage of foreign revenues only.

Do not assume knowledge about another film's agreement and promise the same deal to your investor. Often clients want me to give examples of purchase prices in their business plans. In that case, it is important to note for the investors that the prices announced in the press may be advances against future revenue streams or total buyout prices with no further remuneration to the filmmakers and their investors. For example, an article may say that a film was picked up for $8 million. However, there may be a small or no advance, with the rest contingent on a percentage of the U.S. box office. If the box office is low, then the producers and investors will never see the full $8 million.

The good news is that, with the caveat noted above, there are good stories to tell as a hook for the investors. Sometimes a producer, director, or producer's representative will give useful financial details in an interview. For example, at Sundance 2004 there was a bidding war for the $400,000 *Napoleon Dynamite*. Distributors offered advances as high as $5 million for the film. The winner, however, was Fox Searchlight, which took the prize with $3 million and a commitment to a 1,200-screen release. The big news at Sundance 2005 was that Paramount paid a total of $9 million for *Hustle & Flow*, which was budgeted at $3.5 million. At Sundance 2006 *Little Miss Sunshine* sold for $10.5 million. However, the brakes were put on buying sprees after several big purchases with upfront fees of $8 to $10 million in 2007 and 2008 failed to deliver profits. Nevertheless, films are still sold; but at Sundance 2009, the high prices at film were half of those the previous year. John Pierson, a former producer's rep, says, "Get it up front. That's your bond."

Print and Ad Money

The first step in distributing a film is making copies of it. Prints are copies made from the master, which is made from the original edited negative. For all intents and purposes, the print is the specific motion picture release, as the master does not circulate. (It is kept in a vault for safekeeping and used when additional prints are necessary.) One print usually costs $1,200 to $1,500, depending on the length of the film and current film stock costs. A wide distribution can cost well over $3 million for prints alone. Independent distributors, who have much smaller budgets than studios, usually start with only a few prints—sometimes even one.

Many distributors encourage producers to provide the P&A money, because this limits their risk even more. Producers who do provide the P&A can negotiate a lower distribution fee, often ranging from 10 to 22.5 percent, with the most common fees being 15 to 17.5 percent. These deals—often informally called "rent-a-distributor" or "hired gun"—usually have an escalator clause to give the distributor an incentive. For example, the fee might be 15 percent until net revenues to the producer equal the cost of the film or some multiple of the cost of the film, at which time the distribution fees escalate to 17.5 percent. On the other hand, some distributors just negotiate a flat fee for working this way.

There are varied opinions as to whether it is practical for a producer to pay P&A costs. By putting up the money, the producer lessens the amount that the distributor will receive from the total revenues. On the other hand, many believe that the greater the distributor's share of the incoming revenues, the harder the company will work to maximize them. The producer may also be cast in the role of monitoring the value of the distribution process; without experience, how will you be able to judge? How to handle the P&A question is one issue you have to decide for yourself. In the end, however, having to ask an investor for several million dollars in addition to the production costs may help you decide to forgo this choice.

Distributor as Financier

Chapter 9, "Financing," discusses financing in detail, but let's look here at the situation that arises when the distribution company is the provider of funds. If the distribution company produces a minimum guarantee, it is taking on greater risk, and therefore the fees are higher. Sometimes the deal may give the distributor an equity participation in the film on the backend. The distribution fee is taken off the top, expense reimbursements are second, and then the revenues are split on some percentage basis. The distributor is now on the hook for providing a minimum amount of money no matter what the film does. If the company has provided a bankable guarantee for the producer, the distributor has to make good on the bank loan.

DISTRIBUTOR STRATEGIES

The marketing of the film to the general public is the distributor's job. He makes decisions regarding the representation of the film in terms of genre, the placement of advertisements in various media, the sales approach for exhibitors and foreign buyers, and the "hype" (word-of-mouth, promotional events, alliances with special-interest groups, and so on), all of which are critical to a film's success. Because marketing is part of the distribution company's area of expertise, it usually is unwilling to give the filmmaker a say in the sales strategy, the poster design, or how the film is portrayed.

This comes as a shock to many filmmakers, who assume that they are going to have significant input or even a vote on how the posters look and where the film is opened. Many producers and directors expect a studio to ignore them, but they are under the impression that small distributors run their businesses as cooperative ventures.

Look at this from the distributor's point of view. Too many people involved in the decision-making process could be a nightmare. Formulating a marketing plan by committee could result in the proverbial camel. Artistic people tend to feel that they know the best way to present their project. After all, it is their baby, and they know it more intimately than anyone else. And how hard could advertising really be?

Franklin Delano Roosevelt once said, "If I were starting life all over again, I would go into the advertising business; it has risen with ever-growing rapidity to the dignity of an art." We are all specialists, and marketing is the forte of the distributor. The filmmaker's task is to check out the distributor by researching other films the company has sold and the methods they used in the process. It is hoped that the distributor and the filmmaker will meet each other's standards and that a marriage will be made. Doing your own research to find the best distributor for you should head off a divorce later down the line.

What the Distributor Looks For

In acquiring a project, the distributor looks at many of the same elements discussed in Chapter 3, "The Films":

- Uniqueness of storyline
- Genre
- Ability of the cast members to attract audiences or buyers on their names alone
- Past successes of the producers or director
- Name tie-in from another medium, such as a best-selling novel
- Special audience segment for the type, or genre, of film
- Attached money

Being able to sell a film involves a mix of elements, although the story is always the first concern. The people to whom the distributors sell must see something in the film that will appeal to their audiences. This varies from country to country and depends on the perspective of the buyer. No two buyers necessarily think the same. It is difficult to define why one distributor will buy a particular film, yet the distributor in the next room at the American Film Market will not. It often boils down to a gut feeling—a notion that the distributor knows how to sell and profit from the movie. Every company operates in its own particular niche, but on any given day some distributors are likely to find your film appealing.

As a producer, you cannot count on miracles or on someone's gut feelings, however. Your best bet is to make your product and your approach as strong as possible. The more components that you bring to the table with the film, the more ammunition your distributor has. Negotiating is their business, but they need something to bargain with.

To complicate your life even more, the definition of a saleable commodity can change from year to year or from market to market. While distributors are in the thick of the battle getting the latest information, the rest of us might be a year behind. This situation makes meeting and talking to distributors crucial. One year, when I was new to this business, I arrived at the American Film Market with a client to promote his already finished film. The director had convinced a well-known actress to do a 15-minute wraparound (inserting a well-known person into the film purely to make it more saleable). She had been popular at previous markets. Unfortunately, the most recent European market had seen a glut of films with this person, and when we arrived at AFM to make our pitch, there were yawns all around. The distributors knew she was old news, because it is their business. We had not thought to check beforehand to see if the star's popularity had changed.

Presales are another area that filmmakers often assume (and include in their business plans) is a given. However, you cannot count on such a sale until the deal has been completed. For example, when a film called *The Soldier's Wife* appeared at the 1992 AFM looking for presales, it already had attached elements with track records. Each of these elements was known in some markets, but not all; for example, the American population was not familiar with the British stars. In addition, no one wanted to take a chance on the script at that time. Eventually, a consortium of British Screen Finance, Nippon Film Development, and Channel Four (from Britain) provided the financing, but the name had been changed to *The Crying Game*. The presales were important, because they were needed for the film to be made. At what point the "secret" in the film's plot was included is not clear. However, getting the film made and to market was delayed by taking at least a year longer than expected to find financing.

Approaching a distribution company with a finished film has advantages. The distributor knows what you can do and how it will look on the screen. The company's risk level is lowered, and its financial output is less. A finished film also puts you in a stronger negotiating position. Many distributors say that they prefer even partially completed films to scripts because they can see the film's quality and the production date gives less chance of being sued for stealing someone else's film.

Festivals are another way to secure distribution. If you can get your film accepted at one of the primary festivals (Sundance, Toronto, Cannes), you have a chance of attracting distribution. Individually, those festivals tend to attract more distributors than other festivals. Being at a competitive festival is good. You will find the psychology of the herd at work. If an audience likes a film or if one distributor becomes interested, all of a sudden a distributor feeding frenzy can start and prices will go up.

Methods for Releasing Films

Few people invent new release strategies; they just refine the old tried-and-true ones over time. Some are in fashion, and some are out of fashion. When I first started in the business, the late Peter Myers, then Senior Vice-President of Twentieth Century Fox Entertainment, told me that there were essentially two ways to distribute a film— fast and slow. That says it in a nutshell. All of the distribution books that you read (and you should learn as much as you can) will give names to procedures that are variations of fast and slow. I've added another speed, moderate, for our discussion.

Fast

The fastest way to release a film is to release it wide. Studios use this strategy for releasing many of their films by opening thousands of prints simultaneously around the country.

The wide release allows for a big opening weekend, which could have one of two outcomes. First, suppose a lot of people go to see the film, like it, and tell their friends. Assume the film opens on 3,800 screens. The average mall theater seats around 500 people, and the film shows three times a day. You have five to six million people leaving the theater on a Saturday and telling their friends to see the film. The film develops excellent "legs," which means that it runs for a long time with good box office. The studios often use the results of the opening weekend as a measure of how much effort to put into promoting the film in the ensuing weeks.

The second possible result of a big weekend is that the same people leave the theater and tell their friends, "Terrible film. Stay home." The film doesn't have legs, or doesn't get extensive pro-motion. However, it does have that crowd of people who came opening weekend to see the star. The studio can use that in whatever advertising they do to lure more moviegoers into the theaters, before they hear any bad word-of-mouth.

Moderate

In several standard patterns of release, a film opens in more than one theater at a time but in fewer than 500 overall. The standard definition for an independent used to be one that opened in 475 theaters or less. "Saturation," "platform," "rollout," and "sequencing" are variations on this theme. The film starts in a few selected theaters and moves on in some sort of pattern. A particular film may work best in one market because of the makeup of the population, because the film was shot there, or because the locals will go to see almost anything.

Films with difficult themes or at least an unknown audience usually open in New York City or Los Angeles. The cosmopolitan nature and the size of the populations in those cities are an advantage. With good reviews, a film will continue to move through the country in one of several fashions. It might move to contiguous states, open in successive theaters based on a certain schedule, or cascade into the markets that are most likely to produce revenue. Whatever method is used, the film will continue to open in more and more theaters. Eventually, the number of theaters will decrease, but the film will remain in distribution as long as it attracts audiences. These methods have several advantages. They give unique films special handling, and they allow a popular genre, small-budget film to move at the limit of its advertising budget. For example, if your film has a Native American theme, you can open in a moderately large city that also has a significant Native American population, such as Seattle. In this instance, the film plays to a special-interest audience in a town where the initial box office dollars probably will give you a good start.

The goal of moderate-speed distribution is to realize sizeable opening audiences (relative to the budget and theme of the film) and good reviews and, then use the money and reviews to continue distribution. Clearly, no one expects a $3 million film to sell $17 or $20 million in tickets during the first weekend. The distributor may start with a few prints and fund the copying of more out of the revenues from the first few theaters. Advertising works the same way. Ads in a major city newspaper can run anywhere from $1,000 to $10,000. As a moderately budgeted film earns money, it finances the advertising in the cities to follow. For example, *Juno,* made for $7.5 million, opened on seven screens on December 5, 2007. In mid-December, it received nomination for both the Critics' Choice Award and for three Golden Globes. By December 25, the film was on more than 1,000 screens. When it arrived at the Academy Awards, the film had grossed over $130 million in the United States alone. By the end of its run, the film grossed over $200 million worldwide.

Word-of-mouth is important in all release strategies. Had the initial audiences not liked *Juno,* it would have been pulled early and re-released after the nominations. Paul Dergarabedian, president of the box office tracking firm Exhibitor Relations Co., told *Daily Variety,* "Positive word-of-mouth is the manifestation of the positive feelings people have for a movie. You can buy an opening weekend, literally, with enough marketing hype. But the word-of-mouth is what is going to make or break a movie in the long-term."

Slow

The difference between slow- and moderate-speed distribution is not necessarily the type of sequencing but the budget of the distributor. A very small distribution company may be able to afford only one print. Therefore, the film will start in one theater, and the distributor will "bicycle" it from theater to theater. Low-budget and "no-budget" films are promoted with this kind of marketing budget—exceedingly small. If a film attracts a larger audience than expected, they may sell the distribution rights to another independent with greater funds. I've seen a small company pick up a film at the Sundance festival and "flip" it to a larger company for a profit before the week is over.

"Four-walling" is another tactic that sometimes works with lower-budget films. In this case, the distributor rents a theater for a flat weekly fee and takes all the receipts. The gamble is that the total box office dollars will be significantly greater than the guaranteed minimum to the exhibitor. To double-check the receipts, you may have to stand at the box office and count the "house" as people buy tickets. Four-walling is used infrequently now, although occasionally a producer will self-distribute and revive this strategy.

Over the past six years, numerous alternative distributors have come into the market. Rather than mention the individual companies, many of whom may not be in business by the time you are reading the book, I'm just going to speak briefly about their methods. Companies will scour the various festivals looking for films that are not picked up. Some are trying direct-to-DVD at the same time that they do a small theatrical distribution. Whether you or the company pays for the distribution costs varies. They take the same rights retentions as traditional distributors, and there is no standard backend for the filmmaker. Other companies will give the filmmaker total control over where the film plays, how many screens it hits, marketing, and press screenings. In this case, there is a significant upfront cost to the filmmaker; however, you are still getting professional advice and guidance on what to do.

Self-Distribution

When no distributor wants your product, there is self-distribution. I generally try to dissuade most clients from self-distribution. Many don't have enough (or often any) previous business expertise to understand the dynamics. Sometimes filmmakers have no choice. No distributor wants the film. The filmmaker wants to gain better ancillary deals by exhibiting the film in a few theaters. As we have seen, occasionally the distributor runs out of money and can't afford to live up to an agreement for theatrical distribution. Investors will be very upset if the film is never seen anywhere. However, even a small theatrical distribution usually will mollify them.

There are several ways to approach this. Many filmmakers will put extra money into their budgets for marketing. If any of these funds haven't been spent, they can be used to get the film out. If the film is appropriate for a specialty theater, you may be able to screen the film for very little cost during one of the theater's down times. Localized publicity, such as flyers or the theater's newsletter, may get enough people into the theater to interest another distributor in picking it up. Or the original distributor may suddenly find that money is available that hadn't been accessible before.

Be aware. The exhibitors have been in business a long time and are experienced negotiators. You are not. Trying to work with them yourself puts you at a disadvantage. They are going to offer you a deal that benefits them, not you. Distributors may be difficult, but they know what the best deal is and how to negotiate it. If you want to do this yourself, learn the rules first.

Do not confuse self-distribution with self-marketing as described in Chapter 5, "The Markets." When no one picked up *What the Bleep Do We Know?*, the film's investor paid for initial releasing. Once it was clear that there was a substantial audience for the film, the Samuel Goldwyn Company picked it up. The free screenings that were done for spiritual groups are a form of self-marketing that built word-of-mouth for the film. The former costs money; there are many free ways to do the latter.

FILMMAKER STRATEGIES

David versus Goliath

Many filmmakers let fate determine which way they will go in terms of distribution: studio or independent. This decision has no right or wrong answers, only options. The studio brings with it deep pockets, backup advice from experienced producers, strong marketing, and the ability to retain screens. Independent distributors bring an intimate knowledge of the low-budget market, the ability to disseminate films carefully over time, and a willingness to take a chance. Weigh your options carefully before making a decision.

There is a certain wisdom to the thought, "Just get the film made." Over the years, though, I have come to believe that raising money and making the film may actually be the easy part. Getting a good distribution deal for the film and financial deal for yourself and your investors is where the real work begins.

One filmmaker's meat is another's poison. Before going into any negotiations, be clear on your goals. The distribution decision is the major reason that you went through the exercise of listing your wants and desires in Chapter 2, "The Company." You may seek advice and counsel from others, but in the end, you must make your own decisions. Table 7.1 helps you identify the pros and cons of studio and independent distribution.

The studio's backup system is a safety net for the new filmmaker. There are experienced producers on the lot, and executives are often dispatched to location to solve problems. This might be an advantage or a disadvantage. The independent filmmaker, on the other hand, usually completes the film before finding a distributor

TABLE 7.1

Pros and Cons: Studio versus Independent Distribution

ELEMENT	STUDIO	INDEPENDENT
Greenmail	Often	Seldom
Backup	A Lot	A Little
Upfront Money	Generous	Small
Types of Films	Homogeneous	Eclectic
Overrun Financing	Yes	Not Likely
Distributor Cutoff	Quick	Moderate
Bureaucracy	Heavy	Moderate
Acquisitions	Sometimes	Preferred
Net Profits	Seldom	Sometimes
Producer's Capital	None	Some

and thus has far more freedom during the filmmaking process. Distributors generally do not have extra people to hang around the set and tell you how to direct or produce.

The nature of independent distribution supports smaller-budget films. In the studios, it is hard to make a film with a smaller budget. They've got union salaries, overhead, and extra costs galore. Independent distributors have to run a tighter ship. Certainly, when looking for financing, their goal is a small budget. The size of the budgets for studio films usually leads to less imaginative and less chancy films being made. The independent system, meanwhile, embraces new and eclectic films. Studios maintain large bureaucracies, which make reaching a decision very difficult and time consuming. The less cumbersome independent process enables quicker decisions because there are fewer chefs in the kitchen.

The studio's financial resources generally favor generous salaries for producers, directors, and cast. With independent films, above-the-line money is often cut to lower the budget to make it doable. Most studios assume a certain level of budget overrun with pictures and have the resources to support it. Conversely, private equity investors expect the budget you give them to be the final number. Underestimating can be dangerous because investors may not make up the shortfall. (More on this subject in Chapter 9, "Financing.")

Studio distribution, as we have seen, is generally "get 'em out fast and wide." Historically, the studios have had neither the time nor the inclination to pamper a film through its release. It goes out everywhere with a lot of publicity. In addition, the studios have a short attention span. Films that fail to find their audiences quickly enough are pulled to make room for other titles that might have broader appeal. Independent distributors, on the other hand, often have the knowledge and patience to give special care to eclectic or mixed-genre films. Many are geared to let a film find its audience slowly and methodically. Of course, there are some independent distributors whose forte is the mass-appeal genres. Most independents, though, have an expertise for releasing films with smaller budgets and lesser-known names.

Historically, the studios' desire to share in the small-film market used to last for only a brief time. Studios have gone through cycles of acquiring smaller films, then forgetting about them. By buying indie companies, the studios now manage to keep a hand in the niche market. Many of these specialty divisions essentially act as they did previously, just with lots more buying power. For independent companies, the niche markets are their business.

Earlier, we noted that your chances of a net profit on a studio film are low. There is a greater chance of having a real net profit at the end of the day with an independent film, although it is not guaranteed. The best policy in the movie business usually is to get what you can in the beginning—just in case.

The Control Factor

Filmmakers are well aware of the fact that studios retain the right to change anything they please—title, director's cut, and so on—and sometimes they assume that independent distributors will not want control over these things. Wrong! All distributors want to control the title and the cut. The only way to have total control over your film is to finance and distribute it yourself.

With the studios, the filmmaker's lack of control over projects is the stuff of which legends are made. Once your project goes into the system, it may be the last time you see it. If you are the writer, the finished picture may bear little resemblance to your original. Normally, there is far more control in independent filmmaking, but absolute control is a myth. An independent distributor will not allow you to have your way with everything. Novice filmmakers often are surprised at their lack of control. If only to protect themselves, distributors feel that they need these rights. Their biggest concern is to have a salable product, and, especially with neophyte producers and directors, they have no idea what they may be getting. A film that is too long, that drags in various places, or that includes scenes that were not approved in the original script will be a problem. Most independent distributors would rather deal with a finished film. That way, they know what they are getting before making an agreement, and they can request certain changes before obtaining the film. The latter is why turning over a finished film is no guarantee for the filmmaker of retaining the elusive "final cut."

Be Aware

When going into a distribution negotiation meeting, know what items are important to you. Talk to your attorney and get a feel for your deal-breakers—that is, the points on which you will not negotiate. No matter what someone says to you verbally, written agreements are what count. For example, if having a hand in the marketing is important to you, be sure that it is included in the contract. Be advised that many distributors will not concede this item. They may listen to what you have to say, but they want the final decision.

Learn from the experiences of others. One novice filmmaker sent his distributor 40 minutes of finished film and 45 minutes of dailies. Although the distributor had said that they wouldn't change a frame, they used the dailies to change the film to meet their standards. In addition, they took a frame from a scene that was not in the finished film to use for the poster. This allowed the distributor to promote the film as belonging to a different genre than it actually did. Will the average distributor do this? Probably not, but it is your responsibility to check out the people you will be dealing with to see how they have handled other filmmakers' projects.

In the final analysis, you must enter into the distribution agreement with care. Make sure your rights are spelled out. If you see the term *standard agreement*, ask for a definition. Finally—and this cannot be said too strongly or too often—get the advice of an attorney who specializes in your area before signing anything. Whether that area is film, television, music, book publishing, multimedia, or some other area, be sure that your attorney has experience specific to your needs.

Deliverables

While there isn't room in this book to go into all the aspects of distribution, I want to mention the delivery items. When you see the initial distribution contract and a small advance, remain calm. You have additional expenses. The filmmaker is responsible for delivering certain items to the distributor—another reason for having that detail-oriented attorney. Your lawyer will know whether or not those items are normally the expense of the filmmaker. They will include such things as 35mm print, one-inch videotape, M&E tracks, music cue sheets, continuity script, MPAA rating certificate, E&O insurance policy copyright certificate, still photographs, and copies of all contracts and agreements. This is not a complete list but gives you an example. Often you have to provide multiple prints in different formats, as European countries use PAL. Before you sign, figure out what all this is going to cost you.

WHAT DO YOU TELL INVESTORS?

The salient facts are here, but you must decide how much explanation to include in your plan. Always keep your description short and to the point. The Distribution section of your business plan should run two or three pages at most.

On the other hand, do say something useful. Your investors may know even less than you do about distribution; as with other subjects, you have to dispel any wrong impressions they might have. Many investors think that their production financing gives them control of the distributor, too. In addition, some have been known to assume that the distributor will repay them all the production costs upfront before the film is released. These notions may prevent you from finding a distributor; in that case, no one will ever see your film.

Before you propose to take charge of all the marketing and promotional strategies yourself or decide to self-distribute your films, ask yourself a question: Who is going to make decisions? The idea may sound great—it will give you control—but there may well be pitfalls. Remember: If you do not know how to drive a car, you're not going to get far even after you turn on the ignition.

Getting a distribution deal is never a given. I make a point of saying that the specifics of the distribution deal and the timing of all money disbursements depend on the agreement that is finally negotiated. In addition, the timing of the revenue and the percentage amount of the distributor's fees differ depending on the revenue source. You must always remind investors that you are making estimates based on general industry formulas.

If you leave investors with the impression that distribution automatically comes with making the film, you may end up with a bigger problem than you ever imagined. I have seen many business plans that have a single statement—"We will get a distributor."—as the entire Distribution section. As you should realize by now, this approach is not the best. Never leave your investors in the dark, but don't attempt to talk about something you haven't looked into yourself. Do your research before writing your plan and explain the essentials.

By the way, attorneys will warn you that a phrase like "We expect to negotiate with a distributor" can create some difficulties for you down the road. Rather, it is best to say "aim" instead of "expect to" (or, worst of all, "will"). Then you will be in good shape to give investors confidence while shielding yourself from later legal problems.

8

Risk Factors

A little uncertainty is good for everything.

HENRY KISSINGER
Former Secretary of State

Every business plan requires a statement of risk, in which you tell investors what a high-risk investment this is. Make it clear that nothing is guaranteed. No entrepreneur likes a risk statement, but it is a protection for you. In an LLC or limited partnership, your attorney will insert one whether you like it or not. You are well advised to do this in any proposal for funds. With a risk statement included in your business plan, investors cannot later claim that they did not know that the investment was unpredictable. Even though it seems obvious to you, and probably to them, assume nothing and state the facts anyway. If things should go awry and people lose money, they tend to sue.

A risk statement can be a very short statement or a long explanation. In the business plan for one limited partnership, the risk statement ran 14 pages; this was a bit excessive. Where should you include the risk statement? I normally create a separate section. Please download the one at Focal Press's companion web site for this book. It is a statement that has been vetted by numerous attorneys. Normally your attorney will have a very long risk statement in an offering. In such a case, you can simply put in your Executive Summary a short paragraph, such as the following:

> *Investment in the film industry is highly speculative and inherently risky. There can be no assurance of the economic success of any motion picture, since the revenues derived from the production and distribution of a motion picture depend primarily upon its acceptance by the public, which cannot be predicted. See the "Risk Factors" section of the Investor Offering Memorandum for further particulars.*

153

9

Financing

*Raising money for a movie is like hitchhiking—It could be
the first ride, it could the thousandth. But you have to stay
out there with your thumb out and just wait. And you also
have to know when not to get into the car.*

JOHN SAYLES

Director

Shuffle a pack of playing cards. Now spread them out face down
and pick one card. If it is the ace of spades, you win; if it is not, you
lose. Your chances of getting the right card are 1 out of 52. These
odds are better than the odds of finding independent money for
your film. Do not be discouraged, though. Many filmmakers face
these odds each year—and win.

Film is probably the worst investment anyone could ever
make. It is considered risky and capricious. If risks were measured
on a scale of 1 to 10, movies would rate a 15. One might as well
go to Las Vegas and throw the dice—in fact, those odds are probably better. Why would anyone invest in films, then? From a purely
financial standpoint, it is a gamble for which there is a big payoff. In addition, there are many subjective reasons for investing in
films, such as personal ideals, creative participation, and being part
of the glitter and glamour. The specific people and firms that are
likely to fund films change, but the modus operandi remains the
same. Some of the different sources of financing will be relevant for
your situation; others will not. Some are dynamic; some are static.
As studio executives and production companies go through cycles,
so do forms of financing.

By this point, you are well on your way to a finished proposal.
You have explained the basic information—your company, your

film(s), the industry, the market, and the distribution process. You have your goals and objectives well in hand. Now here is the kicker. Popular agent lore (spread by agents) is that if a script is not interesting after the first ten pages, it gets thrown onto the "forget it" pile. Something similar can be said of investors and business plans. Investors typically read the Executive Summary first and the Financing section second. If they are still interested, they read all the delicious text between the two. This does not mean that all the in-between material is irrelevant, just that the primary emphasis is on the ins and outs of financing and how the numbers look.

When thinking about investors, most people picture a singularly rich person who swoops in and says, "Here's an extra $10 million I found in my drawer. Go make a film—no strings attached." Or they imagine a country suddenly passing a law guaranteeing you 100 percent of your film costs just for showing up. This is the stuff of which movie plots are made. Not impossible scenarios, but improbable ones. You may get lucky early on, but it is more likely that there will be false starts, dashed hopes, and months or years of frustration.

As the saying goes, "If it were easy, everyone would be doing it." The truth is that finding financing is hard work. If you think otherwise, forget it. There are almost as many ways to finance a movie as there are people reading this book. We will look at specific methods, but note that the full financing of your movie may be a combination of several methods.

With a business plan for a new filmmaker or company, there is an additional struggle. Whether you are asking a money source to invest in one film or several, creating a feeling of confidence is not easy. Any anxiety on the part of the investor about funding one of your films is magnified when committing to finance an entire company. Besides making successful films, you have to be able to run that company. The investor will be looking with great care, therefore, at the production team.

In your Financing section, you will discuss how your films will find financing, but you should do this without restating this entire chapter. Only certain financial strategies will be appropriate for your particular projects or for the type of investor you are going after. Too much irrelevant information will only confuse your reader.

This chapter examines some of the specific sources of money: single investors (rich people), presales, co-production and below-the-line deals, negative pickups, limited partnerships, and limited liability companies. In addition, it takes a brief look at bank loans.

This chapter is meant to give you general knowledge of how film financing works; the intention is to make a complex subject easy to understand and to give you material for your business plan. It is not meant to be the complete and final word on the subject. For your own knowledge, do additional research on the specific financing techniques that you plan to use.

BEFORE YOU START

Before writing the Financing section of your business plan, there are several guidelines to think about and follow. These concern the following:

- Seeking reality
- Finding the best fit
- Being careful what you promise
- Being careful what they promise
- Being able to explain it
- *Seeking reality*

The way that one person financed a film yesterday may not be relevant to you today. This statement may appear to contradict what was said earlier about learning from other filmmakers, but it does not. We said it was sometimes the same formula, not necessarily the same people. For example, suppose a filmmaker moves to Cincinnati, goes to play miniature golf, and meets a corporate executive. That very day, the corporation had decided to finance a film, so a deal is struck. That corporation may never fund another film. In fact, no one in Cincinnati may ever fund another film. Do not assume that you will find money in the same place. Learn from the other filmmaker's method, however; it may prove useful for you.

Finding the Best Fit

Filmmakers often believe that all money is equal; it isn't. Each source sets different requirements or conditions for the delivery of funds. You will be able to live with some of these, but not with others. For example, there may be too many fingers in the pie. Three intermediaries later, you will be paying out large sums to finders. Or prospective investors may have requirements that make getting the money not worthwhile. There may be content, length of time, or rate of return demands you cannot meet.

Worse, at the eleventh hour, Ms. Investor may inform you that her husband has to play the lead in the film. Don't be discouraged. The right source for you is out there somewhere; seek until you find it.

Being Careful What You Promise

Making statements of absolute fact about financial conditions may be dangerous. An investor will hold you to whatever you promise. You might say, for example, "We will seek presales in order to recover at least some of the production financing upfront." That is not a promise, only a statement of intent. On the other hand, saying to people, "We will obtain presale commitments," is a promise. Unless you have commitments already in hand, you may be making a promise that you cannot keep. And be careful of implied promises. If you want to tell potential investors the reported Sundance purchase price of *Hustle & Flow* ($9 million) or *Napoleon Dynamite* ($3 million), be sure to say that these are festival prices, which tend to be higher than what distributors might pay at an individual screening in Los Angeles or New York. Also, be sure to point out that we don't always know what the actual deal is in reference to the figures quoted. I have seen investors refuse to approve a distribution deal because they assumed that "normal" purchase prices were twice the negative cost of the film. The typical verbiage that I use is:

> *Deals at festivals vary greatly. The prices announced in the press may depend on specific boxoffice results, be advances against future revenue streams, or be total buyout prices with no further remuneration to the filmmakers and their investors. For most of the publicized dollar amounts, the negotiated agreement is not made public.*

Being Careful What They Promise

Always take the stance that you have to see it to believe it. People do not have to be con artists to lead you astray; many just like to hear themselves talk. Even investment bankers are seen bragging at cocktail parties about financing films they didn't. If a money source (finder or actual) is saying, "The check is in the mail," your mantra should be, "Do not spend any money until the cash is in the production account." This warning applies to family and friends as well as bank executives. Check the paperwork. If you are not knowledgeable about financial terms and clauses, find someone who is. Look carefully in the fine print for how much cash this source is keeping. Do they have the resources to meet your needs, or are they making a promise on behalf of some other entity that has never heard of you and probably never will?

Being Able to Explain It

If you cannot explain a financing scheme, do not include it. To my constant amazement, I often receive business plans to critique that are based on a complicated financing structure, usually in a foreign country, that the producer does not understand or cannot find someone who has successfully used it. Not just inexperienced filmmakers but longtime professionals will base entire companies on such schemes. Frankly, not only are many of these too complex for me, but a majority either don't work or were fictional to begin with. Be especially wary if an intermediary wants a substantial amount of money in advance. A finder gets paid when you have the money in the bank, not before. Remember to request to see all the documents first. If you have to find an investor to make a deal work, you can bet your bottom dollar that your investor will ask for details about the financing, with examples of films financed. They'll also want a meeting with a principal (person who actually controls the other funding), so be prepared.

RICH PEOPLE: THEM THAT HAS THE GOLD

Investors are gamblers no matter what their reasons, and film is one of the biggest gambles you can find. Others have personal reasons for investing in film. Private investors are equity players.

They take a portion of the profits in exchange for their capital. Until you take in partners, you own the whole pie. As partners come in, you start to slice the pie into little pieces, and as the old saying goes, "Them that has the gold makes the rules." The nature of an entrepreneur is to be filled with passion to accomplish a certain end. The hardest job for you may be your own emotional involvement when attempting to see things dispassionately from the investor's point of view.

Who Are They?

The first string of the investment team comprises friends and relatives. Raising development money and the negative cost of films under $1 million is very difficult. Professional investors do not see enough of a return on such small investments. Mom and Uncle Harry are more likely to be willing to give you a chance. Kevin Smith funded the $26,575 budget for *Clerks* with credit card advances, the sale of his comic book collection, and a loan from his parents. Filmmakers Alex and Stephen Kendrick raised the $100,000 budget for *Facing the Giants* as donations from church members and others.

Entrepreneurs

Private money comes most often from people in businesses other than entertainment. Entrepreneurial types who have made a killing in almost any industry may feel the lure of film. It takes a high roller at heart to start a firm and prosper with it. You can try the annual Forbes 400 for a listing of billionaires; however, you may have to travel to Hong Kong or Taiwan to speak with them. You don't have to go that far for what you need.

Investors have all sorts of reasons for taking this risk. Some are after big bucks, some are personal fans, and some want to give back to the community. Despite their reasons, investors are seldom seeking to lose money. I have seen scores of creative people forget their dreams rather than face the reality that, whatever the content, these are business deals as well.

There have always been wealthy people attracted by Hollywood. Many of them invested with studios in the early years. One of the first investors in DreamWorks was Paul Allen, co-founder of Microsoft. Over the past 15 years, however, a growing number of communications, real estate, Internet, sports, finance, and other billionaires have made pacts with experienced producers to start independent production and distribution companies. Phillip Anschutz, chairman of Qwest Communications International, has started several production companies, now combined into Walden Media. He also bought United Artists, Regal Cinemas, and Edwards Cinemas, which currently controls over 6,000 theater screens. Jeff Skoll, a co-founder of eBay, founded Participant Media, which has invested in both studio and independent films. Mark Cuban and Todd Wagner, the founders of *www.broadcast.com*, formed 2929

Productions and Magnolia Distribution, and bought the Landmark Theaters. The partners in Google have co-financed a film; they are also early investors in various areas of high-definition entertainment. Bob Yari, a real estate developer, formed several independent production companies that were combined into the Yari Group in 2005. Gary Gilbert, co-owner of the NBA's Cleveland Cavaliers, along with Usher and the chairman and vice chairman of Quicken Loans, has financed several movies, among them *Garden State*. Sidney Kimmel, a founder of Jones Apparel Group, has formed Sidney Kimmel Entertainment, which has produced several films and has more in development. Beastie Boys' Adam Yauch formed Oscilloscope Laboratories, which became a film producer and distributor in 2008. Bill Pohlad, the son of self-made billionaire Carl Pohlad (owner of the Minnesota Twins baseball team), formed River Road Entertainment and in 2009 financed Bob Berney's new distribution company (still unnamed in June 2009).

These are only a few of the people who have come into the business because they have a commitment to films with a message, because they want to develop new technology frontiers, or because it is fun and they can. However, they are all individuals spending their own money. There are many in other countries of the world; and, presumably, there are more out there waiting for the right opportunity. How do you find them? I wish I could tell you. One thing I do know is that these are people who recognize that film operates on a different risk level than the businesses that made them rich. Over the years, several finders working with real estate investor groups have approached me about film, thinking that they could sell the idea to their syndicates. They couldn't. As a group, real estate investors are putting their funds into projects with less risk than film. However, individuals from those syndicates have expressed interest in investing in LLCs and limited partnerships on their own.

Art

Some investors want to be associated with "art." What constitutes art is in the eye of the beholder. Normally, the term is assigned to films that appear to be based on a higher level of expression and writing, but also with a limited level of audience appeal. Over the years people have held up Merchant-Ivory's *A Room with a View* as an example of an art film compared to film with more mainstream appeal. Even now, they will tell me that they want to finance a film like the Merchant-Ivory classic *A Room with a View*. Unfortunately, they want to make it at 1986 prices ($850,000) and reap the box office of *My Big Fat Greek Wedding* ($600 million worldwide), which is an entertaining and successful film but not art. Using standard inflation rates, the *View* film would have cost $1.5 million to make in 2005. In such a case, the investor's goals are unrealistic. Even if they made the film, having a windfall like $600 million goes into the extraordinary category. You should make an attempt to create realistic expectations for him. If you are lucky, his desire to be associated with quality will outweigh the high return he wants for his investment. On the other hand, if he cannot afford more money and does not want to join with additional investors, move on. Put your energy into finding partners whose outlook and resources are a match for your project.

Special Interests

The line between business and altruism can be a thin one. Few people will become involved in a feature film without considering its commercial possibilities, but investors often have other reasons for funding. If you can find an investor whose sensibilities agree with the theme or purpose of your film, you may be able to create a workable collaboration. Jeff Skoll, for example, formed his company to make films on current social and political topics with the express purpose of inspiring social change. On the other hand, the company intends all films to be profitable.

Then there are nonprofit organizations. Many foundations and similar organizations have funded all or part of fiction feature films that fit with their particular mandate. The increase in the number of inspirational films with themes of good versus evil and redemption have brought more charity-based religious and nondenominational organizations into the market. Having been involved with writing several business plans for filmmakers who were seeking money from such organizations, I caution you to be careful. In order to get a substantial number of people to see your film, your first goal should be to entertain. Paul Haggis, director of *Crash*, said, "Film is an emotional medium, not an intellectual medium, so you have to move people. You can't just lecture them."

Foreign Investors

We hear a lot about European and Japanese investment in the American film community. In the early to mid-1990s, most of the foreign money went to studios or the formation of large production companies with experienced studio executives; $100 million was a favorite startup amount. From the late 1990s to 2002, German investment funds grew like crazy. Investors looking for prestige, profits, and extraordinary tax breaks began funding as much big-budget output as they could. Some funds existed to fund studio films; others financed independent companies, such as the UK firm Intermedia (*Iris, K-19: The Widowmaker, The Quiet American*). As some high-budget films failed and the economy started to collapse worldwide, many of these funds closed. However, new ones came along to take their place. Any detail presented here would be out of date before you bought the book.

Generally, this money doesn't go to novice filmmakers. In tracking foreign money, you often run into finders who claim to have a special relationship with foreign money. Some do; many do not. Remember to check these people out. A finder should be paid a percentage of the money you receive from the investor, and only after the cash is in your bank account, as in any interaction with an intermediary. And, at the beginning of this journey, ask how many people there are between the finder and the money. If that person is going through two other people to obtain the money, have them agree to split one fee. For example, if your finder's fee is 5 percent, then all three split that money; otherwise, you are paying 15 percent in finders' fees. Naturally, this is always your choice. But don't get backed into a corner to pay out three times what you intended simply because you didn't get the facts straight upfront. And I can't stress enough, *do not* give them any money in advance.

Where Are They?

Your own backyard is the first place to look for financing. Few filmmakers are born in Los Angeles; they migrate there. Nor are all the investors born in Los Angeles. They are born and live in Ohio, Michigan, Iowa, Oslo, Sydney, Hong Kong, and so on. At least those are areas where many of my clients have found investors. (Don't call me for a list; it's proprietary—nonpublic, company-owned—information.) You may find untapped markets of entrepreneurs with lots of money from very unglamorous businesses, to whom the lure of the film world may be irresistible. Your best chance is in an area where there is not a lot of competition from other filmmakers—if there still is such a place. The entire financing deal can be conducted without anyone living in Tinsel Town.

Giving a party is another strategy that I have seen some producers use to find interested investors. Since I am not an attorney, check the details with yours before proceeding. I have paraphrased some of the rules set out by Morrie Warshawski in his book *The Fundraising Houseparty* (available at *www.warshawski.com*). Although Morrie is focusing on raising money for nonprofit events, the same principles can be used for film fundraising:

- Potential investors receive an invitation to come to a private home.
- The invitation makes it clear that this is a meeting to launch a film.
- Participants arrive and are served some sort of refreshments.
- The host or hostess explains why they personally feel it is a worthwhile project.
- Participants sit through a brief presentation—appearances by actors in the films, script reading, etc.
- A peer (we might say shill) in the audience—someone articulate, respected, and enthusiastic—stands up and explains why she wants to be part of the project.
- Once you have established an individual's interest, you can contact her later with your documents about investing.

What You Get

Equity investors will want at least a 50 percent cut of the producer's share in the film; some may even want a higher percentage. In recent years, filmmakers have offered the incentive with a return of 110 to 120 percent of the original investment before any split of net profits. No matter how many years you spent writing the scripts or how many hours you spent talking deals, it is their money. Before you start complaining, be glad your investors don't want 80 percent. Venture capital companies and professional film investors often require that much equity to put in seed money.

Filmmakers have a habit of promising "points" and film credits to people for their work in finding investors, making introductions to potential actors, or other steps involved in getting the project made. Directors and stars who are too expensive for the film's budget often are given points as a deferment of part of their salary. These points all come out of the filmmaker's share, unless an agreement is reached with investors. Besides points, filmmakers like to give away credits. Be careful what you promise. If you have one investor for the entire budget, he may want the title of executive producer (and deserves it). Some may want to remain anonymous, so all the other filmmakers wanting money don't contact them. In addition, be careful about the producer title. When your film is nominated for the Best Picture Oscar (I never said you couldn't indulge yourself with some fantasy), only three people can be listed according to the 2007 Academy of Motion Picture rules.

Reasonable Risk

Entrepreneurs often want money from investors with no strings attached as a reward for their creative genius. They do not want to be responsible for how the money is spent or for whether investors realize a gain. No doubt, you are a genius. But do not expect to get financing without showing the investor what kind of risk she is taking.

Early in this business, I tried to get financing for an entrepreneur who had a new idea for making films that would have a nontheatrical distribution in malls. One investor thought the idea was "sexy" and that the films could be taken national but that the business plan was so-so. The investor proposed to invest $5 million and then raise additional money from other investors; however, he wanted a revised business plan. My client would have none of this. "After all," he said, "investors are supposed to take a risk. If these people are not willing to take one, who needs them? I'm not going to waste all this time. Big guys in New York are interested." You can probably guess what happened. The client never heard from the "big guys," never got the first film made, and went back to his old job, never to be heard from again.

The moral here is not that people in New York are unreliable. Serious investors, whether they are in New York or Des Moines, will seldom make a final decision based on flash and dash. They want to see substance and detail. Even if someone likes your project, chances are you will hear, "Come back when you have a business plan."

The Big Payoff

The low-budget, big-return films are the hooks that lure many high rollers into the film business.

Films like *Once, Fireproof,* and *Napoleon Dynamite* can be irresistible. Very few other ventures, outside of Las Vegas, offer the potential of a 500 to 1,000 percent return on investment. At a lower percentage rate but nevertheless as alluring are *Slumdog Millionaire, La misma luna,* and *Juno.* As a filmmaker you must be ready to show prospective investors that the chance of making a killing may outweigh the risk of losing their money. Remember, though, that you can never promise a risk-free investment. And you do not want to tell them, "Ten million dollars is typical of advances and/or buyouts for $1-million films."

When all is said and done, it is the projected bottom line that builds the investor's confidence. You need to find similar films and track their dollar returns. Whether you are looking at a single film or a company, you must project your revenues and expenses, box-office grosses and rentals, and cash flows over the next three to five years. (You will learn how to do that in the next chapter and through doing the exercises provided in the Financial files on Focal's companion web site for this book.)

PRESALES

There are two main activities at markets like AFM and Cannes: seeking presales for as-yet-unmade films in order to finance production, and selling finished films. We are concerned here with the former. The seller (you or your U.S. distributor) has a booth or room and entices the buyers from each territory and medium (theatrical, DVD, VOD, satellite, broadcast, and so on) to buy the ancillary rights (domestic or foreign) to your film in advance. (This is also called a *prebuy.*) In return, you receive a commitment and guarantee from the prebuyers. The guarantee includes a promise from that company to pay a specific amount upon delivery of the completed film. If deemed credible by one of several specialized entertainment banks that accept such "paper," the contract can be banked. Then the bank will advance you a sum, minus their discount amount.

In exchange for the presale contract, the U.S. or foreign buyer obtains the right to keep the revenue (rentals) from that territory and might also seek equity participation. The agreement can be for a certain length of time, a revenue cap, or both. The time period can be anywhere from 5 to 15 years, with 7 being customary.

Many filmmakers are under the impression that "in perpetuity" (forever) enters into this negotiation. These terms are not unheard of, but they are more likely to surface if you are transferring the copyright, or ownership, of the film. There is nothing to keep people with money in their hands from demanding as much as they can get. The buyer tries to make the length of time as long as possible, and the seller tries to make it as short as possible. Be careful of the stance you take. Some foreign companies have told me that if the filmmaker balks at 7 years, they will change the term to 10.

The "revenue cap" is a certain amount of money in sales, up to which the buyer gets to keep all the money. When negotiating these terms, buyers try to estimate the highest amount that the movie will make and then try to make that amount the cap. After the revenue cap is reached, the seller may start receiving a percent of the revenue or may renegotiate the deal.

Being the sole source of financing gives people much more power than if they are one of a group of funders. Yet any of these negotiations still depend on the "eye of the beholder." Any leverage depends on the desire of the buyer for the film.

Advances

In the past, cable, home video, and television syndication companies were major sources of production financing. Through advances, they funded all or part of a film's production in exchange for an equity participation and the rights to distribute the film in their particular medium. Although advances do not occur as frequently as they did in the early 1990s, particularly in video, they are still a potential form of production financing. As noted earlier, most domestic distributors prefer not to see fractionalized rights.

Always weigh this fact against the benefits of having an ancillary company as your main investor. The advance for a finished film is another matter. It may be a total buyout, have a revenue cap, or combine any number of characteristics common to presales.

Advantages and Disadvantages

The primary advantage of presales is that they offer you the chance to make your film. This source of money continues to be a workable one for new filmmakers. In addition, if you manage to reach your production goal over several territories, it lessens the impact that someone else can have on your film. Presumably, the fewer territories in which you presell or from which you receive advances, the more money you will be able to keep on the back end after distribution.

There are two disadvantages to this source of funding. First, you sacrifice future profits in order to make the film. Selling your film in advance puts you at a negotiating disadvantage. Companies that use presale strategies often give away much of the upside cash flow and profit potential from hit movies. Second, not all paper is bankable. You have to do a lot of research before accepting this kind of contract. Things change quickly, particularly in difficult economic times.

INTERNATIONAL CO-PRODUCTION

International co-production deals are the result of treaty agreements between countries. Qualifying films are permitted to benefit from various government incentives provided by the country in which production will take place. However, co-production agreements are not a charity event. A number of requirements may be imposed on the film by government treaty, including the following:

- The producer must be a resident of the host country.
- A certain percentage of above-the-line talent must come from the host country.
- A certain percentage of the technical crew must be residents of that country.
- Distribution must be done by a company located in the host country.
- A percentage of the revenues from the film must remain in that country.

Advantages and Disadvantages

The first advantage of co-production is that the total budget may be smaller because of the advantages of filming in a cheaper locale. Second, because of the readjusted budget, you will have to find a smaller amount of hard cash. The right deal will cover most, if not all, of your below-the-line costs. Many films would still be only a gleam in the producer's eye if part of the actual cash burden had not been removed by a co-production deal. In terms of disadvantages, you will still need to have hard cash for the above-the-line payroll—that is, the cast, director, writer, and production office staff. No film is made without these people, and they will not take I.O.U.s, although some take deferred salaries. Another disadvantage is that finding enough skilled personnel in a host country could be a problem. If you end up having to fly key technical people from the United States to another country, you may end up with a budget burden that offsets the advantages of the co-production deal.

FILM INCENTIVES

Federal Film Incentive

In 2004, Congress passed the American Jobs Creation Act. Section 181 of that act provides for an incentive for film and television productions. The incentive was to end in December 31, 2008; however, it was extended until December 31, 2009. Attorney Hal "Corky" Kessler is currently working with the government on a possible further extension and additional amendments. He has contributed the following explanation of the incentive to include in your business plan.

> Under Section 181 of The American Jobs Creation Act, 2004, any taxpayer, company or individual who invests in a qualifying film or television project under the act can deduct 100 percent of the investment as a loss in the year or years the money is spent. Regardless of budget, filmmakers can take advantage of the first $15 million (or $20 million in specific depressed areas). For Television it is either $15 or $20 million dollars per episode for the maximum of 44 episodes. The triggering effect is when the money is spent. The original act has been extended to the end of 2009. This applies to films beginning January 2008. As to how to characterize the loss, you should check with your tax advisors or attorney. In addition, under Section 199 and not dependent on Section 181, you can adjust your taxable income as follows for any taxable revenue you receive as a return on an investment in a film. From now until 2010 you can deduct 6% from your taxable income received from a film or television project and only pay tax on 94% of the taxable income. Starting 2010 the deduction increases to 9%.

The paragraph is also downloadable from Focal's companion web site for this book. Check there for any future revisions.

State Film Incentives

Currently, 37 states and Puerto Rico have incentives for certain qualified films. The incentives vary from rebates, tax credits for the film company, transferable tax credits (for local individuals/companies enabling them to deduct all or a portion of their investment in the film), and other refunds of expenses. What line items are covered (salaries, below-the-line production spending) and the amount of the incentives (normally expressed as a percentage of the costs covered) differ from states to state. As states have been very competitive in trying to draw films to their communities, similar legislation is being drawn up in many of the remaining states. In addition, some states have assigned all their money for the next two to three years. If you know in which state(s) you want to film, go to their web site to check all the details of the incentives. Print off the files and go over them with your line producer/unit production manager (UPM) and your attorney to see if the fit is good for you. If you aren't familiar with which states have incentives, consult the web site of the Association of Film Commissioners International (*www .afci.org*).

A checklist of items to consider:

1. When will the incentive be paid? Most states do an accounting at the end of production before agreeing to a specific dollar amount; therefore, you need to raise your entire budget before you start filming.
2. If bringing crew from another part of the country is necessary, how does that cost mesh with the amount of incentive you hope to receive?
3. What has been the experience of other filmmakers dealing with the state's incentive regulations?

NEGATIVE PICKUP

In the days when film companies had more cash, there were many negative pickups. The premise is that a studio or independent production company promises to pay the cost of the film negative (production costs) upon delivery of the completed picture. This agreement is taken to the bank, which then provides cash for production at a discount to the total value of the agreement. A discount is a reduction in the stated value of the note.

The catch-22 here is that the bank has to believe that the studio or distributor will be able to pay off the loan upon delivery of the film (often a year from the date of the agreement). In the past, this was not as difficult to do as it is now. In the late 1980s, banks could count on the Majors, a few of the mini-Majors, and a very small number of distributors to make good on negative pickups. The entire situation has changed in the past several years. The financial problems of many of the large production companies are well known. In addition, the troubles and, in some cases, complete collapse of many financial institutions have created an even more dismal picture. Nothing can be taken for granted. Although there are still companies that will give you negative pickups, this is not a financing strategy that I would count on. As with distribution deals, show the documents for your negative pickup to a bank to see if the deal is acceptable.

Advantages and Disadvantages

One advantage of negative pickups is that the film is made without giving away a share of the company to someone else. In addition, a negative pickup with a major studio or distributor removes the angst of searching for a distributor.

On the other hand, the standard negative pickup agreement contains two loopholes that favor the distributor. First, the agreement has a built-in escape clause that says, in effect, "You must deliver the film we were promised." Any change in the script, even if it seems minor to you, can cause cancellation of the contract. Second, the contract also states that the finished film has to meet the distributor's standards of quality. Even if the movie is, shot-for-shot, the same as the script, the distributor can always say that the film's quality is not up to standards.

LIMITED PARTNERSHIPS

Until the mid-1980s, limited partnerships were all the rage. Subscribers could deduct losses calculated at many times the amount of their original investment; taxwise, therefore, the losses sometimes were more beneficial than making profits. In 1986, the Tax Reform Act removed most of these benefits, however, and now the investors have to pray for successful films.

A limited partnership has two kinds of partners. The general partner has unlimited liability with respect to the obligations of the partnership and is active in management. The general partner chooses the investments and does not have to ask for the advice or agreement of the other partners. The limited partners, who provide all of the capital, share any profits or losses and are not actively involved in management. In addition, their liability is limited to the amount of their investment. Gains and losses flow through directly to the limited partners.

A public limited partnership must be registered with the SEC (Securities and Exchange Commission), and, in the case of a public or private limited partnership, there must be a properly prepared prospectus that includes all the facts about the partnership. The overall package should include a business plan (be still, my heart!) and offering with subscription documents.

DO NOT WRITE YOUR OWN LIMITED PARTNERSHIP. In order not to pay attorneys, film producers are fond of cutting and pasting someone else's partnership agreement. I think I just emphasized that this is a bad idea. When it comes to fraud, working with unofficial documents is only one aspect. Any misrepresentation about the company's plans also constitutes fraud. The SEC and the Internal Revenue Service are not known for their sense of humor, and ignorance is not an acceptable defense.

Advantages and Disadvantages

On the plus side, the limited partners have no right to interfere with the creative process. Private placements provide a means to raise funds from multiple investors without having to negotiate different deals with each one. The subscription documents contain all the deal information.

There are disadvantages as well. Because of the complicated nature of all SEC regulations and the differences between public and private offerings, participating in one of these formats requires research and expert advice from an attorney. The law is complex, and ignoring any filing regulation (each state has its own requirements) may bring an order for you to cease and desist in your sale of the offering. Another disadvantage is that the producer or the purchase representative must have a previous relationship with the investor before approaching her with a specific offering.

Limited Liability Companies

In the past few years, a new financial structure, the limited liability company, has become widely used. LLCs are a hybrid combination of the partnership and corporate structures. They are an attractive alternative to partnerships and corporations because the LLC provides limited personal liability to the investors, who are referred to as "members." They have a share in the profits as outlined in the offering document. The LLC also provides a single level of tax. In the standard limited partnership, general partners (read "filmmakers" here) have personal liability for partnership debts, whereas limited partners in an LLC have no personal liability. Theoretically, the worst thing that happens is that they lose their investment. In addition, the limited partners cannot participate in management without jeopardizing their limited liability status.

In addition, an LLC member can participate in the entity's management without risking loss of limited liability. For federal tax purposes, the LLC generally is classified as a partnership. The same is true in most states—the operative word here being "most." I have clients who have formed an LLC in Michigan, for example, but not in Florida, where the LLC is taxed as a corporation. As there is no uniformity in the LLC statutes across states, creating an LLC with members in more than one state may be complicated.

The same rule that I stated for limited partnerships exists here: DO NOT WRITE YOUR OWN. Can I say that too often? From what I have seen, the answer is a resounding "No!" When you hire an attorney, however, be sure that he is someone with experience with both film and the particular form of Investor Offering that you are using. You do not want to pay for an attorney's learning experience.

When pass-through of revenue is of primary concern, strict conformance to IRS and state revenue accounting criteria should be considered before the LLC is chosen over other organizational structures. With new tax credit schemes (both state and federal) appearing on a regular basis, you also may need to consult with a CPA familiar with IRS statements.

Los Angeles attorney Michael Norman Saleman prefers the limited partnership structure to limited liability companies (see below). As he explains,

The reasons that I prefer the limited partnership to the LLC have to do with the fact that the law does not adequately protect the LLC Member investors by limiting them to their investment as the total amount of their potential losses, as it does for the limited partner investors in a limited partnership. For example, California law creates personal liability for LLC members if the LLC "veil" of protection is pierced, in the same manner as a corporation. That cannot happen to a limited partner. Also, there is nothing in the law that separates the control of the business from the managers and the members in the LLC as it does between the general partner and the limited partners in a limited partnership. In a limited partnership, should the limited partners attempt to involve themselves in the day-to-day operations of the partnership (i.e., production of the film), they would, by law, run the risk of assuming unlimited liability. With this safeguard in place, the producer may make the picture without having to worry about investor interference or attempts to wrest the production from the producers.

Limited Liability Companies

The limited liability company has become one of the most favored business structures for independent film investment. Producers frequently set up their own production companies separately as closely held corporations in which investors do not participate. LLCs are a hybrid combination of the partnership and corporate structures. The LLC is an attractive alternative to partnerships and corporations because the LLC provides limited personal liability to the investors who are referred to as "members." The LLC owns all distribution rights to the film and investors have a share in the profits as outlined in the offering document. The LLC also provides a single level of tax like a partnership however unlike a formal partnership the filmmakers as managers of the LLC have no personal liability for business debts. The worst case for investors is the loss of their investment but there is no liability for any business debts. Limited partner investors cannot participate in management without jeopardizing their limited liability status, but if an investor becomes a manager, the member can participate in the entity's management without loss of limited liability. For Federal tax purposes, the LLC may elect at the time of its formation to be treated as either a corporation or as a partnership. Most states afford the same tax treatment to an LLC as its Federal status. The operative word here is "most." As there is no uniformity in LLC statutes across states, creating an LLC with members in more than one state may be complicated.

The same rule that I stated for limited partnerships is applicable to the formation of an LLC. DO NOT CREATE YOUR OWN. The Operating Agreement for an LLC, which governs its business operations, is a complex document far more complicated than simply filing basic Articles of Organization and must be drafted with the assistance of legal counsel and often accounting advice.

Being Fair to Your Investors

When people invest in an LLC or a limited partnership, there is a payback schedule that is agreed to by both the filmmaker and investors. The investment agreements which are included in the financing package include the budget which you have prepared. Production Attorney and Producer William L. Whitacre of Orlando, whose clients include Haxan Films (*The Blair Witch Project* and *Altered*) and the Pamplin Film Company, says,

> *In a limited liability company investors are passive; however, once the investment structure is determined and funds have been accepted, there can be no change in that structure, since doing so would dilute the interests of the initial investors. Accordingly, it is extremely important to budget accurately in the beginning, and to establish an investment structure that will get you to the finish line (including postproduction and completion of an answer print or master) before accepting investment funds into a limited liability company, since your only alternative to raise additional capital would be to sell your own Producer's shares.*

BANK LOANS

Bank loans are not associated with business plans per se. However, this discussion focuses on what you will tell potential investors, and bank financing may be relevant to your situation.

Banks are in the business of renting money for a fee. They have no interest in the brilliance of your potential films; they do not care that you are a nice person and have a sparkling reputation. By law, commercial banks (the ones that give you checking accounts) can only lend money based on measurable risk, and the only credit they can take is the collateral, or the assets being offered to secure the loan. The contracts that have already been discussed—negative pickups, distribution agreements, and presales—are such collateral (assets offered to offset the bank's risk). The bank does not have to worry about when you deliver the film or how the box office performs; it is the distributor who has that worry.

The cost of the loan is tied to the prime rate, which is the rate of interest that banks pay to borrow from the Federal Reserve. It is a floating number that may fluctuate significantly. Home lending rates, also based on the prime rate, are a good example. When the prime rate falls, everyone rushes to refinance their mortgages. In most commercial lending, loans to "low-risk" firms (e.g., major studios) can be 0.5 to 1 percent above the prime rate. On the other hand, a small production company, which represents a higher risk, would pay up to 3 percent above prime. Let's say that the bank is going to charge 2 percentage points above prime and that prime is 9 percent. The total would be 11 percent. On a $1-million loan, therefore, the bank removes $110,000 ($1 million multiplied by 0.11). To hedge their risk, the bank also retains another 1 or 2 percent in case the prime rate goes up. If the bank charges 1 percent, another $10,000 is added to their retained amount. Now you are down to $880,000 for the film. The bank is not through with you yet, however. It also charges you for its attorneys' fees, which can range from $15,000 for a simple contract to six figures if several companies are involved. Of course, you will still have to pay your own legal fees.

Once again we come back to the subject of attorneys. The one who represents you must know the ins and outs of all these contracts, so you should hire an experienced entertainment attorney. Costs go up drastically if your attorney is charging you an hourly rate to learn how the entertainment industry works. General corporate attorneys may mean well, but they can be an expensive choice.

Advantages and Disadvantages

The first advantage of bank loans is that the producer is not personally liable for the loan; the bank can't take your house. A company is established for the production of the film, which is its only asset. In addition, many producers prefer to pay back a loan rather than give up equity. On the down side, the process to obtain a loan is expensive, and several parties and miles of paperwork are involved. Also, if the distributor defaults on the loan, the bank takes possession of the film.

COMPLETION GUARANTORS

Misunderstood by neophyte filmmakers is the role of the completion guarantor. This is not the person you go to for the rest of your
production money; the guarantor's role is to provide an assurance
that the film will be completed and delivered to the distributor. The
contract with the producer or distributor allows the guarantor to
take over the film to complete it, if need be. For the bond itself, the
guarantor charges a fee based on the film's budget. The charges
have been flexible over the past few years, depending on the state
of the completion business. The bond is not issued until after funding is in place, however, and this fact is often difficult to explain
to investors. To make matters worse, small films have trouble getting bonded anyway. The risk is too great for most guarantors to
bond low-budget films. In the past few years, several of the biggest bond companies lost their financing from insurance companies when high-budget films failed. The active companies had their
hands full with major productions, leaving them little time or inclination to consider your $1-million film. New companies have come
into the market, making the completion bond more accessible for
some smaller films. However, their staying power depends on the
insurance companies that back them.

In many business plans for low-budget films, I no longer mention a bond, as I know they have no chance of getting one. Bonders
seem to be constantly going in and out of the market and changing their requirements. Check the market before deciding what to
say in your business plan. One suggestion is that you say you will
"seek" a bond. If you say that you "intend" to get a bond, it implies
a promise to the investor. Never promise what you don't already
have, whether it is a financial document, an actor, or a director.

A completion bond is always desirable to protect both you and
your investors financially. Accidents and bad weather can happen, but
investors have the right to decide what exposure they want to have.
As always, honesty is the best policy with your investors and yourself.

WHAT DO YOU TELL INVESTORS?

A section on financing assumptions is required as part of your
business plan package. Give investors only relevant information,
not everything in this chapter. Based on the assumption that

your readers are not film sophisticates, you should explain what constitutes a presale agreement, a negative pickup, or whatever form of financing you will pursue. Be prepared to answer investors' questions.

They may ask you about the forms of financing that you have not included. You should be conversant enough with the pros and cons of various strategies to explain your choices intelligently. As mentioned earlier, it is unproductive to include financing methods that you do not plan to use. If you plan to use a limited partnership, for example, the business plan will be part of the offering; otherwise, there is no reason to discuss this form of financing. To do so would be to create a red herring for investors, confusing them with a nonexistent choice.

Along the same lines, you should be careful about considering options that may no longer exist. What Canada or Australia is doing in 2006 may not be relevant in 2008 or later. Financing patterns, like everything else in our culture, can be in or out of vogue from year to year. It is important to keep current with the business climate through the trades and other sources while writing your plan.

FILMMAKERS SHARE THEIR INVESTOR EXPERIENCES

I asked a group of filmmakers and fundraisers to relate their experiences when raising money from equity investors. The participants included Joslyn Barnes, co-founder of Louverture Films with Danny Glover; Joel Eisenberg and Tim Owens, EMO Films; Patricia Payne, NoHo Films International; April Wade, Woman On Top Productions; and Jay Spain, producer, *Moving Midway*.

LL: What are the top questions that investors asked?
Joslyn: Who's in the film from a talent standpoint? How are you going to get my money back and when? More recently we've been getting sophisticated questions about soft monies, tax incentives, and various gap and super gap lending frameworks. Investors are quite savvy that their equity participation is a hard thing to find at this time, and therefore equity financing is becoming more expensive.

Joel and Tim: Our potential investors didn't know what questions to ask. Since they had already worked with Tim in real estate investing, they had a comfort level with him and his advice. As experienced investors, however, they wanted to know all the risks. Joel spoke several times about studio films and independent films. He did general education about film and the entertainment industry being sure they knew all the risks in independent film. He also told them there were several thousand films a year that don't get any distribution, and the worst-case scenario that they might not make any money.

Patricia: Who are the actors? Who is the director? Have your previous projects made money for investors? Give me reasons why I'd want to invest in films. Why do you want to make this film? Who is your audience? Do you have a distributor? They also ask about what type tax write-off or benefits they will get; will there be any income generated from the project and when will it start and how much to expect. Is there information available to substantiate their backgrounds? Is there a prospectus and material supporting this project, and is it currently available? As an investor, do I get the first right of refusal on any subsequent projects? Would there be a role for my daughter/son/wife?

April: These are basic, but they are pretty much the *only* questions I get asked when looking for money: Who is in it? Who is directing it? Where are you shooting? They don't ask me about myself, and they ask about the movie only generally. I find that with the one that I am currently working on getting funded, they have a lot of specific questions about the mood of the piece, since it is a "nontraditional rock-film" about a very dark topic. Otherwise, "who is the audience," "what are your plans for distribution," etc. has not really been asked of me yet.

Jay: Most of our investors are North Carolinians. *Moving Midway* had tremendous local appeal to them. They either knew the family or wanted to participate in history, or both. Having said that, the questions we got most were: How much money do you need? How much have you raised so far? Who else has invested? How much did this or that person invest? During the first round of fundraising, we told everyone we had a business plan—with, of course, your credentials, the LLC paperwork, and who our attorney was. I know a few of them read the paperwork, but I don't think most did. Only a few asked about return on investment. I don't think most cared. One of them told me that he thought it was just the right thing to do.

Otherwise, there were a lot of reasons: the Academy Award potential, preserving history, education, and race relations. There were a lot of reasons that were not about making money. I think our biggest investor did it mainly for the arts.

During the second round of fundraising after we asked you to update the plan, more people read it and commented. Most of the questions then were making sure they understood what was there. Between the plan and the LLC and the distribution deals, I feel like I got an Entertainment Law degree. [LL: As happens in many documentaries, events prevented finishing the project in the original timeframe planned; therefore, we updated the financial tables.]

LL: Is there a difference between U.S. and European/Asian investors?

Joslyn: Yes, mainly it is the expectations that are quite different. U.S. investors expect to recoup against all world sales on *a pro rata pari passu* basis, and expect to be in first position behind only the standard P&A expenditures, sales fees, and taxes. They also expect a premium on their investment upfront and to see their names prominently displayed in the credits.

European investors expect to recoup against specific territories and are used to international co-productions with many producing partners. There does not seem to be as much of an emphasis on personal credits, though there are arguably many people interested in being involved with quality, prestige vehicles, red carpet opportunities, and networking with film stars. This last applies to the United States, as well.

The other significant difference is the approach to content. European and American investors and filmmakers have cultivated different tastes and audience bases over the decades. Europeans are used to auteur-driven filmmaking as much as they can also appreciate a Hollywood blockbuster. I don't think the reverse can be said of Americans, and American audiences are notoriously allergic to subtitles and dubbing—English language rules, despite emerging successes in the Spanish-language market, which is finding its clout. As a result, U.S. investors tend to shy away from foreign films. And the American indie market, with its white bourgeois male 20- to 30-something bias, has also shrunk dramatically.

On the doc side, you will find engaged U.S. equity investors ready to put up monies for issues they sincerely care about if they feel the films have a chance of being distributed/seen. In Europe equity investors for docs are extremely rare, as most docs are for broadcast and funded via broadcast networks and the many soft monies available to filmmakers in Europe. U.S. filmmakers do not have access to as much soft money, few foundations support film at a level that really makes a difference, and those that do tend to fund at the seed stage or the outreach stage rather than to fund production itself. This is actually I think a smart approach given the limited funding available and the demonstrable need; but the lack of soft money in general in the United States to support the arts is egregious and frankly outrageous when compared with other industrialized nations.

LL: How did you find your investors?
Joslyn: When we launched our company we were quite clear about our intentions, and we have been fortunate to work with producer colleagues and superb filmmakers who have realized those intentions successfully. We have been able to attract investors as a result.

We are of course in a privileged position as Mr. Glover is a well-known and well-respected film star, so it has been easier to navigate the usual channels of social networking than would likely have been the case otherwise. The key, however, has been building a brand, and we have done that through clarity of intent, adhering to certain principles, and sheer sweat equity!
Joel and Tim: We didn't solicit investors at the group. The first person who put money in came up to us after the meeting. That led to another and to another, etc.
Patricia: That's a difficult one for me to be specific. Having been in the industry for many years working in several countries I have gathered contacts both in and out of the film industry. I never ask a relative or friend to invest in my own projects. It's been doctors, dentists, real estate developers, hoteliers, actor/estate agents, government film agencies, an advertising company, commercial radio, and television stations. I also have approached banks for gap financing. There were professional fundraisers at a brokerage firm (in Australia) where I worked some time ago who raised several million dollars for me from 147 investors. In the latter deal there were a few substantial investors seeking a tax break and many smaller investors along for the ride and a tax break. However, the tax structure has changed in Australia since this project was funded. They didn't solicit investors at the group.

Jay: Our investors were mostly friends of the executive producer, Bernie Reeves, or Godfrey's [Cheshire, the director] or mine. Many also came in by word-of-mouth from our investors. Each had to have a net worth of $1 million minimum. We did have some donations also through our fiscal sponsor, the Southern Documentary Fund in Durham.

LL: What suggestions do you want to make to filmmakers in approaching investors?

Joslyn: Do your due diligence. Make sure that your project is sound. Do you have a great script, a feasible production schedule, an accurate budget? Do you have people with the necessary talent and skills to execute your project at a professional level? Are you sure of your financial model insofar as possible? Have you tested your sales estimates? Have you vetted your investors? Are you 100 percent sure they are for real? Do they have the monies they say they do? What is their reputation? Have they worked in film before or not? What business do they work in?

Seek investors with common interests and goals to your own so that expectations at all levels dovetail. Most people in a position to invest monies in films have made those monies because they are quite savvy businesspeople. In our experience, such investors appreciate down-to-earth, informed presentations where risk is laid out honestly alongside efforts to mitigate that risk. You may need to educate them about the film business and the kind of flexible mindset it requires.

Build long-term relationships. Don't focus on short-term quick fixes. If you burn through investors, you are not helping anyone, including yourself. Building long-term relationships implies honesty, respect, transparency, delivery, and accountability.

Joel and Tim: You have to know what you are doing or work with someone who understands and can explain the business and marketing of film. Before we took any money, we had an operating agreement for our LLC and a PPM with subscription docs. We also decided to become investors by leaving our finder's fees for raising the money in the film. [LL: As executive producers, they raised the money for *April Showers*, a film that April Wade produced. It is coincidental, however, that I have answers from all three. Patricia, who has known her for a long time, asked her to participate in this section.]

Patricia: Know your stuff, and be able to present it cogently. Many potential investors invest for a living or a tax break. The filmmaker's responses should be substantial and relevant; your enthusiasm for the project should be coherent. It helps to have name actors, a director with some experience, and personnel—creative and production—on board who have track records. Not only do these people help get the film finished, but also they are pitch points up front when raising money. Less detail about the script itself is better, as it often loses something in the telling particularly to nonindustry folk. Just hit the main pitch points and know them backward. If the investors want to know more about the script, they'll ask.

Other potential investors may be real estate developers, doctors, dentists, or a neighbor. Many of these folks don't know much about the film or television industry other than viewing the finished product. Be prepared to explain the project and the deal in terms each individual can understand.

When dealing with tax incentives, you are dealing with governments and taxpayer funds. Film commissions need to answer to their state or federal government as to why this production and investment is worthwhile for their state or country. All government agencies want to see the merit of investing taxpayer dollars, and they want all the reassurance they can get.

Jay: Three words: DO YOUR HOMEWORK!

EUROPEAN FILM FINANCING*

*This section is courtesy of and written by Thierry Baujard and Frauke Feuer, Peacefulfish, a consultancy for financing the Content Industry, Berlin, Germany.

In Europe, co-production is the most used option to finance projects within a country or with other countries. The term can be misleading as co-production can simply be a collaboration between two companies or a collaboration that follows very strict rules that are indicated in an official contract between two or more countries.

This chapter is trying to give some background information and issues on how to develop co-production financing in Europe for independent producers. Peacefulfish, a consultancy based in Berlin, Germany, can help you better understand the process, identify the right partners to raise the money, and develop the right business and finance plans that will make the most of the co-production opportunities in Europe.

For more information, please log on to *www.pecefulfish.com* or contact *thierry@peacefulfish.com*.

Co-Productions

One way to finance your film is to look for a co-producer. Co-production means sharing production costs, rights, and profits with another production company either from the same country or a foreign country. In the case of a foreign country there are two possible reasons: either the co-producer can access additional funding in the form of public subsidies such as grants, interest-free loans, or tax incentives, or the co-producer offers very low production costs.

If the main goal is to access public funding in the foreign territory, then there needs to be a co-production agreement or a treaty between your country and the foreign one. Regarding Europe, there are two types of agreements to keep in mind: the European convention and bilateral treaties.

European Convention on Cinematographic Production (Council of Europe[1])

The European Convention aims to support European co-production by enabling a film production to benefit from all national

[1] The Council of Europe is *not* the European Union/European Commission; these are two completely different organizational entities.

supports available through the participating producers. There have to be at least three established producers from different countries. Only these countries are relevant, which have ratified the Convention. If a producer from a nonmember country is involved, her contribution must not be more than 30 percent of the total budget.

Bilateral Treaties

There are numerous bilateral treaties between European and non-European countries, which also enable co-productions to benefit from both countries' support schemes. For the latest information visit:

- United Kingdom: *http://www.culture.gov.uk/what_we_do/ creative_industries/3269.aspx* (accessed May 19, 2009).
- France: *http://www.cnc.fr/Site/TemplateA2.aspx?SELECTID= 35&id=36&t=1* (accessed May 19, 2009, French only).
- Germany: *http://www.bundesregierung.de/nn_25188/Webs/ Breg/DE/Bundesregierung/BeauftragterfuerKulturundMedien/ Medienpolitik/Filmfoerderung/InternationaleFilmfoerderung/ internationale-filmfoerderung.html* (accessed May 20, 2009, German only).
- Canada: *http://www.telefilm.gc.ca/04/43.asp?lang=en&* (accessed May 20, 2009).

Public Subsidies

In Europe, subsidies are playing a key role in film production. There are state-funded grants on three levels: the European level (provided by the European Union and the Council of Europe), national level, and regional level. Subsidies have to be applied for and are granted if a project is approved by a board or commission depending on business and creative criteria.

European Level

At the European level there are two relevant schemes: the MEDIA 2007 program (EU, duration 2007 to 2013) and EURIMAGES (Council of Europe). The European Union (EU) is a community of currently 27[2] European member states that collaborate to a level where some national sovereignty is handed over to EU bodies in order to make democratic decisions on specific matters of joint interest. The Council of Europe (COE) is an organization of currently 47[3] European states that aims at increasing the awareness of a European identity and providing control and monitoring for human rights and democratic processes. The COE has no legislative powers.

Media 2007 (EU)

The MEDIA 2007 program supports the audiovisual industry in Europe in the areas of training, development, distribution, promotion, and cinematographic festivals. For aspiring filmmakers, the areas of interest are mainly support for development. To be eligible for support, the applying company has to be registered in a country that participates in the MEDIA program. Currently the MEDIA 2007 program has 32 members. The scheme could therefore also work for non-European companies in case they enter into co-production with an eligible company. Apart from geographical eligibility there are also requirements regarding the existence of the applying company (registered for at least 12 months) and proof of previous experience. However, there are no specific requirements of a company's turnover or profit. The amount of support granted can be up to 50 percent or even 60 percent of a part of the budget, depending on the kind of support and the respective threshold. For application forms as well as more information and deadlines, visit the EU's MEDIA website at *http://ec.europa.eu/information_society/media/overview/2007/index_en.htm* (accessed May 26, 2009).

Preparatory Action Media International/MEDIA MUNDUS

The PREPATORY ACTION is a funding scheme by the EU for audiovisual activities between EU and third countries. It is undertaken in preparation of the MEDIA MUNDUS program, which is planned to run from 2011 to 2013 with a budget of EUR 15 milion for funding of submitted projects. It is a broad international cooperation program for the audiovisual industry to reinforce the cultural and

[2]Source: *http://europa.eu/abc/keyfigures/index_en.htm.*
[3]Source: *http://www.coe.int/aboutCoe/index.asp?page=quisommesnous&l=en.*

commercial relations between Europe's film industry and filmmakers from third countries. For more information, visit *http://ec.europa.eu/ information_society/media/mundus/index_en.htm* (accessed May 26, 2009).

Eurimages (Coe)

EURIMAGES is a funding program initiated by the Council of Europe aiming to support co-production, distribution, and exhibition of European cinematographic works. Support is divided between co-production, distribution, and exhibition for feature films, documentaries, and animation projects of at least 70 minutes in length. To be eligible for co-production support the project needs at least two producers from different EURIMAGES member states and has to have a European origin. Financially that means that at least 51 percent of the funding has to derive from EURIMAGES member states and no more than 30 percent of the funding can originate from non-European sources or one non-EURIMAGES country. For filmmakers outside EURIMAGES member countries this means that the program becomes only of interest in the case of minority a co-production. For more information, visit *http://www .coe.int/Eurimages* (accessed May 26, 2009).

National Level

Throughout Europe most countries provide state support for the audiovisual industry. Foreign filmmakers can benefit from these support schemes through being part of a co-production with one or more of these countries. If the participating countries have agreements with one another, national subsidies are accessible for international co-productions as well. In the following, different schemes are outlined based on their support budget, eligibility and selection criteria, funding aspects, and recoupment strategies.

United Kingdom: UK Film Council

The UK Film Council has an annual budget of about GBP 55 million derived from the National Lottery and Grant-in-aid. Support is available in the areas of development, feature film production, distribution and exhibition, and short films, as well as in a range of other related fields. Applicants need to be production companies based in the United Kingdom or the EU. In case of an EU applicant, if funding is awarded it can only be paid to a limited liability company registered in the United Kingdom (either a company incorporated in the United Kingdom or a company incorporated in the European Economic Area and registered as a branch in the United Kingdom). For non-EU applicants co-production is an option taking into account the requirements above.

For feature films the UK Film Council offers two schemes: the Premiere Fund and the New Cinema Fund. The Premiere Fund invests (usually up to 35 percent of the budget[4]) in mainstream, commercially driven films, and encourages the participation of British creative talent. The New Cinema Fund finances films (participation between 15 and 50 percent of the budget[5]) that "communicate unique ideas, demonstrate an innovative approach or showcase new voices" but are still commercially viable. The budgets of the two funds have so far been about GBP 8 million (Premiere Fund; support for eight to nine films per year[6]) and GBP 5 million[7] (New Cinema Fund).

The Film Council's executives assess eligible projects for their creative merit and, depending on the scheme, also on commercial prospects. Once funding is offered, the actual amount granted depends on the individual project depending on the support scheme and the individual case. In most cases funding will not be higher than 50 percent of the budget. All support is given in the form of an equity investment and will be recouped on a *pro rata pari passu* basis with those offered to other equity investors. For more information, visit *http://www.ukfilmcouncil.org.uk/* (accessed May 26, 2009).

Germany: FFA (German Federal Film Board) and DFFF (German Federal Film Fund)

The German Federal Film Board is funded by a film levy from video exhibitors and distributors and has an annual budget of about EUR 76 million.[8] Support is available in the areas of production, script development, and distribution, as well as in a range of other related

---

[4]Source: *http://www.ukfilmcouncil.org.uk/media/pdf/i/q/Premiere_Fund_-_guidelines__updated_ March_2009_.pdf* (page 2).
[5]Source: *http://www.ukfilmcouncil.org.uk/ncfavailable*.
[6]Source: *http://www.ukfilmcouncil.org.uk/premiere*.
[7]Source: *http://www.ukfilmcouncil.org.uk/media/pdf/5/8/HC_714_web_PDF.pdf* (page 10).
[8]Source: *http://www.ffa.de/start/index.phtml?page=profil*.

fields for feature films of at least 79 minutes or children's films of at least 59 minutes as well as short films. To be eligible the responsible producer or the production company has to be registered in Germany, or in the case of an international co-production, the German co-producer has to have the majority. Furthermore, the producer has to come up with at least 15 percent of the budget. Support is only granted if the project deems to improve the quality and profitability of German cinema. The decision is made by a board on the basis of screenplay, budget, financing plan, cast and crew lists, and, if applicable, the distribution contracts. Selected projects can receive EUR 250,000 on average and up to EUR 1 million in special cases. The grants are conditionally repayable, interest-free loans, and recoupment sets in at 10 percent of the revenues accruing to the producer after his initial recoupment of 20 percent of the FFA-recognized production costs from the film's exploitation.

The FFA has also been responsible for running the German Federal Film Fund (DFFF) since January 1, 2007. It was initially planned for three years until 2009 and has since been extended until the end of 2012.[9] This local spend-based funding model for theatrical feature films that can qualify as "German"[10] was initiated by the federal government and provides annual subsidies of EUR 60 million. For more information, visit *http://www.ffa.de/* (accessed May 26, 2009).

France: CNC

The National Centre for Cinematography (CNC) offers support in the areas of development, feature film production, distribution, and short films, as well as in a range of other related fields. For first-time feature projects, a selective support scheme is available. Applying projects need to be shot in French and are either completely produced by a French production company or they can be international co-productions. The CNC's executive director and a commission of industry professionals assess eligible projects. Funding is offered either as an advance against takings before completion or an advance after completion and amounted to about 12 percent of the budget on average. The actual amount granted depends on the individual project, and the conditions of repaying

[9]Source: *http://www.ffa.de/start/index.phtml?page=dfff_start*.
[10]Based on a cultural test similar to the British and French tests.

the advance are also based on the individual case. There is also a support scheme for foreign-language films, which still demands a French production company to be involved but can be shot in a language other than French. For more information, visit *http://www .cnc.fr/* (accessed May 26, 2009).

Regional Level

Most European countries also have film-supporting agencies on a regional level. In the following, the biggest three regional agencies in the three biggest markets—United Kingdom, Germany, and France—are outlined.

United Kingdom

The United Kingdom has nine English regional support agencies and one each in Scotland, Northern Ireland, and Wales. Among the biggest are Northern Ireland Film & Television Commission (up to GBP 600,000 per project[11]), Screen Yorkshire (up to GBP 350,000 per project[12]), and EM Media (up to GBP 250,000 per project[13]). Mostly eligibility depends on local money spent and/or residence in the area while the involvement of local talent/cultural relevance is often preferable but not obligatory. Selection is made by the funding agencies and individual contracts are then set up. Most agencies do not give grants, so money has to be repaid. All film boards also help with other aspects of production such as location scouting. For further information, visit *http://www.ukfilmcouncil. org.uk/contactscreenagencies*, *http://www.northernirelandscreen.co.uk/*, *http://www.screenyorkshire.co.uk/*, and *http://www.em-media.org.uk* (all accessed May 27, 2009).

Germany

There are nine regional film agencies plus other regional institutions that support film and audiovisual production. The biggest three are Filmstiftung North-Rhine-Westphalia (EUR 36 million

[11] Source: *http://rsu.ukfilmcouncil.org.uk/?pf=&low=&c=16&y=2007&s=.*
[12] Source: *http://rsu.ukfilmcouncil.org.uk/?pf=&low=&c=16&y=2007&s=.*
[13] Source: *http://rsu.ukfilmcouncil.org.uk/?pf=&low=&c=16&y=2007&s=.*

annual budget[14]), FilmFernsehFonds Bavaria (EUR 30 million[15]), and Filmboard Berlin-Brandenburg (EUR 29 million[16]). Who can apply for support differs between funds. Requirements can include a German-registered company, a certain percentage of money spent in the region, a certain percentage of the budget invested by the producer, etc. Eligible projects are then assessed for their cultural, artistic, and commercial value by the board and a selection is made. Selected projects mostly receive an interest-free loan, which is repaid only on the basis of success. All film boards also help with other aspects of production such as location scouting. For further information, visit *http://www.filmstiftung.de/*, *http://www.fff-bayern.de/*, and *http://www.medienboard.de* (all accessed May 27, 2009).

France

There are 19 local and regional supports in France. The biggest three are Ile-de-France (EUR 14,550,000 annual budget in 2008[17]), Rhône-Alpes (EUR 3,771,500[18]), and Nord-Pas-De-Calais (EUR 2,657,240[19]). Support is available for screenplay writing, development, production, and postproduction of feature and short films as well as other formats. Only French companies can apply and the application needs to be in French as well. Support ranges from subsidies over co-financing to co-producing and is mostly granted before principal shooting has begun. The actual conditions and obligations depend on the region and individual project and will be stated in a contract between the applying (and selected) company and the administration. When planning to produce or fund your project in France, it is very handy to know the French language since a range of web sites are available only in French so far. For more information, visit *http://www.filmfrance.net*, *http://www.centreimages.fr//production_guide.php*, *http://www.iledefrance.fr/cinema*, *http://www.rhone-alpes-cinema.fr/*, and *http://www.crrav.com/* (all accessed May 27, 2009).

---

[14]Source: *http://www.filmstiftung.de/fist/download_pdf/diverses/die_zahlen_2008.pdf*.

[15]Source: *http://www.fff-bayern.de/fileadmin/user_upload/FFF_Bayern_Jahresbilanz_2008_Factsheet.pdf*.

[16]Source: *http://www.medienboard.de/WebObjects/Medienboard.woa/wa/CMSshow/1436390?wosid=*.

[17]Source: *http://www.centreimages.fr//Syntheses2008.pdf* (page 304).

[18]Source: *http://www.centreimages.fr//Syntheses2008.pdf* (page 304).

[19]Source: *http://www.centreimages.fr//Syntheses2008.pdf* (page 304).

Tax Incentives

Besides state subsidies, many European countries have set up tax incentives to attract film production to their territories. In the following, some of the most popular schemes are introduced from the United Kingdom, France, Hungary, and Ireland.

United Kingdom

In 2006 the popular sale-and-leaseback scheme, also known as "Section 42" and "Section 48," was replaced by the new tax relief system for film. For lower-budget films (< GBP 20 million) there is a net tax relief of 20 percent; for higher-budget productions (> GBP 20 million) it is 16 percent. Both reliefs only apply to the qualifying UK spend of the budget. There is also a threshold of minimum UK spending, which is 25 percent of the budget. In addition, there is an enhanced deduction available of 100 percent of qualifying UK spend for lower-budget productions and 80 percent for higher-budget productions. The payable cash element is 25 percent of surrendered losses for lower budgets and 20 percent for higher budgets. Furthermore, in order to get support, films have to pass a test in order to qualify as culturally British, which is composed of cultural content, cultural hubs, and cultural practitioners. For more information, visit *http:// www.ukfilmcouncil.org.uk/qualifying*, *http://www.ukfilmcouncil.org.uk/ taxrelief*, *http://www.hmrc.gov.uk/manuals/fpcmanual/Index.htm*, and *http://www.culture.gov.uk/what_we_do/creative_industries/3269.aspx* (all accessed May 28, 2009).

France

The French have set up two schemes, one called *SOFICA*, which are film investment trusts aimed at tax deduction, and the other called *credit d'impot*, which is a tax credit. Individuals or companies invest in SOFICA to qualify for tax deductions. The SOFICA invest in production or production companies on the basis of individually contracted recoupment conditions. The credit d'impot aims at nourishing production and postproduction activities in France; thus the production or postproduction has to take place in France. French producers can choose between a cash rebate or a lowering of corporation tax of up to 20 percent of below-the-line costs.

In December 2008, the French Parliament passed a new law creating the Tax Rebate for International Production (T.R.I.P.). It is aimed at film production and postproduction services of movies of which the "dramatic content" has links with the "culture, heritage or territory of France." To fulfill these conditions a cultural test has to be passed. In addition, shooting has to span at least five days in France and EUR 1 million of eligible costs in France have to be incurred. Although the procedure is not yet official by the time of writing (June 5, 2009), producers whose activities have started after January 1, 2009, and that qualify under the scheme can claim the benefit. The rebate, worth 20 percent of all eligible costs, is capped at EUR 4 million (U.S. $5.3 million[20]). For more information, visit *http://www.filmfrance.net/telechargement/FranceCoprodGuide08.pdf* and *http://www.filmfrance.net/v2/gb/home.cfm?choixmenu=taxcredit* (both accessed May 28, 2009).

Hungary

The Hungarian tax incentive scheme is service production oriented. The model involves a service agreement or co-production agreement between a foreign and a Hungarian production company and a Hungarian corporate company. The corporate company sponsors up to 20 percent of the Hungarian production budget and qualifies for a reduction of its corporate tax. In order to qualify the production has to be registered at the National Film Office (NFO) in Hungary, which assesses the Hungarian production costs. If approved, the NFO gives out a tax certificate to the Hungarian corporate company. Due to European legislation on state aid, film projects also have to pass a European cultural test to qualify for this scheme. For more information, visit *http://filminhungary.com/object.ed29a811-0146-4ef1-81ce-202d4be8f428.ivy* and *http://www.nemzetifilmiroda.hu* (both accessed May 28, 2009).

Ireland

The Irish tax incentive scheme for film and television is called "Section 481" and was set up in 1993. It is spend based and worth up to 28 percent of eligible spending. The incentive is paid up front

---

[20]Rate: €1 = U.S. $1.32838 (April 9, 2009).

in cash on the first day of principal photography, net of all fees, and has a cap of EUR 50 million of eligible spending. The way to access this incentive is through an Irish co-producer, and a list of producers is available on the Irish Film Board website: *http://www .irishfilmboard.ie/filming.php?id=7* (Los Angeles, CA, office) and *http:// www.irishfilmboard.ie/filming/Tax_Incentives/18*.

Distribution

Regarding distribution in Europe there are similar structures to the United States in terms of theatrical distribution. In addition, the TV broadcasters play an important role. Most TV broadcasters are buying finished films or are involved in presales. Thus, when looking for funding, take the relevant TV markets into consideration.

United Kingdom

In the United Kingdom the most important player in the TV market is the BBC. Through its film production arm, BBC Films, it supports British productions and British-International co-productions. Film4 has also played an important role in film financing. However, due to the financial crisis in 2008/2009 the parent organizations of both entities have been facing budget reductions and/or restrictions. For more information, visit *http://www.bbc.co.uk/bbcfilms/ who/* and *http://www.channel4.com/film/ffproductions/team.html* (both accessed June 2, 2009).

Germany

The German TV market is the largest in Europe and the second largest in the world. In Germany there are about 30 nationwide free TV broadcasters, among them 15 TV channels under public law and 8 private ones. One channel, which is especially active in film co-production, is "arte," itself a co-production between Germany and France aimed at cultural understanding. Language is not an issue, presuming that the production budget of an English-language film includes dubbing into German. Subtitling is occurring but rarely on main channels and during primetime. For more information, visit *http://www.arte.tv/fr/70 .html* (French and German available) (accessed June 2, 2009).

France

All European countries are held to dedicate the majority of air-time to European productions following the European directive "Television without Frontiers" from 1989, revised in 1997 and 2005. In France, the government even set the quota to 60/40 in favor of European works. This also enhances French-International co-productions. The main player in production is Canal Plus. For more information, visit *http://www.canalplus.fr/* (French only) (accessed June 2, 2009).

Banking

Only the five big European countries have developed film banking markets: France, Germany, United Kingdom, Spain, and Italy. The main film banking services that are provided are Interim Finance, Tax-Incentive Financing, Gap Financing, Working Capital/ Corporate Finance, and Bank Guarantee.

Due to the financial crisis in 2008/2009 many financial institutes across Europe are reconsidering their engagement in film financing, which has led to the closure of some divisions (temporarily).

In the United Kingdom, Barclay's Bank, Coutts, and Allied Irish Bank were still active in film financing in the middle of 2009.

Two French credit institutions specializing in the audiovisual sector are Cofiloisirs S.A. and Natexis Coficiné S.A. As a security for the banks there is the Institute for the Financing of the Cinema and Cultural Industries (IFCIC). Banks can apply for a financial guarantee of 50 to 70 percent of the loans they are granting to production companies. The IFCIC assesses the film projects and issues the guarantee if the project is approved.

There are also activities in other countries such as Germany (namely Commerzbank, Deutsche Bank, and HypoVereinsBank) or Hungary (mainly aimed at prefinancing funds based on the Hungarian tax credit), even though these activities are moderate in the latter case.

On a European level there is a development, which sees the European Investment Bank getting involved in film financing. So far it is active in France, but support for specialized banks in other European countries is possible.

CASE STUDY (FICTIVE)

Let's do a short walk-through example of how you could fund a film project in Europe. Before we flesh out the example with some numbers, here is a list of questions you may like to consider when looking at co-productions:

1. Where is the main production company located? If you are located in the United States, consider co-producing with Canada, since Canada has a range of agreements with European countries.
2. Is your country part of a bilateral agreement of a European country or member of the European Convention on Cinematographic Production?
3. Is your country part of the European Union?
4. Has your country signed the EURIMAGES agreement?
5. Are there national subsidies in your country?
6. Are there regional subsidies in your country?
7. Are there tax incentives in your country?
8. Are there broadcasters involved in presales or co-production in your country?
9. Are there banks specialized in film financing in your country?
10. Which countries are most promising in entering into a co-production with (choose your candidates and go through the previous questions for each of them)?

The Example

Our fictive film project involves four production companies from France, Germany, Canada, and the United States. The budget is EUR 4 million.

As in every co-production, be it national or international, involved companies have to decide on their individual share of rights, territories, profits, recoupment positions, revenue corridors, etc. In a traditional co-production, the co-producer from a certain country normally received the rights for that particular country and neighbor countries using the same language. The co-producer can also look for distribution (theatrical and TV) in the country.

France and Germany both have a bilateral agreement with Canada and are members of the European Convention on Cinematographic Production.

The bilateral agreements and the convention secure the same option: to benefit from the co-producing countries' national supports. But if the convention is applied, the share of the total budget (and thus shares of rights, profits, etc.) for the United States and Canada can only be up to 30 percent (EUR 1.2 million). Through the co-production treaty, you will be able to access funding from the other country but do not forget that you will have to spend at least 150 percent in the country or region where you will get the subsidies from.

That might not be enough considering the efforts such a multi-international production causes. However, even under the bilateral agreements with European countries, the obligation is that the majority needs to be held by European producers.

France and Germany are both part of the European Union as well as members of EURIMAGES and are thus eligible for European subsidies. Both have national and regional subsidies. France has a tax shelter and two tax credits. Germany has the German Federal Film Fund. Both countries have cultural tests linked with their subsidies. The German-French broadcaster "arte" could be involved in presales or co-productions. France and to a lesser degree Germany have banks involved in film financing.

This is only a very rough idea of the complexity of international co-productions.

Don't forget that there are extensive rules and obligations for each country referring to each financing tool. Due to local spend, majority requirements and cultural relevance finance might not be as easy to get as it seems at first glance. Many funds on a national level are selective aids; however, this can also be an advantage for producing in Europe since funding is not primarily aimed at commercial projects.

In addition, there are excellent production facilities and professional staff capacities available in central Europe for a fraction of the price of the ones in established countries. If you are going to produce in or with Europe it will be wise to get some professional help in dealing with the business plan, the financing strategy, and the legal aspects involved, as well as to benefit from an already established network of contacts in the European film industry. For more information, visit *www.peacefulfish.com* or send email to *contact@peacefulfish.com*.

After this initial financing strategy, the next step is to work on the cash flow for the project, which is basically the same as in American productions and explained in the "Financial Worksheet-Instructions" on Focal's companion site for the book.

10

The Financial Plan

Get your facts first; then you can distort them as you please.

MARK TWAIN

FORECASTING WITHOUT FEAR

Predicting the future has been popular since the days of Nostradamus. No one can afford to run a business without looking ahead. Only when you have a clear picture of your film's potential results or company's future can you proceed with a feeling of confidence. In the past 500 years, little has changed except the technology. For filmmakers, predicting the revenue of films yet to be made is a necessity. This chapter reviews how to find data, what to do with it after you find it, and how to create your own financial forecasts.

Students often object to looking up boxoffice grosses for a class assignment. Their idea of a business plan is a description of their films and, possibly, general market and distribution information. Although important, these items pale in importance to projected income. Remember the investors? They are going to read the Executive Summary first and then go quickly to the revenues and expenses. Money is the glue that holds these building blocks together.

A filmmaker recently asked me if all my business plans showed films making a profit. The short answer is "Yes." Before investors hand over hard cash, they want to believe that your project will be profitable. In rethinking the Mark Twain quote at the beginning of this chapter, I became concerned about the phrase "as you please." Partially, this is true. However, keep in mind that whatever the forecast, it has to look reasonable to the "he who has the gold."

199

Forecasting is an art, albeit not a precise one. Sophisticated business writers like to say that the one sure thing about a prediction is that it will be wrong; they are probably right. The value of a forecast is as a guide for making decisions; the better informed the forecaster, the closer to actual events the forecast will be. By researching history, obtaining the best data possible, looking for relationships among the data you find, and making assumptions about the future based on those relationships, you hopefully have a rational basis for your forecasts.

When writing your proposal, you have to decide which group of numbers tells your story best. The most recent data may be a year or two behind because of the flow of revenues. You therefore have the opportunity to forecast to the current period, putting whatever spin on these statistics you can justify with current events. Remember our discussions about investors in the previous chapter? They value two things most of all: facts and common sense. Your goal is to show that the independent film market is robust and that profits can be made.

Anyone Can Do It

There is no mystery to forecasting revenues and expenses. You do not have to be an accountant or hold an M.B.A. You do not need previous knowledge of trend and regression analysis or internal rate of return. This jargon is used by financial whiz kids to speak to one another; life can go on without it. The information that you uncover can be used to create the numbers that make a company look feasible. You will take the elements that seem to influence the outcome of a film—genre, stars, director, distribution, ancillary returns—and analyze how much you think each will influence the resulting revenue. I used to say that the only math skills you will need are adding, subtracting, multiplying, and dividing. Mix these skills with a little gut feeling, and you have a forecast. If you can balance your checkbook, you can create a forecast.

FINDING THE DATA

What Are Comparative Films?

Forecasting requires that you use films that reasonably can be compared by theme, budget, and release date. Due to inflation, audience tastes, numbers of screens, and other film business trends, the industry standard has been five to seven years including the current one. I have always used five years.

What makes a comparative (comp) film is a combination of factors. The fact that you are making an independently financed film does not mean that you can only use independent films. For low budgets, most of the films within a reasonable budget range are likely to be the only ones available. If you were making a film like *Knowing*, for example, with a budget of $37 million, it is likely that a majority of your comparative films will have been made by studios.

What is a reasonable budget range? With a $2-million budget, I would like all comp films to be at $6 million or below on the high side. Any film with a lower budget that shows a gross profit is fine. However, to find enough films you may have to move the upper limit of budgets that you are using. Be aware though that production quality and cast become important the higher you go. As talented as you may be, you can't use films with $15-million budgets in this financial comparison.

With the advent of digital film, the concept of having a budget that includes a transfer to 35mm is important. I have found it is often difficult for filmmakers to comprehend. At this point, of course, there aren't enough films to compare. As discussed earlier in the book, despite the number of digital screens, all the profitable low-budget films that I have found were released theatrically in both digital and 35mm. When your $30,000 is upped to 35mm, what will it really look like? Is it really going to look like $5 million on the screen? Will it have the same cast that a $5-million film will have? When comparing your film to other movies, remember that the audience doesn't care how you made the film; they care about what the film looks like and who is in it.

On a statistical basis, I feel that at least four to five films are required over the three for which worldwide data is available. In 2009, for example, those years are 2005 to 2007. Now that you have decided your time span and budgets, you can then start looking for films that fit.

Matching Your Film

Do they all have to be just like your film? Films can be similar in genre and subthemes; however, it is unlikely that at any budget you will find 15 films "just like yours." After all, your film is going to be unique. Therefore, start with your overall genre. You may have a crime drama. The film also could have action, romance, gay themes, coming-of-age, or a host of other themes.

The goal is to use films that relate to at least one of these. To fill out your list, budget also is a consideration. Since you are likely to be asked by an investor why you used certain films, have a reason for each film that you use. All you can do is your best to have a rationality for each film. There isn't a rule as to what will seem reasonable to a given investor.

The data that you gather about previously released films will serve two purposes: (1) show the profits of films recently released, and (2) supply a basis for estimating the revenues *and* total costs for your films. The first part of your numerical story consists of showing what has happened with films that have already been produced and released. You use these examples to build a case for the ultimate success of your film. Select recent films that have a relation to your planned production in terms of genre, budget, or other common factors.

Genre is a common way to group films; however, use whatever characteristic you feel links these films together. But whatever your rationale for grouping films, use budget clusters that make sense.

The films you include in your business plan depend on what is available. It is your choice whether to include films that have lost money. There is no database that includes all the films ever made, so you can't have a "fair" sampling no matter what you do. However, if you use only five films and three of them are films with extraordinary results—for example, *The Blair Witch Project, My Big Fat Greek Wedding, Napoleon Dynamite*—any projection you make will be unrealistic and recognized as such by most investors. Of course, if your budget is in the range of these films, you can't use *Lord of the Rings*.

For example, recently I did a business plan for a sci-fi action faith-based film. It is hard to find sci-fi in a low-budget film due to the special effects requirements. I went to *www.imdb.com* and used the "power search" feature to look for films with sci-fi in them. A list of 1,901 films came up. There were two films that I felt I could use for forecasting in this particular business plan. Of course, there were more that I could use in the Markets section, where you can use a film of the same genre regardless of budget. For the comps, there still were action, inspirational/faith-based, and other films in a reasonable (notice how often that word pops up) budget range that fit this particular synopsis.

Whatever tact you take, heed this warning: **DO NOT INVENT NUMBERS**. If lying does not bother you, getting caught in a lie will. Then the game will be over.

Where Do You Find Information?

Your first trip is to trade papers and free online data collectors such as *www.boxofficemojo*, *www.imdb.com*, *www.thenumbers.com*, and others. Film markets, seminars, and other industry meetings also help give you information on what films you will want to use. Let's look at some specific data that you can uncover in your research. Much has changed since the last edition of this book was published in 2006. I will be describing what sources you will use today. Those may change again by the time you buy this edition; however, the overall methodology will not.

Both *Variety* and the *Hollywood Reporter* have the full list of boxoffice grosses online every week for the current period and cumulative year-to-date. The grosses are reported to *Variety* by Rentrak and to the *Hollywood Reporter* by Exhibitor Relations Co., Inc. Previously, the full *Daily Variety* list was only available by subscription; those data is now free. The same list is available online at the *Hollywood Reporter* but only with a subscription. The boxoffice grosses in these tables equal the total domestic gross sales for the film. Since they include Canada and Puerto Rico, I refer to the grosses as domestic or North American rather than United States. The majority of the films on the list used to be studio productions. Over the past ten years, however, a vast majority of films on the list fit this book's definition of "independent." Both sources have virtually the same boxoffice numbers. Once you have picked the films you want, *www.boxofficemojo.com* is another credible source.

Finding budgets can be another question. Hopefully, most of the films you want to use will have budgets at the sites indicated above. Interviews with filmmakers in the public press are another good source. Check the week or two before release. For recent film releases, check television and radio shows for the appearance of a filmmaker. Young filmmakers appear often on the daytime and evening talk shows. Watch CNN, E! Entertainment Channel, *Oprah*, *Charlie Rose*, and all the news programs, especially on the all-news channels. In recent years, the Independent Film Channel and the Sundance Channel have gone on air in selected markets; naturally, they are dedicated to information about independent films.

The film festivals are another place where you can gather extensive financial information. Many producers and directors of independent films attend, and they will usually answer questions about not only the cost of their films, but also the source of their financing. People often feel more comfortable about revealing proprietary data when face-to-face. Also watch the Oscar telecast and the Cannes Film Festival Awards (broadcast on Bravo). You never know what you might learn.

Revenues from cable, free television, DVD, and other ancillary sources; foreign; and the prints and ads (P&A) costs are harder to find. Some DVD data may be published, although currently the only credible free site is Box Office Mojo. Be careful that you are looking at dollars, however, and not a rental index as listed on *www.imdbpro.com*. Note that Box Office Mojo was acquired by IMDb.com, Inc. in July 2008.

In previous editions, I had a separate section for *average foreign revenues*. The section included a table of typical revenues from individual foreign territories for a $1.5-million film. With presales in flux and foreign territories giving more and more screens over to their locally made films, I don't feel it is appropriate to put together such a table at this time. Distributors either are giving very low numbers or saying that there aren't any foreign sales at all for low-budget independent films. As always, the foreign value of any film depends on the story, cash, etc. In addition, the trade papers have been reluctant to estimate such sales in 2009. Normally, during Cannes or AFM, the *Hollywood Reporter* has had a table called "The Going Rate," which shows average sales of films by territory. Likewise, once or twice a year *Variety* has had a table called "Global TV Price Spread," which shows average prices paid for feature films as well as televison movies, dramas, reality shows, sitcoms, and a combination category of documentaries and children's programming. The last of those charts appeared in 2007. Note their names, as I am sure they will reappear when the world economy gets on a better footing. When I feel there are real numbers, I will include my chart on the book's companion web site.

If you do use the tables from the trades, the range of likely prices is based on the distributors' experience in selling low-budget films. When forecasting, you always want to be conservative, so you would use the average return of dollars. For example, if in Japan, you see that the high is $70,000 and the low is $20,000.

This does not mean that all distributors will pay you $70,000; generally, the most they will pay is 10 percent of the budget. Use the average figure, which is $45,000.

Eventually, to find all the data you will need for your three years of worldwide numbers, you will need to buy the information. I recommend Baseline StudioSystems (*www.blssi.com*) as the current best source. Once you go to the web site, click on "Baseline Research" to learn about purchasing films.

You have to go with the best information you can get. **DO NOT MAKE UP THE NUMBERS.** If telling the truth isn't reason enough, you may have investors check some of your sources, which will be listed at the bottom of your tables. Or, as I have seen many times, some friend of theirs will claim he saw "something somewhere that was another number." Worse yet, your potential investor may have a relative or friend in the film business who can check the data. All sources will not necessarily have the same information; however, you want to be able to point to your sources as the most credible you could find.

ANALYZING THOSE PESKY NUMBERS

Did I say without fear? You must analyze the data before putting it into your proposal. Be strong. You can do it. When collecting and analyzing, keep in mind the words of Mark Twain: "There are three kinds of lies: lies, damned lies, and statistics."

The discussion of financing and your presentation of comparative films, projections, and cash flows is the single most important section of your business plan. Most investors will read your Executive Summary first and then go straight to the tables. The filmmaker's job is to be honest and use common sense.

I have said it before, but filmmakers have convinced me that I cannot say it too often. This analysis is your job, not the investor's. Do not expect the investor to accidentally happen upon useful information while browsing through the 15 or 20 pages you have photocopied from newspapers and magazines. It is your duty to find useful information and present it in an easily understandable way.

Tables 11.3 through 11.6 included with the sample business plan (see Chapter 11) are examples of methods for presenting comparative films. The films listed in these tables are fictional but are based on the results of real films. These sample tables include the following items:

1. *Domestic theatrical rentals:* Domestic rentals are the portion of the North American theatrical box office that reverts back to the distributor (or producer). (The tables in the trades include Canadian boxoffice figures in this total.) There has been confusion in recent years, as we also refer to DVD rentals. The term *domestic theatrical rentals* is the industry standard and should be used.

   As mentioned above, when working with numbers, you should avoid factoring in exceptional movies that would make all your averages too high. If you want to include *My Big Fat Greek Wedding*, list it and indicate in a footnote that it is in your chart for reference only. Just as on any given day any team can win, it is theoretically possible for any film to be a breakout hit.

2. *Domestic ancillary revenue:* The ancillary revenue includes all nontheatrical sources, such as cable, DVD, video, free television, syndicated television, and pay-per-view. Distributors have been trying various formulations of revenue sharing as opposed to paying per unit. However, it is too early to know the effect on independent film. Pay-per-view (movies on demand) is growing, although not as quickly as analysts have expected. Specific numbers do not exist for individual films, so some analysts use a general estimate. Those estimates are derived mostly from studio films, so they are more appropriate for budgets over $15 million than for other films.

   Although release times (windows) into home video have become shorter for studio films, the windows for indies have remained the same. Cable and the premium channels are getting movies sooner than they used to, also. Be aware that although a few of the indie films financed by cable networks have had a U.S. theatrical release, most do not. In the past, PBS has also financed documentaries that have had a theatrical release prior to being shown on television.

3. *Foreign theatrical revenue:* The distributor is responsible for collecting money from the foreign box office, which includes all countries except the United States and Canada as well as Puerto Rico. Generally, the industry assumes that the North American box office drives all

the other windows. If a picture does not perform well in U.S. theaters, therefore, all other theatrical and ancillary venues may be worth less money. On the other hand, some films that do only moderately well in the United States do much better overseas. To make the picture even murkier, there are films that do very well at the domestic box office and in domestic ancillary revenues but have virtually no foreign revenues that are recorded. Depending on the gross profit of those films, they can still be used.

The type of film and the stars often have a lot to do with these results. Certain U.S. television stars continually appear in movies of the week, for instance, because they have large followings in foreign markets. This fact does not mean that distributors will accept them in your feature films.

4. *Foreign ancillary revenue:* Foreign ancillary presents a great opportunity. Television companies often buy exclusive product. In addition, markets have opened up in Eastern Europe and Asia. The studios have established their own distribution arms in India and China. The potential revenues for English-language films, even small ones, in other countries remain much stronger than for foreign-language films in the United States.

5. *Total revenue:* This is rentals plus domestic ancillary plus foreign equal total revenue. The foreign dollars are assumed to have the exhibitor portion removed and, therefore, can be added to the domestic dollars to find total revenue. Always be sure that you are comparing apples to apples.

6. *Negative cost, prints and ads, and total costs:* We have already discussed finding the production, or negative costs, of the film. These are not the total costs, however. Prints and ads are an important expense. It is necessary to include these costs to get a total profit picture. As films stay in distribution, the P&A costs grow. Therefore, if you are forecasting the initial release cost, indicate it. The most credible source for this type of information is still Baseline.

7. *Gross profit (loss):* Gross profit (loss) equals the revenue minus the direct expenses before the company operating expenses. In this case, direct expenses are the negative and P&A costs. They relate directly to your film, as compared to the company overhead costs, which exist whether a film

is in production or not. Notice the parentheses around the word *loss*. When preparing financial statements, use parentheses rather than minus signs to indicate negative numbers. Both words can be written on the profit line. However, if there isn't a projected profit, you may want to rethink the whole idea.

Forecasting While Keeping One Foot on Earth

Now we come to your films. Here are two guidelines for projecting your revenues. First, be conservative. The rule of thumb is to forecast your income on the low end and your expenses on the high end. Probably all filmmakers who have ever done a budget have padded it to be sure that they did not run out of money. You want to take the opposite path for revenues. If you are making a $1-million Indian-themed film, you would be fooling yourself to assume that the film will gross $141 million, as Oscar-winner *Slumdog Millionaire* did. It is nice to aspire to be an Oscar winner, but you can't plan on it.

Second, be honest. As long as the data of your historical films are as accurate as possible and the films you choose are comparable to those you plan to make, you should be all right. The comment made to me most often by distributors and investors is, "Tell them not to include *Napoleon Dynamite* and *Facing the Giants* as an average film." Feel free to discuss them in your analysis as an example of an exceptional result to hold out the brass ring as a hook for the investor.

Assumptions

Before seizing your calculator, you should write down your assumptions. Unless you have concrete reasons for the forecasted revenues in your tables, people may assume that you invented them. There has to be a thought process leading to these numbers. If you have just written 15 or 20 pages for the preceding sections, you have already gone through the thought process. In most cases, the crucial elements have already been mentioned, and the list is a recap for your benefit and for the investor's. Do not expect readers to remember the specifics from the body of the business plan; this is not a game of hide and seek with the investor.

Explain your assumptions at the end of your Financing section, directly before the tables, to be sure that the reader knows how you came to your conclusions. If you do not do this, it may look like you have no rationale. Review the assumptions in the sample business plan both in the book and the files you have downloaded from the companion web site before continuing.

Revenue and Expenses (Income Statement)

The *Projected Income Statements* (Tables 11.7 through 11.9 in Chapter 11), also known as the Statement of Revenues and Expenses, is the profit statement for each film. Likewise, the *Summary Projected Income Statement* (Table 11.1) indicates the bottom line for the company.

As I say in a preamble to the sample business plan, whether you are doing a business plan for one film or a company, the methodology is the same. In a one-film plan, you won't have summary tables. In the downloaded files, you will find a complete Financing section for one film using *Len's Big Thrill* from Chapter 11.

The sample shows a straightforward production company in which all the income is from films. If you are planning to produce other products or have additional divisions, such as direct-to-DVD or distribution, you will need other methodologies and types of tables for those items. You will have to provide separate assumptions and cash flows for those products because they function differently from film. Then make a combined statement that includes all the products.

Looking at our numbers, you can take the average or the median (the point above and below which half the films fall) of all the films, or you can give more weight to the more recent films. (Do not panic. The "how-to" is contained in the downloaded files.) It depends on whether you feel that the genre is gaining more audience approval or has been drawing the same amount of boxoffice dollars for the past few years. You have to look at the available data and use good judgment.

Note that these tables show worldwide results. As you will not have these for the two most recent years, you want to include a table for each film (Tables 11.4 and 11.6) that shows the box office and budgets only for those years.

The net profit (loss) line is the sum of the company's revenues and expenses. Commonly, the phrase "before taxes" is added to indicate that this is a preliminary income forecast. Do not let these phrases throw you. An accountant can easily prepare these statements for you.

Cash Flow Statement

A cash flow statement shows the timing of incoming revenue and outgoing cash. The dollars will not come in all in one week or one month. Table 11.10 shows the cash flows for the individual films, and the summary is Table 11.2. Notice that in the columns for the table, I have used generic terms Year 1, Year 2, Year 3, and so on. If you are looking for the production money, your year starts when that money is in the bank. To specify the first year—for example, 2010—could create a problem. What if you are still wandering around two years later looking for money? Finding money is hard; no need to announce it to your current prospect.

In addition, each year is further divided into quarters. This seems to make the most sense for showing cash flow. I would shy away from individual months. There is no way to actually track each month. Unless you have the distributor's monthly accounts for various films in front of you, there is no way to track such data accurately. You have to give your investor a readable document, even if you aren't crazy about the idea.

In the sample cash flow statements all of the production money is outgoing in Year 1. I have assumed one year from the beginning of production to the end of postproduction. (The exception in my cash flows is animated films for which experienced filmmakers want two years for production.) If you are an experienced filmmaker, you may be able to shorten this timeframe. Release of the film is scheduled for six months after the end of postproduction.

An independent filmmaker won't know the actual timing in advance, unless she is doing her own distribution. Even if you already have a distribution agreement in place, you won't know. (I am making an assumption that vertically integrated companies like Lionsgate and DreamWorks aren't buying this book to find out how to calculate cash flows.) In order to make the table readable, I skip two quarters before distribution starts and make it clear that the plan is not promising a specific interval. Note there is the following comment at the bottom of the table: "For reference only.

How and when monies are actually distributed depends on contract with distributor."

The first rentals are shown during the quarter in which distribution begins. Throughout the year, we track domestic grosses week
to week to find trends in the number of theaters and the amount of
grosses. Going through that exercise will reveal a pattern that you can
use. Average release "windows" give you an idea of the money flow
from other sources. Most films don't stay in the theaters longer than six
months; however, due to some long stays in the theater, I have a small
amount of revenue still coming in a third quarter. The median stay for
both independent and studio films is about four and a half weeks.

We can track when films go into DVD but not necessarily how
long they are there. In addition, there may be a different method
on how the dollars flow back to your distributor, the head of your
revenue food chain. Therefore, I have chosen to include them, as
the distributor normally does the accounting for money that is
owed to the filmmakers and their investors—once a year.

For foreign revenues, all sources are grouped into one number.
Not all films are released the same way. Some countries actually
legislate the time period; in other cases, the distributor negotiates it.
Some films go directly to DVD or satellite, which is a more popular
distribution method in Europe and Asia. Trying to figure this out
country by country would be excessive. The timing has been very
fluid lately, so it is a good idea to research the topic to keep current. The films go into foreign release in the third quarter of Year 2,
approximately seven months after the domestic release date.

The total line is the sum of the incoming cash minus the outgoing cash. Do not panic over minus totals. The amount of eventual
profit is the deciding factor. In companies the minus total may last
longer than in a one-film plan. As in Table 11.2, depending on how
often you plan to start preproduction on the next film, the costs for
the next film coming in as well as the P&A money spent by the distributor may keep a negative number in the cumulative total for several years. In a multipicture company, the cash flow statement allows
you to see whether you will have enough money coming in to keep
production going.

Overhead (Administrative) Expenses

The cumulative total is simply the sum of the totals from quarter
to quarter, showing the position in profit and loss. These numbers

represent the profits and losses from the films only. To keep the table simple for our purposes, assumed overhead numbers have been included in Table 11.21. In the overhead table (Table 11.11), however, I have not included specific numbers. It is meant to show you what line items you may have to use. These differ from city to city and country to country. While the films are clearly fake, I don't want to take the chance that someone will copy my overhead sample. You must research what those costs are in your community. In addition, add anything that is specific for you, and leave out line items that don't relate to your film.

An ongoing company has its past history to report, along with a statement of its present position. Your accountant will do the serious reports for you, such as Sources and Uses of Funds, Balance Sheet, and so on. These go into your Financing section along with the other tables. As new companies have less to report, don't worry. Just report what there is. There may or may not be a bank account worth mentioning. Present information that must be included in the business plan, even for a very small company.

If you are setting up a company, you will have ongoing expenses, far less than those of the studios, of course. These general administrative costs include salaries that are not attributable to a specific film budget as well as all of the company's tools of the trade—office equipment, telephone charges, entertainment costs, and so on. Your company may have fewer people or no salaried employees at all. Before Year 1, there are generally startup expenses. You may rent an office, option a script, buy a computer, or scout locations in the Dardanelles. Any expenses that are necessary to get your company going are shown in this table. Even if you wait for investment funds before doing any startup, list these costs separately. Some of them—like the computer—are one-time costs.

Like everything else, administrative costs are projected over the time period of the business plan. Look ahead to the number of films that you plan to make three or four years down the road. You may need additional office staff, more office space, or increased development money. Everyone knows that these numbers are guesstimates; however, as a general rule, you should include all the expenses you can think of. On the other hand, do not give yourself a salary of $1 million. I see this item in a lot of companies that never get funded. Because you are partners with the investor, your salary should be moderate.

What If I Have Only One Film?

No matter how often I mention it in the book, some people still are confused about the sample business plan in Chapter 11, which uses three films, because they only have one film. As a filmmaker (producer, director), you are the manager of a small company. The difference is that any expenses need to be in the budget of the film. Don't overburden this poor film with your car and house payments. Include only those things that belong in a film budget. You will be splitting those massive (let's be positive) profits with your investors.

The layout is the same for one film as for multiple films, but fortunately you have less number crunching. Your first table will be comparative films for the past three years (or four if you need them) for which you have worldwide numbers. Your second table will be the two years for which you only have U.S. box office and budgets. Then you have an income statement (without the overhead) and a cash flow statement, which will be similar to any of the individual films in the sample business plan.

DOCUMENTARIES

Due to the limited number of films and the lack of some information, I break my own rules in forecasting docs. There is more responsibility placed on you, the filmmaker, to be sensible and logical throughout the process. I know that many of you would rather never think about numbers. However, your investors do. How you do a forecast has to look rational to them.

In the past, I had only one table of comparative films. Since the last edition was written, however, there are more feature docs to use in a business plan. Consequently, the first two tables are similar with one major difference. Due to the relative lack of docs with worldwide data, I may go back as far as 2002. Therefore, instead of breaking the films into three years for running numbers, I use one long table. There is a sample documentary forecast in the companion files to show you the details.

Which documentaries to use and which not to use is a choice you will have to make. Clearly, political films don't fit with a sports or music documentary. They reach a broader audience, particularly with all the turmoil that has been going on around the world. I can't give you a hard-and-fast rule for which documentaries to use; it has to be your choice. Depending on the total story you are telling, you could be telling the true story about a well-known performer who was active in political and socially relevant subjects. Therefore, you may be able to use most of the successful feature docs that you want to.

As when making a table of the traditional feature films, list the extraordinary films when they are appropriate (e.g., *Fahrenheit 9/11*, *March of the Penguins*), but do not include them in your forecasting process. Even though it is tempting to use their high revenues, remember that your investor probably will know better. You want him to have confidence in you.

Note that fiction films cannot be mixed into a forecast for a documentary. They have a wider audience appeal and usually wider distribution. All of the revenue windows for a fiction feature are going to show higher grosses. Using them would mean that you are fooling not only your investor with an unlikely net profit number but yourself as well.

On the other hand, a successful documentary in the same budget range as your feature film can be used. For example, *Enron: The Smartest Guys in the Room* can fit in a low-budget film plan that deals with corporate greed and corruption, a theme that has become more prevalent in the financial turmoil of recent years. Since we always are looking at a conservative revenue projection for our "Moderate" column, using a film that has done well with a lower net profit result is not a problem.

Next, go through the forecasting process in Focal's companion web site for this book. Apply that process to your films with worldwide numbers. Taking into account those results and what you know about the boxoffice results for the other documentaries, make a reasoned estimate of the box office for your film. Then forecast the rest of the dollars.

THE NEXT STEP

Review Chapter 1, "The Executive Summary," and then study the sample business plan in Chapter 11. Work through the sample in the downloaded files from the companion web site. Feel free to use this format as a guide in writing your own plan.

Have fun, and good luck!

11

Sample Business Plan for a Fictional Company

The sample business plan in this chapter shows the forecasts and cash flows for a company planning to produce three films. Due to space considerations, it is not practical to include separate business plans for both a single film and a company plan. They both follow the same format. However, a one-film plan has only four tables, as the summary tables and overhead are not necessary. All of the costs for a one-film plan should be included in the budget. Of course, the reader also has to modify the text as shown in the book to relate to one film. For more information and detail on how to create the forecasts and cash flow, please refer to the "Financial Worksheet Instructions" on Focal's companion web site for the book.

The format for an overhead table is included (see Table 11.11). It is only meant to show some of the line items that you need to consider and has no data to match the Company Overhead numbers in Table 11.1. Not all companies will need all the line items, and some may have more. In addition, the place that the filmmaker lives and/or is filming will make a difference in the specifics for each expense. For example, rent in New York will not be the same as rent in Missoula or Berlin. One-film plans do not have an overhead table, as all your expenses are in the budget.

Tax incentives for films are not included in the sample business plan. Whether in the United States or other countries, incentives change on a regular basis. In some cases, they may be discontinued altogether or simply run out of funds to apply for a period of time. If you plan on accessing an incentive, include it after the section on Strategy but *before* Financial Assumptions. Be sure to state that investors need to check with their own tax advisors to see how a specific incentive would affect them. In addition, do not subtract potential incentives from your total budget. In the case of most U.S. state incentives and many of those in other countries, there is an accounting done by the governing body before the actual dollars are awarded.

215

CRAZED CONSULTANT PRODUCTIONS:

THE BUSINESS PLAN

This document and the information contained herein is provided solely for the purpose of acquainting the reader with Crazed Consultant Productions and is proprietary to that company. This business plan does not constitute an offer to sell, or a solicitation of an offer to purchase, securities. This business plan has been submitted on a confidential basis solely for the benefit of selected, highly qualified investors and is not for use by any other persons. By accepting delivery of this business plan, the recipient acknowledges and agrees that: (i) in the event the recipient does not wish to pursue this matter, the recipient will return this copy to Business Strategies at the address listed below as soon as practical; (ii) the recipient will not copy, fax, reproduce, or distribute this confidential business plan, in whole or in part, without permission; and (iii) all of the information contained herein will be treated as confidential material.

CONTROLLED COPY

Issued to: _____

Issue Date: _____

Copy No.: _____

For Information Contact:

Louise Levison

Crazed Consultant Productions

c/o Business Strategies

4454 Ventura Canyon Ave. #305

Sherman Oaks, CA 91423

Phone/Fax: 818-981-6857

TABLE OF CONTENTS

1 / THE EXECUTIVE SUMMARY

Strategic Opportunity

- North American boxoffice revenues were $9.8 billion in 2008.
- The independent film share of the North American box office was $3.5 billion in 2008, or 36 percent of the total.
- Worldwide revenues from all sources for North American independent films were over $8 billion in 2008.
- Worldwide boxoffice revenues were $28.1 billion in 2008.
- The overall filmed entertainment market is projected to reach $44.0 billion in the United States in 2011 and $103.3 billion worldwide.

The Company

Crazed Consultant Productions (CCP) is a startup enterprise engaged in the development and production of motion picture films for theatrical release. CCP's goals are to make films that will raise the consciousness of the American public about the importance of household cats and that will be commercially exploitable to a mass audience. The Company plans to produce three films over the next five years, with budgets ranging from $500,000 to $10 million. At the core of CCP are the founders, who bring to the Company successful entrepreneurial experience and in-depth expertise in motion picture production. The management team includes President and Executive Producer Ms. Lotta Mogul, Vice President/CFO Mr. Gimme Bucks, and Producer Ms. Ladder Climber.

The Films

CCP owns options on Jane Lovable's first three *Leonard the Wonder Cat* books and has first refusal on the next three publications. Currently, one book is in print, another is about to be published, and a third is still in the writing stage. The first book has created an established audience for the films. The movies based on Lovable's series will star Leonard, a half-Siamese, half-American shorthair cat, whose adventures make for entertaining stories that incorporate a strong moral lesson. CCP expects each film to stand on its own and to produce profits to finance each successive film. The movies are designed to capture the interest of the entire family, building significantly on an already established base.

The Industry

The future for low-budget independent films continues to look impressive, as their commercial viability has increased steadily over the past decade. Recent films such as *Juno, Napoleon Dynamite,* and *Eight Below* are evidence of the strength of this market segment. The independent market as a whole has expanded dramatically in the past 15 years, while the total domestic box office has increased 80 percent. At the 2005 through 2009 Academy Awards, four of the five films nominated for the Best Picture Oscar were independently financed. Technology has dramatically changed the way films are made, allowing independently financed films to look and sound as good as those made by the Hollywood studios, while remaining free of the creative restraints placed upon an industry that is notorious for fearing risks. Widely recognized as a "recession-proof" business, the entertainment industry has historically prospered even during periods of decreased discretionary income.

The Markets

Family films appeal to the widest possible market. Films such as the *Spy Kids* series, *Garfield*, and the *Stuart Little* films have proved that the whole family will go to a movie that they can see together. For preschoolers, there are adorable animals, while tweens and teens get real-life situations and expertly choreographed action, and parents enjoy the insider humor. The independent market continues to prosper. As an independent company catering to the family market, CCP can distinguish itself by following a strategy of making films for this well-established and growing genre.

Distribution

The motion picture industry is highly competitive, with much of a film's success depending on the skill of its distribution strategy. As an independent producer, CCP aims to negotiate with major distributors for release of their films. The production team is committed to making the films attractive products in theatrical and other markets.

Investment Opportunity and Financial Highlights

Crazed Consultant Productions is seeking an equity investment of approximately $13.5 million for development and production of three films and an additional $2.0 million for overhead expenditures. Using a moderate revenue projection and an assumption of general industry distribution costs, we project (but do not guarantee) gross worldwide revenues of $244.9 million, with pretax producer/investor net profit of $93.6 million.

2 / THE COMPANY

Crazed Consultant Productions is a privately owned California corporation that was established in September 1999. Our principal purpose and business are to create theatrical motion pictures. The Company plans to develop and produce quality family-themed films portraying positive images of the household cat.

The public is ready for films with feline themes. Big-budget animal-themed films have opened in the market over the past five years. In addition, the changing balance of cat to dog owners in favor of the former is an allegory for changes in society overall. The objectives of CCP are as follows:

- To produce quality films that provide positive family entertainment with moral tales designed for both enjoyment and education.
- To make films that will celebrate the importance of the household cat and that will be exploitable to a mass audience.
- To produce three feature films in the first five years, with budgets ranging from $500,000 to $10 million.
- To develop scripts with outside writers.

There is a need and a hunger for more family films. We believe that we can make exciting films starting as low as $500,000 without sacrificing quality. Until recently, there was a dearth of cat films. We plan to change the emphasis of movies from penguins, pigs, and dogs to cats, while providing meaningful and wholesome entertainment that will attract the entire family. In view of the growth of the family market in the past few years, the cat theme is one that has been undervalued and, consequently, underexploited.

Management and Organization

The primary strength of any company is in its management team. CCP's principals, Ms. Lotta Mogul and Mr. Gimme Bucks, have extensive experience in business and in the entertainment industry. In addition, the Company has relationships with key consultants and advisers who will be available to fill important roles on an as-needed basis. The following individuals make up the current management team and key managers.

Ms. Lotta Mogul, President and Executive Producer

Lotta Mogul spent three years at Jeffcarl Studios as a producer. Among her many credits are *Lord of the Litter Box*, *The Dog Who Came for Dinner*, and *Fluffy and Fido Go to College*. These films all had budgets under $10 million and had combined grosses of more than $600 million worldwide. As President and Executive Producer, her considerable experience will be used to create our production slate, manage the CCP team, negotiate with distributors, and plan future strategies.

Mr. Gimme Bucks, Vice President and CFO

Gimme Bucks will oversee the long-term strategy and financial affairs of the company. A graduate of the University of California at Los Angeles, Mr. Bucks has an M.B.A. He worked in business affairs at XYZ Studios and has been a consultant to small, independent film companies.

Mr. Better Focus, Cinematographer

Better Focus is a member of the American Society of Cinematographers. He was Alpha Numerical's director of photography for several years. He won an Emmy Award for his work on *Unusual Birds of Ottumwa*, and he has been nominated twice for Academy Awards.

Ms. Ladder Climber, Producer

Ladder Climber will assist in the production of our films. She began her career as an assistant to the producer of the cult film *Dogs That Bark* and has worked her way up to production manager and line producer on several films. Most recently, she served as line producer on *The Paw* and *Thirty Miles to Azusa*.

Consultants

> Samuel Torts, Attorney-at-Law, Los Angeles, CA
> Winners and Losers, Certified Public Accountants,
>   Los Angeles, CA

3 / THE FILMS

CCP currently controls the rights to the first three *Leonard the Wonder Cat* books, which will be the basis for its film projects over the next five years. In March 2009, the Company paid $10,000 for three-year options on the first three books with first refusal on the next three. The author will receive additional payments over the next four years as production begins. The Leonard series, written by Jane Lovable, has been obtained at very inexpensive option prices due to the author's respect for Ms. Mogul's devotion to charitable cat causes. Three film projects are scheduled.

Leonard's Love

The first film will be based on the novel *Leonard's Love*, which has sold 10 million copies. The story revolves around the friendship between a girl, Natasha, and her cat, Leonard. The two leave the big city to live in a small town, where they discover the true meaning of life. Furry Catman has written the screenplay. The projected budget for *Leonard's Love* is $500,000, with CCP producing and Ultra Virtuoso directing. Virtuoso's previous credits include a low-budget feature, *My Life as a Ferret*, and two rock videos, *Feral Love* and *Hot Fluffy Rag*. We are currently in the development stage with this project. The initial script has been written, but we have no commitments from actors. Casting will commence once financing is in place. As a marketing plus, the upcoming movie will be advertised on the cover of the new paperback edition of the book.

Len's Big Thrill

This film is based on the second Leonard book, which is currently in the prepublication stage. In the story, Leonard accompanies Natasha while she auditions for a movie role. When Len struts across the room, the director—Simon Sez—is captivated by Len's natural ease in front of a camera. Simon makes a deal for both Natasha and Leonard to be in the film, rewriting the script to feature Leonard as the cat who saves his mistress from a burning building. The film is a smash with audiences and two sequels are made. Finally realizing they are in love, Natasha and Simon marry, giving Len the biggest thrill of all.

Ultra Virtuoso is set to direct this feature also. Development on this project will start after we are in production on *Leonard's Love*. Current estimates place the budget at $2.5 million. We plan to interview screenwriters as soon as the shooting script for the first film is finalized.

Cat Follies

The third book in the series is currently being written by Ms. Lovable and will be published in late 2010. The story features a dejected Leonard, whose films aren't drawing the audiences they used to. No matter what Natasha and Simon, his human parents, do, they can't cheer up our cat. Desperate to find something to encourage Len, they take him for ice skating lessons. Amazed at Leonard's agility on skates, his teacher contacts the Wonderland Follies, who sign Leonard to a contract. He is an immediate hit with the audience, especially the young people. As luck would have it, one night film mogul Harvey Hoffenbrauer is in the audience. Seeing the reaction of both kids and adults to Leonard, he decides to make a film of the follies. Soon Leonard is back on top.

4 / THE INDUSTRY

The future for low-budget independent films continues to look impressive, as their commercial viability has increased steadily over the past decade. Recent films such as *The Visitor*, *Hot Fuzz*, and *Under the Same Moon* are evidence of the strength of this market segment. The independent market as a whole has expanded dramatically in the past 15 years, while the total domestic box office has increased 80 percent. At the Academy Awards from 2005 through 2009, four of the five films nominated for the Best Picture Oscar were independently financed, with *Crash, No Country for Old Men*, and *Slumdog Millionaire* winning in 2005, 2007, and 2008, respectively.

The total North American box office in 2008 was $9.8 billion. The share for independent films was $3.5 billion, or 36 percent. Revenues for independent films from all worldwide sources for 2008, from both box office and ancillary markets, are estimated at more than $8 billion. PricewaterhouseCoopers projects that the overall filmed entertainment market will reach $44.0 billion in the United States in 2011 and $103.3 billion worldwide. Once dominated by the studio system, movie production has shifted to reflect increasingly viable economic models for independent film. The success of independent films has been helped by the number of new production and smaller distribution companies emerging into the marketplace every day, as well as the growing interest of major U.S. studios in acting as distributors in this market. In addition, there has been a rise in the number of screens available for independent films.

Investment in film becomes an even more attractive prospect, as financial uncertainty mounts in the wake of Wall Street bailouts and international stock market slides. Widely recognized as a "recession-proof" business, the entertainment industry has historically prospered even during periods of decreased discretionary income. In 1987, the year the stock market experienced one of the biggest crashes in history, the motion picture industry enjoyed its highest gross receipts ever. This trend is continuing in 2009. At the industry's annual ShoWest Convention at the end of March, Motion Picture Association of America (MPAA) Chair-CEO Daniel Glickman reported that the thriving worldwide box office makes the U.S. film business a powerful growth engine. For the first quarter, domestic boxoffice revenue was up 18 percent over the same period last year, according to industry analyst *www.boxofficemojo.com*.

Motion Picture Production

The structure of the U.S. motion picture business has been changing over the past few years at a faster pace as studios and independent companies have created varied methods of financing. Although studios historically funded production totally out of their own arrangements with banks, they now look to partner with other companies, both in the United States and abroad, that can assist in the overall financing of projects. The deals often take the form of the studio retaining the rights for distribution in all U.S. media, including theatrical, home video, television, cable, and other ancillary markets.

The studios, the largest companies in this business, are generally called the "Majors" and include NBC Universal (owned by General Electric), Warner Bros. (owned by Time Warner), Twentieth Century Fox Film Corporation (owned by Rupert Murdoch's News Corp.), Paramount Pictures (owned by Viacom), Sony Pictures Entertainment, and the Walt Disney Company. MGM, one of the original Majors, has been taken private by investors and currently functions as an independent distributor. In most cases, the Majors own their own production facilities and have a worldwide distribution organization. With a large corporate hierarchy making production decisions and a large amount of corporate debt to service, the studios aim most of their films at mass audiences.

Producers who can finance independent films by any source other than a major U.S. studio have more flexibility in their creative decisions, with the ability to hire production personnel and secure other elements required for preproduction, principal photography, and postproduction on a project-by-project basis. With substantially less overhead than the studios, independents are able to be more cost-effective in the filmmaking process. Their films can be directed at both mass and niche audiences, with the target markets for each film dictating the size of its budget. Typically, an independent producer's goal is to acquire funds from equity partners, completing all financing of a film before commencement of principal photography.

How It Works

There are four typical steps in the production of a motion picture: development, preproduction, production, and postproduction. During development and preproduction, a writer may be engaged to write a screenplay or a screenplay may be acquired and rewritten. Certain creative personnel, including a director and various technical personnel, are hired, shooting schedules and locations are planned, and other steps necessary to prepare the motion picture for principal photography are completed. Production commences when principal photography begins, and generally continues for a period of not more than three months. In postproduction, the film is edited, which involves transferring the original filmed material to a digital media in order to work easily with the images. Additionally, a score is mixed with dialogue, and sound effects are synchronized into the final picture, and, in some cases, special effects are added. The expenses associated with this four-step process for creating and finishing a film are referred to as its "negative costs." A master is then manufactured for duplication of release prints for theatrical distribution and exhibition, but expenses for prints and advertising for the film are categorized as P&A and are not part of the negative costs of the production.

Theatrical Exhibition

There were 40,194 theater screens (including drive-ins) in the United States out of approximately 150,000 theater screens worldwide in 2008, per the most recent report of the MPAA. Film revenues from all other sources are often driven by the U.S. domestic theatrical performance. The costs incurred with the distribution of a motion picture can vary significantly depending on the number of screens on which the film is exhibited. Although studios often open a film on 3,000 screens on opening weekends (depending on the budget of both the film and marketing campaign), independent distributors usually tend to open their films on fewer screens. Film revenues from all other sources usually are driven by theatrical distribution. Not only has entertainment product been recession-resistant domestically, but also the much stronger than expected domestic box office has continued to drive up ancillary sales, such as DVD and soundtracks, as well as raising the value of films in foreign markets.

Television

Television exhibition includes over-the-air reception for viewers either through a fee system (cable) or "free television" (national and independent broadcast stations). The proliferation of new cable networks since the early 1990s has made cable (both basic and premium stations) one of the most important outlets for feature films. Whereas network and independent television stations were a substantial part of the revenue picture in the 1970s and early 1980s, cable has become a far more important ancillary outlet. The pay-per-view (PPV) business has continued to grow thanks to continued DBS (direct broadcast satellite) growth and significant NVOD (near video on demand) rollouts by cable operators. Pay-per-view and pay television allow cable television subscribers to purchase individual films or special events or subscribe to premium cable channels for a fee. Both acquire their film programming by purchasing the distribution rights from motion picture distributors.

In addition to NVOD, video on demand (VOD) user growth is projected to grow at a healthy rate over the next several years. Total worldwide users are forecasted to reach 34 million by the end of 2009. In a recent report, Informa Telecoms & Media, a London-based market analysis firm, indicates that by 2012, 909 million homes will have access to true VOD or NVOD technology. That is equivalent to 78 percent of the world's television households. The report also indicates that North America and Europe will account for a combined 83 percent of global on-demand revenue by 2012, and that North America will lead the way with close to 50 percent of the world's VOD revenue and 25 percent of the world's combined VOD/NVOD. While true VOD operators still use a free-content model to promote high customer awareness of the technology, there are now signs that these services are successfully converting users into revenue generators, according to report author Adam Thomas.

Home Video

Home video companies promote and sell DVDs to local, regional, and national video retailers, which then rent the discs to consumers for private viewing and also sell directly to consumers in what is termed the "sell-through" market. DVD sales and rentals totaled $21.6 billion in 2008, according to the Digital Entertainment Group (DEG). Adding in Blu-ray and near-negligible VHS sales, overall consumer spending totaled $22.4 billion. With game consoles that also use Blu-ray taken out of the comparison, the adoption rate of standalone Blu-ray players is similar to that of DVD players at the same point after their introduction. Between consumer confusion over formats and the effect of the economy on player sales, overall disc sales have been declining for two years in a row. Analysts feel that, although the growth of Internet downloads and movie-streaming services will be an additional factor in slow growth in sales, Blu-ray should manage to supplant DVD as the main disc format in the next couple of years. Industry analyst SNL Kagan projects that the high-definition (HD) piece of the pie will grow to almost 19 percent by 2011, when Blu-ray revenue is projected to reach \$3.53 billion, and to reach \$13.0 billion by 2014, when it expects HD to account for 60 percent of segment revenue.

International Theatrical Exhibition

Much of the projected growth in the worldwide film business comes from foreign markets, as distributors and exhibitors keep finding new ways to increase the boxoffice revenue pool. More screens in Asia, Latin America, and Africa have followed the increase in multiplexes in Europe, but this growth has slowed. The world screen count is predicted to remain stable over the next nine years. Other factors are the privatization of television stations overseas, the introduction of DBS services, and increased cable penetration. The synergy between international and local product in European and Asian markets is expected to lead to future growth in screens and box office.

Future Trends

Revolutionary changes in the manner in which motion pictures are produced and distributed are now sweeping the industry, especially for independent films. Companies like Movielink (owned by Blockbuster), Amazon's Video on Demand, CinemaNow, and Apple's iTunes Store are providing films and other entertainment programming for download on the Internet. New devices for personal viewing of films, including the PSP, Xbox, video iPod, and iPhone, are gaining ground in the marketplace, expanding the potential revenues from home video and other forms of selling programming for viewing. Although there may not be a significant impact of the new technologies at present, their influence is expected to grow significantly over the next five years.

5 / THE MARKET

The independent market continues to prosper. The strategy of making films in well-established genres has been shown time and time again to be an effective one. Although there is no boilerplate for making a successful film, the film's probability of success is increased with a strong story, and then the right elements—the right director and cast and other creative people involved. Being able to greenlight our own product, with the support of investors, allows the filmmakers to attract the appropriate talent to make the film a success and distinguish it in the marketplace.

CCP feels that its first film will create a new type of movie-goer for these theaters and a new type of commercial film for the mainstream theaters. Just as *My Dog Skip* found a home in both art houses and malls, so will *Leonard's Love*. Although we expect our film to have a universal enough appeal to play in the mainstream houses, at its projected budget it may begin in the specialty theaters. Because of the low budget, exhibitors may wait for our first film to prove itself before providing access to screens in the larger movie houses. In addition, smaller houses will give us a chance to expand the film on a slow basis and build awareness with the public.

Target Markets

Family-Friendly Films

Family-friendly films appeal to the widest possible market and have been among the most profitable. Crazed Consultant Productions' projects have a multigenerational audience from tweens to grand-parents. In December 2007, *Variety* and other trade and local papers announced in headlines that "family films boost the box office." John Fithian, President of the National Association of Theater Owners (NATO), said, "Year after year, the box office tells an important story for our friends in the creative community. Family-friendly films sell." Previously thought of only as kids' films, family-friendly movies now offer a new paradigm of family entertainment. Production and distribution companies know that wholesome entertainment can be profitable. We feel that films that offer diversion and feature a strong cat storyline will draw a large audience. Heretofore, studios have made the majority of family films. We believe that the time is right to make cost-effective films on smaller budgets.

Cat Owners

Pet ownership is currently at its highest level since the first study in 1988 with 71.1 million households in the United States owning at least one pet (63 percent of the 113.7 million total U.S. households). The steady increase is up from 69 million households in 2004, 64 million households in 2002, and 51 million households in 1988. The two most popular pets in most Western countries have been cats and dogs. In the United States, 39 percent (44.3 million) of households own dogs compared to nearly the 34 percent (38.4 million) that own cats, according to the 2007 to 2008 survey of the American Pet Products Manufacturers Association. However, there are 83 million pet cats compared to 74.8 million pet dogs. The geographic location of pet owners closely matches that of the U.S. population, with pet owners living in both large cities and rural areas. Comparable numbers are not available for Europe, although an earlier study showed that households in Europe own approximately 50 million cats and those in Japan own 10 million.

The time has finally come for the cat genre film. Cats have been with us for 12 million years, but they have been underappreciated and underexploited, especially by Hollywood. Recent studies have shown that the cat has become the pet of choice. We plan to present cats in their true light, as regular, everyday heroes with all the lightness and gaiety of other current animal cinema favorites, including dogs, horses, pigs, and bears. In following the tradition of the dog film genre, we are also looking down the road to cable outlets.

We believe that cat programs will be the next trend in this medium. Animal films in general, and cat films in particular, have had increasing commercial success. Examples in recent years include *Garfield: The Movie, Cats and Dogs, Stuart Little, Stuart Little 2, Dr. Dolittle,* and *Dr. Dolittle 2.* These films have opened the door for Crazed Consultant's films. As the pet that is owned by more individuals than any other animal in the United States, the cat will draw audiences from far and wide. There is even talk of a cat television channel.

CCP plans to begin with a $500,000 film that would benefit from exposure through the film festival circuit. The exposure of our films at festivals and limited runs in specialty theaters in target areas will create awareness for them with the general public. In addition, we plan to tie in sales of the Leonard books with the films. Although a major studio would be a natural place to go with these films, we want to remain independent.

6 / DISTRIBUTION

The motion picture industry is highly competitive, with much of a film's success often depending on the skill of its distribution strategy. The filmmakers' goal is to negotiate with experienced distribution companies in order to seek to maximize their bargaining strength for a potentially significant release. There is an active market for completed motion pictures, with virtually all the studios and independent distributors seeking to acquire films. The management team feels that the Company's films will be attractive products in the marketplace.

Distribution terms between producers and distributors vary greatly. A distributor looks at several factors when evaluating a potential acquisition, such as the uniqueness of the story, theme, and the target market for the film. Since distribution terms are determined in part by the perceived potential of a motion picture and the relative bargaining strength of the parties, it is not possible to predict with certainty the nature of distribution arrangements. However, there are certain standard arrangements that form the basis for most distribution agreements. The distributor will generally license the film to theatrical exhibitors (i.e., theater owners) for domestic release and to specific, if not all, foreign territories for a percentage of the gross boxoffice dollars. The initial release for most feature films is U.S. theatrical (i.e., in movie theaters). For a picture in initial release, the exhibitor, depending on the demand for the movie, will split the revenue derived from ticket purchases ("gross box office") with the distributor; revenue derived from the various theater concessions remains with the exhibitor. The percentage of boxoffice receipts remitted to the distributor is known as "film rentals" and customarily diminishes during the course of a picture's theatrical run. Although different formulas may be used to determine the splits from week to week, on average a distributor will be able to retain about 50 percent of total box office, again depending on the performance and demand for a particular movie. In turn, the distributor will pay to the motion picture producer a negotiated percentage of the film rentals less its costs for film prints and advertising.

Film rentals become part of the "distributor's gross," from which all other deals are computed. As the distributor often re-licenses the picture to domestic ancillaries (i.e., cable, television, home video) and foreign theatrical and ancillaries, these monies all become part of the distributor's gross and add to the total revenue for the film in the same way as the rentals. The distribution deal with the producer includes a negotiated percentage for each revenue source; for example, the producer's share of foreign rentals may vary from the percentage of domestic theatrical rentals. The basic elements of a film distribution deal include the distributor's commitment to advance funds for distribution expenses (including multiple prints of the film and advertising), and the percentage of the film's income the distributor will receive for its services. Theoretically, the distributor recoups his expenses for the cost of its print and advertising expenses first from the initial revenue of the film. Then the distributor will split the rest of the revenue monies with the producer/investor group. The first monies coming back to the producer/investor group generally repay the investor for the total production cost, after which the producers and investors split the money according to their agreement. However, the specifics of the distribution deal and the timing of all money disbursements depend on the agreement that is finally negotiated. In addition, the timing of the revenue and the percentage amount of the distributor's fees differ depending on the revenue source.

Release Strategies

The typical method of releasing films begins with domestic theatrical, which gives value to the various film "windows" (the period that has to pass after a domestic theatrical release before a film can be released in other markets). Historically, the sequencing pattern has been to license to pay-cable program distributors, foreign theatrical, home video, television networks, foreign ancillary, and U.S. television syndication. As the rate of return varies from different windows, shifts in these sequencing strategies will occur.

Distributors plan their release schedules with certain target audiences in mind. Given the cost of prints ($1,200 to $1,500 each), this release method can create an initial marketing expense of over $1 million, accompanied by an equally high advertising program. Films with lower budgets will often get a "platform" release. In this case, the film is given a build-up by opening initially in a few regional or limited local theaters to build positive movie patron awareness throughout the country. The time between a limited opening and its release in the balance of the country may be several weeks.

7 / RISK FACTORS

Investment in the film industry is highly speculative and inherently risky. There can be no assurance of the economic success of any motion picture since the revenues derived from the production and distribution of a motion picture primarily depend on its acceptance by the public, which cannot be predicted. The commercial success of a motion picture also depends on the quality and acceptance of other competing films released into the marketplace at or near the same time, general economic factors, and other tangible and intangible factors, all of which can change and cannot be predicted with certainty.

The entertainment industry in general, and the motion picture industry in particular, are continuing to undergo significant changes, primarily due to technological developments. Although these developments have resulted in the availability of alternative and competing forms of leisure time entertainment, such technological developments have also resulted in the creation of additional revenue sources through licensing of rights to such new media and potentially could lead to future reductions in the costs of producing and distributing motion pictures. In addition, the theatrical success of a motion picture remains a crucial factor in generating revenues in other media such as videocassettes and television. Due to the rapid growth of technology, shifting consumer tastes, and the popularity and availability of other forms of entertainment, it is impossible to predict the overall effect these factors will have on the potential revenue from and profitability of feature-length motion pictures.

The Company itself is in the organizational stage and is subject to all the risks incident to the creation and development of a new business, including the absence of a history of operations and minimal net worth. In order to prosper, the success of the Company's films will depend partly upon the ability of management to produce a film of exceptional quality at a lower cost that can compete in appeal with higher-budgeted films of the same genre. In order to minimize this risk, management plans to participate as much as possible throughout the process and will aim to mitigate financial risks where possible. Fulfilling this goal depends on the timing of investor financing, the ability to obtain distribution contracts with satisfactory terms, and the continued participation of the current management.

8 / FINANCIAL PLAN

Strategy

The Company proposes to secure development and production film financing for the feature films in this business plan from equity investors, allowing it to maintain consistent control of the quality and production costs. As an independent, Crazed Consultant Productions can strike the best financial arrangements with various channels of distribution. This strategy allows for maximum flexibility in a rapidly changing marketplace, in which the availability of filmed entertainment is in constant flux.

Financial Assumptions

For the purposes of this business plan, several assumptions have been included in the financial scenarios and are noted accordingly. This discussion contains forward-looking statements that involve risks and uncertainties as detailed in the "Risk Factors" section.

1. Table 11.1, **Summary Projected Income Statement**, summarizes the income for the films to be produced. **Domestic Rentals** reflect the distributor's share of the boxoffice split with the exhibitor in the United States and Canada, assuming the film has the same distributor in both countries. **Domestic Other** includes home video, pay TV, basic cable, network television, and television syndication. **Foreign Revenue** includes all monies returned to distributors from all venues outside the United States and Canada.
2. The film's **Budget**, often known as the "production costs," covers both "above-the-line" (producers, actors, and directors) and "below-the-line" (the rest of the crew) costs of producing a film. Marketing costs are included under **P&A** (Prints and Advertising), often referred to as "releasing costs" or "distribution expenses." These expenses also include the costs of making copies of the release print from the master and advertising and vary depending on the distribution plan for each title.
3. **Gross Income** represents the projected pretax profit after distributor's expenses have been deducted but before distributor's fees and overhead expenses are deducted.

4. **Distributor's Fees** (the distributor's share of the revenues as compared to his expenses, which represent out-of-pocket costs) are based on 35 percent of all distributor gross revenue, both domestic and foreign.

5. **Net Producer/Investor Income** represents the projected pretax profit prior to negotiated distributions to investors.

6. Table 11.2 shows the **Summary Projected Cash Flow Based on Moderate Profit Cases**, which have been brought forward from Table 11.10.

7. The films in Tables 11.3 and 11.4 are the basis for the projections shown in Tables 11.7 and 11.8. Likewise, the films in Tables 11.5 and 11.6 are the basis for the projections in Table 11.9. The rationale for the projections is explained in (8) below. The films chosen relate in either theme, style, feeling, or budget to the films we propose to produce. It should be noted that these groups do not include films of which the results are known but that have lost money. In addition, there are no databases that collect all films ever made, nor are budgets available for all films released. There is, therefore, a built-in bias in the data. Also, the fact that these films have garnered revenue does not constitute a guarantee of the success of this film.

8. The three revenue scenarios shown in Tables 11.7 and 11.8—low (breakeven), moderate, and high—are based on the data shown in Tables 11.3 and 11.4. Likewise, Table 11.9 is based on the comparative films in Tables 11.5 and 11.6. We have chosen films that relate in genre, theme, and/ or budget to the films we propose to produce. The low scenario indicates a case in which some production costs are covered but there is no profit. The moderate scenario represents the most likely result for each film and is used for the cash flows. The high scenarios are based on the results of extraordinarily successful films and presented for investor information only.

Due to the wide variance in the results of individual films, simple averages of actual data are not realistic. Therefore, to create the moderate forecast for Tables 11.7 through 11.9, the North American box office for each film in the respective comparative tables was divided by its budget to create a ratio that was used as a guide. The North American box office was used because it is a widely accepted film industry assumption that, in most cases, this result drives all the other revenue sources of a film. In order to avoid skewing the data, the films with the highest and lowest ratios in each year were deleted. The remaining revenues were added and then divided by the sum of the remaining budgets. This gave an average (or, more specifically, the mean variance) of the box office with the budgets. The ratios over the five years represented in the comparative tables showed whether the box office was trending up or down or remaining constant. The result was a number used to multiply times the budget of the proposed film in order to obtain a reasonable projection of the moderate boxoffice result.

In order to determine the expense value for the P&A, the P&A for each film in the comparative tables was divided by the budget. The ratios were determined in a similar fashion, taking out the high and low and arriving at a mean number. For the high forecast, the Company determined a likely "extraordinary" result for each film and its budget.

The remaining revenues and P&A for the high forecasts were calculated using ratios similar to those applied to the moderate columns.

In all the scenarios, and throughout these financials, "ancillary" revenues from product placement, merchandising, soundtrack, and other revenue opportunities are *not* included in projections.

9. **Distributor's Fees** are based on all the revenue exclusive of the exhibitor's share of the box office (50 percent). These fees are calculated at 35 percent (general industry assumption) for the forecast, as the Company does not have a distribution contract at this time. Note that the fees are separate from distributor's expenses (see **P&A** in (2) above), which are out-of-pocket costs and paid back in full.
10. The **Cash Flow** assumptions used for Table 11.10 are:
    a. Film production should take approximately one year from development through postproduction, ending with the creation of a master print. The actual release date depends on finalization of distribution arrangements, which may occur either before or after the film has been completed and is an unknown variable at this time. For purposes of the cash flow, we have assumed distribution will start within six months after completion of the film.

    b. The largest portion of print and advertising costs will be spent in the first quarter of the film's opening.

    c. The majority of revenues generally will come back to the producers within two years after release of the film, although a smaller amount of ancillary revenues will take longer to occur and will be covered by the investor's agreement for a breakdown of the timing for industry windows.

    d. Following is a chart indicating estimated entertainment industry distribution windows based on historical data showing specific revenue-producing segments of the marketplace.

WINDOW	MONTHS AFTER INITIAL THEATRICAL RELEASE	ESTIMATED LENGTH OF TIME
Domestic theatrical	—	3–6 months
Foreign theatrical	Variable	6–12 months
Domestic home video (initial)	3–5 months	6–12 months
Domestic pay-per-view	3–5 months	6 months
Foreign video (initial)	6–9 months	9–12 months
Domestic pay television	12–15 months	18 months
Foreign television (pay or free)	18–24 months	12–36 months
Domestic free television (network, barter, syndication, and cable)	24–30 months	1–4 years

11. Company **Overhead Expenses** are shown in Table 11.11.

TABLE 11.1

Crazed Consultant Productions Summary Projected Income Statement (Millions of Dollars)

FILMS	BOX OFFICE	REVENUE DOMESTIC		FOREIGN	TOTAL	COSTS			DISTRIBUTOR'S GROSS PROFIT	EST. DIST. FEES	PRODUCER/ INVESTOR GROSS	COMPANY OVERHEAD	NET PROD./ INVESTOR INCOME
		RENTALS	ANCILLARY			BUDGET	P&A	TOTAL					
Leonard's Love	2.0	1.0	3.0	4.0	8.0	0.5	1.0	1.5	6.5	2.8	3.7	0.1	3.6
Len's Big Thrill	14.5	7.3	27.6	29.0	63.9	3.0	12.0	15.0	48.9	22.4	26.5	0.6	25.9
Cat Follies	36.0	18.0	57.0	98.0	173.0	10.0	37.0	47.0	126.0	60.6	65.4	1.3	64.1
TOTAL	52.5	26.3	87.6	131.0	244.9	13.5	50.0	63.5	181.4	85.8	95.6	2.0	93.6

TABLE 11.2

Crazed Consultant Productions Summary Projected Cash Flow* Based on Moderate Profit Cases (Millions of Dollars)

FILMS	YEAR 1				YEAR 2				YEAR 3				YEAR 4				YEAR 5				YEAR 6
	QTR. 1	QTR. 2	QTR. 3	QTR. 4	QTR. 1	QTR. 2	QTR. 3	QTR. 4	QTR. 1	QTR. 2	QTR. 3	QTR. 4	QTR. 1	QTR. 2	QTR. 3	QTR. 4	QTR. 1	QTR. 2	QTR. 3	QTR. 4	QTR. 1
Leonard's Love	(0.1)	(0.2)	(0.1)	(0.1)	0.0	0.0	0.2	0.1	1.1	0.9	0.6	1.0			0.3						
Len's Big Thrill					(0.7)	(0.9)	(0.9)	(0.5)	0.0	0.0	(0.8)	(0.5)	9.6	5.9	4.3	7.0	4.0				
Cat Follies									(2.5)	(3.0)	(3.0)	(1.5)	(6.1)	0.0	0.0	(2.1)	23.2	20.2	14.7	23.5	2.0
TOTAL CASH	(0.1)	(0.2)	(0.1)	(0.1)	(0.7)	(0.9)	(0.7)	(0.4)	(1.4)	(2.1)	(3.2)	(1.0)	3.5	5.9	4.6	4.9	27.2	20.2	14.7	23.5	2.0
CUMULATIVE CASH FLOW	(0.1)	(0.3)	(0.4)	(0.5)	(1.2)	(2.1)	(2.8)	(3.2)	(4.6)	(6.7)	(9.9)	(10.9)	(7.4)	(1.5)	3.1	8.0	35.2	55.4	70.1	93.6	95.6

*For reference only. How and when monies are actually distributed depends on contract with distributor. Prints and advertising, which the distributor spends, are paid back first, then the production budget.

TABLE 11.3

Crazed Consultant Productions Gross Profits Of Selected Comparative Films with Varied Genres For Two Films* with Budgets $0.5 to $7.0 Million Years 2005–2007 (Millions of Dollars)

FILMS	DOMESTIC REVENUE			FOREIGN REVENUE (c)	TOTAL REVENUE (d)	COSTS				DISTRIBUTOR'S GROSS PROFIT (e)
	BOX OFFICE	RENTALS (a)	OTHER (b)			BUDGET	P&A	TOTAL		
2005										
Curious Case of Wasps, The	12.0	6.0	20.0	13.0	39.0	0.5	14.0	14.5		24.5
Flypigs	15.0	7.5	24.0	33.0	64.5	3.5	13.3	16.8		47.7
Angel and Me	10.6	5.3	18.9	15.0	39.2	3.0	11.0	14.0		25.2
My Bloody Flamingo	25.0	12.5	45.0	22.5	80.0	6.0	18.0	24.0		56.0
Tropic Spiders	12.0	6.0	28.3	18.0	52.3	4.0	20.8	24.8		27.5
2006										
Dark Bat, The	8.2	4.1	12.0	3.5	19.6	7.0	4.0	11.0		8.6
In Search of Alpacas	8.1	4.0	24.0	10.4	38.4	0.8	6.4	7.2		31.2
Little Miss Gopher	17.0	8.5	20.0	23.0	51.5	5.0	14.7	19.7		31.8
Sex and the Kitty	22.0	11.0	33.6	44.0	88.6	4.0	14.0	18.0		70.6
Space Mice	7.6	3.8	55.0	80.0	138.8	1.5	10.0	11.5		127.3
2007										
Buffy Getting Married	18.4	9.2	60.0	77.0	146.2	6.2	48.4	54.6		91.6
Beverly Hills Butterflies	22.0	11.0	39.0	45.0	95.0	5.0	28.0	33.0		62.0
Escape of the Gila Monsters	15.0	7.5	22.0	39.0	68.5	5.9	8.0	13.9		54.6
Indiana Cobra: The Flicking Tongue	16.8	8.4	44.0	28.0	80.4	4.0	15.0	19.0		61.4
Tell No Bears	24.0	12.0	28.0	18.0	58.0	2.0	20.0	22.0		36.0

*The amounts obtained by these comparable films do not constitute a guarantee that *Leonard's Love* and *Len's Big Thrill* will do as well.
(a) Rentals equal distributor's share of U.S. box office.
(b) Domestic Revenue Other includes television, cable, DVD, and all other nontheatrical sources of revenue.
(c) Foreign Revenue includes both theatrical and ancillary revenues.
(d) Total Revenue equals Domestic Rentals, Domestic Other, and Foreign.
(e) Gross Profit before distributor's fee is removed.
Source: Business Strategies.

TABLE 11.4

Crazed Consultant Productions Selected Comparative Films with Varied Genres for Two Films* with Budgets $1.5 to $8.0 Million, U.S. Box Office and Budgets Only, Years 2008–2009 (Millions of Dollars)

FILMS	BOX OFFICE	BUDGET
900 Horses	6.8	2.7
Chimps and Whales	15.6	7.0
Cocaine Buffalo	15.8	5.0
Ferret Visitor, The	11.2	5.0
Ghost Sheep	62.0	5.3
High School Collies	59.8	8.0
The Mouse Diaries	10.2	1.5
My Big Fat Siamese	18.0	3.5
*Other Lemur, The***	20.0	2.0

* The amounts obtained by these comparable films do not constitute a guarantee that *Leonard's Love* and *Len's Big Thrill* will do as well.

** Still in distribution as of July 5, 2009.

Note: Domestic ancillary and all foreign data generally are not available until two years after a film's initial U.S. release; therefore, this table includes U.S. domestic box office only.

Source: Business Strategies.

TABLE 11.5

Crazed Consultant Productions *Cat Follies* Gross Profits of Selected Films with Varied Genres* with Budgets of $6.0 to $24.0 Million, Years 2005–2007 (Millions of Dollars)

FILMS	DOMESTIC REVENUE			FOREIGN REVENUE (c)	TOTAL REVENUE (d)	COSTS			DISTRIBUTOR'S GROSS PROFIT (e)
	BOX OFFICE	RENTALS (a)	OTHER (b)			BUDGET	P&A	TOTAL	
2005									
27 Beavers	18.8	9.4	30.1	42.0	81.5	6.0	30.0	36.0	45.5
Cat-A-Tonic	45.0	22.5	45.0	55.0	122.5	12.0	40.0	52.0	70.5
Cincinnati Crickets	51.2	25.6	70.0	51.2	146.8	15.0	47.0	62.0	84.8
Last Caribou of Alaska	40.0	20.0	53.7	54.6	128.3	11.0	46.0	57.0	71.3
Revolutionary Geese	22.0	11.0	45.0	35.0	91.0	10.0	26.0	36.0	55.0
2006									
Astronaut Pigeons	33.0	16.5	40.0	50.0	106.5	15.0	40.0	55.0	51.5
Christmas Reindeer, A	18.0	9.0	28.0	43.0	80.0	8.0	32.0	40.0	40.0
Lovebird Sonata	54.0	26.0	104.0	150.0	280.0	12.0	50.0	62.0	218.0
Pekingese Dream	62.0	31.0	98.0	35.0	164.0	20.0	32.0	52.0	112.0
Rika: Mall Cat	21.8	10.9	35.0	55.0	100.9	14.0	25.0	39.0	61.9
2007									
Chronicles of Boujabee, The	70.0	35.0	133.0	240.0	408.0	12.0	50.0	62.0	346.0
Day Without a Cat, A	76.6	38.3	120.0	90.0	248.3	20.0	65.0	85.0	163.3
Helldog: In the Kennel	26.0	13.0	34.0	56.0	103.0	8.0	36.0	44.0	59.0
Last Chance Mabel	38.0	19.0	55.7	94.0	168.7	24.0	40.0	64.0	104.7
Waltz with Wombats	16.4	8.2	33.0	64.0	105.2	8.0	20.0	28.0	77.2

*The amounts obtained by these comparable films do not constitute a guarantee that *Cat Follies* will do as well.
(a) Rentals equal distributor's share of U.S. box office.
(b) Domestic Other Revenue includes television, cable, video, and all other non-theatrical sources of revenue.
(c) Foreign Revenue includes both theatrical and ancillary revenues.
(d) Total Revenue equals Domestic Rentals, Domestic Other, and Foreign.
(e) Gross Profit before distributor's fee is removed.
Source: Business Strategies.

TABLE 11.6

Crazed Consultant Productions' *Cat Follies*
Selected Comparative Films with Varied Genres*
U.S. Box Office and Budgets Only Budgets $7.0 to $23.0 Million,
Years 2008–2009 (Millions of Dollars)

FILMS	BOX OFFICE	BUDGET
Adventures of Beaver, The**	15.0	9.0
Badger Brothers	55.9	20.0
Finding Millie	35.0	15.4
Kung Fu Kitty	43.0	17.0
Mad Hot Marmots	40.0	12.0
P.S. I Love Abyssinians	23.4	7.0
Race to Elephant Mountain	87.0	23.0
Smokin' Poker Shark	36.0	8.5
Traveling Gerbil Show, The	18.0	7.6
Unfinished Unicorn, An	36.0	10.5

*The amounts obtained by these comparable films do not constitute a guarantee that *Cat Follies* will do as well.
**Still in North American distribution as of July 5, 2009.
Note: Domestic ancillary and all foreign data generally are not available until two years after a film's initial U.S. release.
Source: Business Strategies.

TABLE 11.7

Crazed Consultant Productions' *Leonard's Love* Projected Income Low, Moderate, High Results (Millions of Dollars)

		LOW	MODERATE	HIGH
U.S. BOX OFFICE REVENUE		0.5	2.0	15.0
Domestic Rentals	(a)	0.3	1.0	7.5
Domestic Other	(b)	0.7	3.0	22.5
Foreign	(c)	0.9	4.0	30.0
TOTAL DISTRIBUTOR GROSS REVENUE		1.9	8.0	60.0
LESS				
Budget Cost		0.5	0.5	0.5
Prints and Advertising		0.7	1.0	6.0
TOTAL COSTS		1.2	1.5	6.5
DISTRIBUTOR'S GROSS INCOME		0.7	6.5	53.5
Distributor's Fees	(d)	0.7	2.8	21.0
NET INCOME BEFORE ALLOCATION TO PRODUCERS/INVESTORS		0.0	3.7	32.5

Note: Box office revenues are for reference and not included in the totals. These projections do not constitute a guarantee that *Leonard's Love* will do as well.

(a) Box office revenues are for reference and not included in the totals. 50 percent of the box office goes to the exhibitor and 50 percent goes to the distributor as Domestic Rentals.

(b) Domestic Other Revenue includes television, cable, DVD, and all other nontheatrical sources of revenue.

(c) Foreign Revenue includes both theatrical and ancillary revenues.

(d) Distributor's Fee equals 35 percent of Distributor's Gross Revenue.

Prepared by Business Strategies.

TABLE 11.8

Crazed Consultant Productions' *Len's Big Thrill*
Projected Income Low, Moderate,
High Results (Millions of Dollars)

		LOW	MODERATE	HIGH
U.S. BOX OFFICE		3.0	14.5	43.5
REVENUE				
Domestic Rentals	(a)	1.5	7.3	21.8
Domestic Other	(b)	2.3	27.6	82.7
Foreign	(c)	2.8	29.0	87.0
TOTAL DISTRIBUTOR GROSS REVENUE		6.6	63.9	191.5
LESS				
Budget Cost		3.0	3.0	3.0
Prints and Advertising		1.3	12.0	30.0
TOTAL COSTS		4.3	15.0	33.0
DISTRIBUTOR'S GROSS INCOME		2.3	48.9	158.5
Distributor's Fees	(d)	2.3	22.4	67.0
NET INCOME BEFORE ALLOCATION TO PRODUCERS/INVESTORS		0.0	26.5	91.5

Note: Box office revenues are for reference and not included in the totals.

These projections do not constitute a guarantee that *Len's Big Thrill* will do as well.

(a) Box office revenues are for reference and not included in the totals. 50 percent of the box office goes to the exhibitor and 50 percent goes to the distributor as Domestic Rentals.

(b) Domestic Other Revenue includes television, cable, DVD, and all other nontheatrical sources of revenue.

(c) Foreign Revenue includes both theatrical and ancillary revenues.

(d) Distributor's Fee equals 35 percent of Distributor's Gross Revenue.

Prepared by Business Strategies.

TABLE 11.9

Crazed Consultant Productions' *Cat Follies* Projected Income Low, Moderate, High Results (Millions of Dollars)

		LOW	MODERATE	HIGH
U.S. BOX OFFICE REVENUE		10.0	36.0	60.0
Domestic Rentals	(a)	5.0	18.0	30.0
Domestic Other	(b)	15.0	57.0	94.8
Foreign	(c)	20.0	98.0	162.0
TOTAL DISTRIBUTOR GROSS REVENUE		40.0	173.0	286.8
LESS				
Budget Cost		10.0	10.0	10.0
Prints and Advertising		16.0	37.0	50.0
TOTAL COSTS		26.0	47.0	60.0
DISTRIBUTOR'S GROSS INCOME		14.0	126.0	226.8
Distributor's Fees	(d)	14.0	60.6	100.4
NET INCOME BEFORE ALLOCATION TO PRODUCERS/INVESTORS		0.0	65.4	126.4

Note: Box office revenues are for reference and not included in the totals.

These projections do not constitute a guarantee that *Cat Follies* will do as well.

(a) Box office revenues are for reference and not included in the totals. 50 percent of the box office goes to the exhibitor and 50 percent goes to the distributor as Domestic Rentals.

(b) Domestic Other Revenue includes television, cable, DVD, and all other nontheatrical sources of revenue.

(c) Foreign Revenue includes both theatrical and ancillary revenues.

(d) Distributor's Fee equals 35 percent of Distributor's Gross Revenue.

Prepared by Business Strategies.

TABLE 11.10

Crazed Consultant Productions' Combined Cash Flow for Three Films* Based on Moderate Profit Cases
(Millions of Dollars)

	YEAR 1				YEAR 2				YEAR 3				YEAR 4				YEAR 5				YEAR 6
	QTR. 1	QTR. 2	QTR. 3	QTR. 4	QTR. 1	QTR. 2	QTR. 3	QTR. 4	QTR. 1	QTR. 2	QTR. 3	QTR. 4	QTR. 1	QTR. 2	QTR. 3	QTR. 4	QTR. 1	QTR. 2	QTR. 3	QTR. 4	QTR. 1
Leonard's Love																					
Production Budget	(0.1)	(0.2)	(0.1)	(0.1)																	
Prints and Ads							(0.5)	(0.1)	(0.3)	(0.1)											
Domestic Rentals							0.7	0.2													
Domestic Ancillary							1.5														
Foreign Revenue							1.1	1.0	0.6	1.0											
Distributor Fees							(1.3)	(1.5)													
Len's Big Thrill																					
Production Budget					(0.7)	(0.9)	(0.5)														
Prints and Ads									(6.3)	(1.6)	(3.0)	(1.1)									
Domestic Rentals									5.5	1.1	0.7										
Domestic Ancillary											13.8	13.8									
Foreign Revenue											8.4	7.0		4.3	7.0						
Distributor Fees											(10.3)	(12.1)									
Cat Follies																					
Production Budget										(2.5)	(3.0)	(1.5)									
Prints and Ads													(19.6)	(4.8)			(9.3)	(3.3)			
Domestic Rentals													13.5	2.7			1.8	28.5			28.5
Domestic Ancillary																	28.4	23.5	14.7	23.5	7.9
Distributor Fees													(1.8)				(26.2)	(3.3)			(34.4)
TOTALS	(0.1)	(0.2)	(0.1)	(0.1)	(0.7)	(0.9)	(0.7)	(0.4)	(1.4)	(2.1)	(3.2)	(1.0)	9.9	5.9	(1.8)	4.9	27.2	20.2	14.7	23.5	2.0
CUMULATIVE TOTAL	(0.1)	(0.3)	(0.4)	(0.5)	(1.2)	(2.1)	(2.8)	(3.2)	(4.6)	(6.7)	(9.9)	(10.9)	(1.0)	4.9	3.1	8.0	35.2	55.4	70.1	93.6	95.6

*For reference only. How and when monies are actually distributed depends on contract with distributor. Prints and advertising are usually paid back first, then the production budget.

Prepared by Business Strategies

TABLE 11.11

Crazed Consultant Productions' Sample Overhead Expenses
Format First Five Years

	YEAR 1	YEAR 2	YEAR 3	YEAR 4	YEAR 5
President					
Executive In Charge of Production					
Office Manager					
Payroll Taxes					
Salaries					
Travel and Entertainment					
Office Rent					
Office Supplies and Equipment					
Publicity/Promotion/ Advertising					
Dues and Subscriptions					
Legal Fees					
Accounting Fees					
Telephones					
Utilities					
Parking Spaces					
Security					
Insurance					
Repairs and Maintenance					
Freight/Air Couriers					
Other					
Total Non-Payroll					
TOTAL OVERHEAD EXPENSES					

NOTE: I have provided the format only examples of line items. You must choose the line items that are appropriate for your company and fill in the data. One-film plans do not have overhead.

12

Short Film Distribution

Co-written with David Russell,
President, Big Film Shorts

We now can move on to awakening the sleeping giant that is short films.

MARK LIPSKY
Gigantic Releasing

A chapter on short film distribution? Does that mean you can write a business plan for short films? You can't write a traditional business plan quite yet, but short films are the fastest growing and changing market segment in the entertainment industry, a sector of the industry that is changing faster than others. New revenue sources are developing rapidly. As a producer or director of a short film, you need to know everything you can about the business side. We are both getting emails every day asking for information on finding funding for short films.

The whole industry knows about short films. In fact, the industry has *always* known about short films; they invented them. Prior to the last few years of the 1990s, student filmmakers were able to use short films as showcases; however, exhibitors and distributors didn't pay attention. Nor did the audience. Now that some exhibitors are daring to show their audiences short films, there is the emergence of a revenue-producing business.

This chapter can present only the tip of the iceberg. You may be reading it three years after publication. Of course, you will have to add your own research on this subject to be sure you have the most updated information for yourself and to include in the business plan you will write. There are minimal amounts of money for investing in short films now, but the future shows promise. This is only the beginning.

Originally, we contemplated writing an entire book about the business side of short films, but it would have been very short, like the format itself. Why? There was not much to say, partly because the short form has never been fully exploited as a revenue source. People are just beginning to figure out how they can use short films beyond the usual filler. As more money looms on the horizon for makers of short films, we feel we can now make this chapter worth your while.

WHAT IS A SHORT FILM?

There is nothing new about the format or the length. Compared to films today, silent films and talkies were short. The first public film screening by the Lumière Brothers in 1895 included approximately ten short films lasting 20 minutes in total. The majority of their films were documentaries and some were comedies. In the first decade of the 20th century, Edison and others made films that took up only one roll of film, thus earning the format the nickname "one-reelers"; the length of time to play these single-roll movies was 10 to 12 minutes, so, by their very nature, they were short films.

Newsreels were introduced in England in 1897 by the Frenchman Charles Pathé, but became popular in the 1920s. From the 1920s through the 1940s, five companies—Fox Movietone, News of the Day, Paramount, RKO-Pathé, and Universal—made the five-minute-long newsreels for the approximately 85 million people attending films each week. Along with the newsreels, the theaters also showed a variety of short films between 1919 and 1930; for example, Pathé produced a series of short documentaries for film audiences. When projectors were modified to accommodate longer reels, a "short" became 20 minutes long. In addition, Pete Smith, Robert Benchley, and others made popular 15-minute black-and-white featurettes from the 1930s until the television revolution of the 1950s. The cartoons that were shown in addition to the newsreel and specialty shorts were usually 5 to 8 minutes in length.

At one point, a short film could actually run up to 59 minutes. As television became the accepted source for filmed news stories and feature films became longer, short subjects became unnecessary. At the moment, the most acceptable lengths at the more prestigious festivals range from 15 minutes for Cannes to a limit of 40 minutes for Sundance, the Academy Awards, and Clermont-Ferrand, the largest international short film festival.

WHY MAKE A SHORT FILM?

Calling Card

A lot of people want to make a short film strictly as a calling card to introduce themselves to companies for future work or to show to investors for their feature films. Filmmakers often think that a calling card film should be half an hour, in three acts, and an example of why someone should give you $3 million to make a feature. The experience of distributors is that you can't get anyone to watch a half-hour film. What will get their attention is a very successful 5- to 15-minute film that will get buzz like *George Lucas in Love* (8 minutes), *The Spirit of Christmas* (5 minutes), or *Bottle Rocket* (11 minutes). The last film secured a studio deal for Wes Anderson and Owen Wilson, who went on not only to a feature-length version of their short film, but also to *Rushmore* and *The Royal Tenenbaums*, as well as individual projects. Since then, many well-known actors have either appeared in shorts (to help out their struggling friends) or produced and directed them for their own creative reasons. Christine Lahti won an Oscar for her film *Lieberman in Love* in 1995. Other names that have appeared in short films in the past few years are Wentworth Miller, Josie Moran, Sandra Oh, Amy Adams, Eric Stoltz, Karen Black, Sarah Chalke, Michael York, Tippi Hedren, Gordon Clapp, Jim Belushi, Oliver Hudson, James Denton, and many others. None of these films, according to the filmmakers, were made for financial rewards. But they were rewarding creatively and gave the celebrities a chance to try something different.

More than one person has emailed Business Strategies saying that they had an investor with $500,000 to make a short film. Why would you want to do that? These days, with digital movies and the new equipment available, chances are you can make a full-length feature for the same amount of money. In that case, show that you can tell a story and make a feature. If not, make one or several short films for a lot less money.

Raise Money for a Feature

Making a short film that is essentially a promo for that $3-million feature is another useful purpose. The tendency often is to try to tell the entire story of the film, but instead, you want to give the potential investors a short glimpse of what the feature film is about. A short scene will do well, even a partial scene. If the film is intense, include something very dramatic. If the film is a comedy, a short guffaw will do. You don't want to spend a lot of money. For one thing, you don't want the investor to think that you will be wasting his money. For another, you don't want to waste your own.

When making a short for this purpose, keep in mind that the film is essentially a piece of hype, similar to a colorful brochure or a storyboard, meant to entice the investor. The movie has the plus of showing some of the director's skill as well.

Filmmaking Experience

Making a short is the cheapest way to get the experience of going through the filmmaking process. It is better to make mistakes on a $10,000 short than on a $1-million feature. What filmmakers often don't realize is that the steps involved in making a five-minute short are the same that they will be using for the rest of their filmmaking lives. Many inexperienced people leave out important elements in the beginning because they cut many corners, don't know what is essential, or just plain forget things in their first effort. The result is that they end up with a film that is not releasable or is missing needed rights that prevent it from ever being shown. One of our hardest tasks is to convince the filmmaker: Be smart and believe. Distributor T C Rice says,

> Shorts are essentially for the development of filmmakers; it is how they learn their craft. This is the whole process of learning by trial and error. No matter how many film courses anyone takes, they are no substitute for hands-on experience. Shorts are the training ground for the feature film-makers of tomorrow.

Make Money

Making money is another story. Most filmmakers don't start out to make a short film to sell. It never crosses their minds. Until now there have been few good reasons to think about it. The philosophy of the indie filmmaker was "just do it"—just get something made. Well, that was in the good old days, the 1990s. Now there's potential for short films beyond making a calling card or getting experience. If you want to get some of your money back and sell or license your film in commercial markets, be aware of guild rules, distributors' requirements, music, and property rights. As more buyers eagerly anticipate short films, the differences between the short form and long form are the variety of markets and the eventual amount of money the filmmaker is likely to make.

SOURCES OF FINANCING

Probably the question most frequently asked both of us is, "Where do I find the money?" Usually money for short films comes from two places: (1) family and friends and (2) grants. Until more revenue sources open up, the money has to come from people who want to see your film made for either personal or business reasons and who don't expect a return on their investment. Until now, there has been no return to promise them. As we will see, this situation may be changing. At the moment, however, money invested in a short film should be considered a donation.

Family and Friends

If you want to raise money from a private investor, that person is usually a friend or member of your family. The only reason for someone to give you money for a short is to see their name on a screen, or because they love you. At the moment, it is unlikely that investors will make all their money back, much less a profit.

Grants

Getting a grant for a short film is not that different from getting one for a feature documentary. The big difference is that there are fewer foundations and companies that are likely to be interested in shorts. Each grant has to be applied for with an understanding of what the granting body requires. The process can be very complicated. To write a successful grant application, you'll need to understand the granting philosophy of the donor organization and its budget.

One client, for example, applied for $30,000. Since the foundation he applied to had a $10,000 cap, the application was rejected. It would seem rational that they might award part of the budget; however, this foundation didn't work that way. Because they only would fund one project a year, it was all or nothing.

Another short film client submitted this story:

> *The biggest mistake I ever made in regard to trying to get a grant was in submitting what I thought at the time to be a flawless application and essay. Later I learned from the foundation's director that my mistake was not submitting any personal information about myself. I had, in effect, turned in a very professional, comprehensive, and worthy application but forgot that the people reviewing it wouldn't know anything about who I was as a person. Therefore, they felt no emotional connection to me whatsoever. My advice is to be as forthright and transparent as possible so that the people reading your application will want to give you what you're asking for. In the case of grants, they need to not only like and admire your work but like and admire you.*

The grant market is so different from the commercial market that the filmmaker has to do extensive research on every organization to which she wants to apply. The Internet and the library have much reference material. In addition, when you approach a group, ask as many questions as you can.

MARKETS

The market for short films has been very limited. While there are new markets opening up in theaters, television, cable, and DVD, they are not yet mature. Nor do we know to what size they will grow. Still, the filmmaker needs to understand how all the markets work in order to decide how to proceed. Carol Crowe of Apollo Cinema says,

> *The short film market continues to evolve. Apollo Cinema has quadrupled the number of cities where it tours the Oscar Shorts showcase theatrically in the U.S., which is a 300% increase over what we did just two years ago. Our sales to airlines and new media outlets also continue to grow. There are only four companies in the United States that distribute short films and each year we each continue to build and expand our businesses. We are all hopeful that the shorts will be more part of the mainstream and not on the outer edges of the art house arena.*

It takes a long time to sell short films, because there are not large companies, such as studios, taking them for worldwide distribution. Every sale is a one-on-one negotiation that has to be customized individually for the buyer. It is not unrealistic to have a film that will appeal to a majority of the world markets. Nevertheless, it takes as much work as, if not more than, selling a feature film.

Festivals

Film festivals are a good way to get your film seen by a large number of people. There are several reasons to enter: to have your film seen by potential buyers, create a name for yourself with feature film companies and investors, and make your film eligible for the Academy Awards. Distributors; theatrical, television, and cable buyers; critics; and other festival directors attend the major festivals and are always looking for interesting films and the talent who makes them. As with features, the major competitive festivals give the filmmaker more chance for exposure. The competition for all these festivals is still growing at a high rate despite other outlets. At the 2009 Sundance Film Festival, for example, there were 5,632 short film entries for 96 spots. The Tribeca Film Festival received 2,643 entries for 46 slots. However, being in any festival, whether competitive or not, may bring notice for your film.

Worldwide

The markets for shorts are expanding at a more rapid pace than they have in the past 50 years. Bronwyn Kidd, Director of Flickerfest Short Film Bureau (Australia), says,

> *Short film is the truly independent storytelling medium of our generation, devoid of studio interference and filmmaking by committee, it enables the individual to make some really unique insights into the moments, experiences and events that define our modern world. As interest in this independent art form continues to grow, so, too, will the markets for shorts throughout the world.*

Although there has always been a very small theatrical market worldwide for shorts, major theater chains in the United States are beginning to pay attention. At the moment, the United States has the only real theatrical market for shorts. Anything over six minutes generally gets knocked out of the theatrical ballpark, however. The broadcast markets want very short films also. Most buyers pay by the minute, so technically a company would have to pay more for half-hour films. Among cable casters, Starz plans to show shorts on all their channels, but the payment, if any, is not known. This is an example of a company realizing that there are new uses for the short film that people didn't see before. Other cable channels, such as Comcast and Time-Warner, also are gearing up to add shorts to their programming; of course, there is no information yet available on what types of deals they will offer. The filmmaker has to decide if the exposure (and possible loss of future sales) is worth it. For DVDs, the pay may not be by the minute, but it is a new market still finding its structure.

In Europe and the other international markets, currently there is no theatrical distribution for shorts. Even in countries where the government supports the making of short films, the exhibitors choose not to comply with rules to show the films. On the other hand, those countries have a more lucrative ancillary market for shorts than the United States. Jean Charles Mille, general manager of Premium Films in France (one of the top three short film companies in Europe), says,

> *Our main objective is to motivate TV stations to broadcast shorts, and our 140 international shorts from 17 countries are our best asset. The TV and the DVD rights are the sole important revenue for short film producers and the good news is that more and more European TV channels are interested in airing shorts not only as fillers but also in some special short programs—and they don't hesitate to broadcast them on prime time! We are confident in short films in Europe and hope that the digital broadcasting will increase the sales.*

Advertainments/Advertorials

Questions keep coming to us about short films as advertisements or "advertorials." There are two types going on at the moment. Most filmmakers are aware that BMW and a few other companies have commissioned filmmakers to do short films. These films, often referred to as "advertainment," are product promotions disguised as entertaining short films. At the moment, these shorts are commissioned by the company that makes the product. As a rule, these companies have been hiring well-known directors, such as Ang Lee and Guy Ritchie.

Another concept, "advertorials," comes from Regal CineMedia Corp. In October 2002, they announced an agreement with NBC followed by one with Turner in January 2003 to produce "entertainment snippets" to be part of Regal's 20-minute preshows in their theaters. It is still a small market.

No one has yet developed these into a profitable position in the industry. There are many companies still trying to figure it out. It is suspected that they will emerge in a much higher profile at some point down the road. And when that happens there will be opportunities for short filmmakers to work in this arena, developing short series or episodes that incorporate products in an entertaining way. And they won't be going to star directors for the content.

The Internet

The way the market works today, putting a short film on the Internet is a deal-breaker for any possibility of selling the film through other media. Distributors insist on having the Internet rights, because the buyers want them. It doesn't matter whether the buyers have any plans to use the Internet rights; they don't want anyone else to have them, and with good reason. If IFC or Sundance just paid money for a film, they don't want to see it pop up on the Internet.

The big channels are still going to want exclusives, because the Internet is worldwide. For example, IFC may buy the film for the United States but insist on a worldwide exclusive for the Internet rights. If the Internet could be split, then the cable channel would probably only want the U.S. rights. That territory is their only concern. Since the other channels don't pay as much, they either don't ask for the Internet to be included or, if they do, don't ask for an exclusive. Since the distributor doesn't know in advance what the deal will be, Internet rights have to be available.

Remember that the distributor can always negotiate. Continuing this example, if IFC has the rights for a short for distribution in the United States, including the Internet rights, and then a month later Canal Plus wants it for Canal Plus International, which covers a lot of Europe, it is likely that the sale can be done. Canal Plus will discount for the fact that those rights are currently held. If the distributor says that IFC has the rights for the world but has no plans to use them at the moment, the European company might ask how long the contract is. IFC is not going to relicense it, nor does the European company care. The goal of both companies is to keep the film off the Internet. Sometimes they even pay extra for that right. When the IFC contract runs out, it can be licensed to the European company.

Another example is when a distributor has a film for which an American company has nonexclusive rights. There is a buyer in Japan who wants exclusive Internet rights. It can be worked out with the Japanese company by offering them the exclusive for their country and an agreement that it will not relicense the short to any competitors in Japan who are going to subtitle it in Japanese. That is all they are really concerned about. They know that worldwide is worldwide; however, an American company is not going to subtitle the film in Japanese. If the distributor has nonexclusive deals like that, he can make that deal in every country, but each of these contracts has to be negotiated separately with each buyer.

Subscription broadband is an emerging market. It could become a valuable market, when there is some kind of convergence and Internet companies will pay for the privilege. Since most of the films that short film distributors see are "unsaleable" by their description, showcasing on the Internet is a way to go. If it is only a calling card and you have no intention of ever trying to make any money from the film, go ahead. All the Internet sites that feature short films need content, which works in the filmmaker's favor. Read all contracts carefully, however, all the way to the end. Before signing anything, take the contract to your attorney as you would with a feature film.

Ah, the Internet! The Web! This venue has been a bright light for the future that keeps going on and off, then on and off again. The light was getting brighter in the past few years when a lot of the major companies were developing exhibition plans for short films on the Internet—everyone from Sony, Apple, Google, and Yahoo to Viacom (MTV and Comedy Central). They were all trying to figure out how to use these great little entertainments, get them out to the public, and make money on them. Then along came the phenomenon, YouTube. Now everyone is looking at "shorts" of every kind—for free. Granted, most of the stuff on YouTube is not short films as we know them. But the success of this channel has challenged the traditional short form to come up with ways to attract an audience. The initial attempts have been advertiser-based business models that rely on sponsors for the content. That has not panned out yet. Currently there are a number of Web "channels" that will contract for short films. There is seldom any license fee paid upfront. Most of the deals outline various types of revenue sharing from download fees, subscription fees, or ad revenue. But there are little glimmers ahead and someone out there will figure out how to create a business model that will generate enough revenue from short film exhibition to warrant buying films from filmmakers. Some companies are beginning to explore the possibility of contracting with short filmmakers to create series for the Internet.

SHORT DOCUMENTARIES

As with feature-length films, fiction and documentary shorts require different handling. Not all festivals accept short documentaries. Cannes does not accept them in either the short film category or the Cínéfondation, which accepts short and medium-length films from schools. Sundance accepts short documentaries in its short film program, even though the Oscars separate narrative, animated, and documentary short subjects. Which festivals do accept documentary shorts and in what category needs to be checked individually.

Every day brings new opportunities. The cable universe is making more room for short documentaries, for example. The Canadian Documentary Channel buys shorts as well as features. Sundance has said that it is starting a documentary channel, but currently compromises by regularly programming a "Doc Day" on its main channel. In 2003, Japan established a new doc channel that accepts short films of 15 minutes and shorter. They license the films for two months, as opposed to most buyers, who want three years.

The success of recent high-profile feature documentaries has created renewed interest in short documentaries within the industry; however, the market for them has not flourished as was hoped. Nevertheless, several outlets are still working on finding the audience for them and getting them out there.

POTENTIAL REVENUE

If you are making a ten-minute film, the likely return is $5,000. Big Film Shorts uses the formula of $15 to $100 a minute, with a film selling to five different markets on average. Don't interpret this to mean the longer the film, the more money. Ten minutes and under is still the best. The longer a film, the less saleable it is, and the less likely the revenue formula is to be pertinent. As mentioned above, it takes a long time to sell short films, because every sale is one-on-one. But it is realistic to expect that, if you have a film that appeals to most of the world markets, you can make back $5,000; in some cases, you can even make more.

Short films usually show on Cinemax as fillers and interstitials after features. Meaning "in between," *interstitials* are usually 20 to 130 seconds long and were developed as a form of entertaining advertising for television. The term has evolved to mean anything that fits in the space that might otherwise be dead air. The same deal as fillers and interstitials can work with Showtime. Whatever price Showtime pays entitles the company to show your film on its other channels: MTV, Comedy Channel, and the Sundance Channel.

Quality of Product

With short films, as with a feature, how the movie needs to look depends on what you are going to do with it. For theatrical release, the product has to look crisp and clear whether it is on digital or 35mm. Distributors say that they often receive shorts that look grainy. But if you are going into the marketplace, it is still preferable to be on film and look like it is film, no matter what genre. In general, the buyers and the audience do demand the same production quality. The movie has to compete in every way with the other content in a given market. Content is paramount, if the film passes all the other criteria. A slick-looking film with no content, long or short, only seems to work if a Hollywood studio made it.

Unless a short film is going to have a theatrical life, there will be no need for a 35mm print. But all the other formats that will be delivered to the various worldwide markets will look better if they come from a 35mm or high-definition shoot.

Distributors say that most films don't sell because most films are not good. It's all about all the ingredients coming together and making magic. Quality is the end result. If it's saleable, it's watchable; if it's watchable, it's because good talent made it. That doesn't mean that the whole world will love it, but that there's an audience out there for it somewhere.

Documentaries can get away with digital and CGI (computer-generated imaging) animation of anything else created on computers. The audience doesn't demand the same quality as they do with fiction films. They want docs to look more like the creator meant them to look. With a narrative, however, the audience wants it to look like a clean print.

Unfortunately, markets vary. Big Film Shorts had films that were delivered to HBO Latin that were shot on high definition in 16:9 (the digital widescreen format) and transferred to 35mm for festivals. HBO Latin will not accept the 1.85:1 ratio that all the prints and tapes were made with, as they require 4 × 3 (television) format. On the other hand, major European broadcasters have been transmitting widescreen in Pal Plus (analog) and now in digital broadcasting. There isn't any reason it can't work both ways. There are several conversion systems available. It is important to be aware that different buyers have different requirements for delivery. Investigate your target market's specs before making your film. Generally, however, no matter what system you edit on, distributors in the short film business prefer films that have been shot on 35mm.

Even more important than the look is the sound. The reality of the marketplace is that the short has to compete with the highest end feature in terms of sound. Whether on a theater screen or on cable, the film is going to be paired with a feature. It has to fit in the same class of filmmaking as the feature. For example, Big Film Shorts had the experience of having a film that was monosound. Everyone in the theater had just heard the last booming trailer. This little short came on with monosound, and the audience started complaining, thinking that there was something wrong with the theater's sound system. The exhibitor stopped showing the short.

CONTRACTS

Owning Your Film

In order to "own" the copyright, the filmmaker must have releases (signed permission) or contracts for everything in the picture, just as he would have to have for a feature film. This list may include the following:

- *Actors and extras:* Any nonunion actor and even regular people like friends and relatives must sign a release giving you permission to use their likeness and voice in all possible exhibition venues. It is not necessary to get every person on a street or in a crowd to sign a release as long as the camera does not linger on them and is a doing a "drive-by."

- *Sound:* Music, effects. The use of music without permission is the single most abused element in short film production. The producer must get permission from the owners of both the publishing and the sync rights.
- *Locations:* Any private property, public property (usually via permits). You also need releases that give you permission to use someone's private property for filming their car, building, sign, pond, or woods. In other words, if it's not your property, it's theirs. In the case of public property, you need a permit from the local authorities (see your film commission). For drive-by shots, be careful not to "establish" a building, or even a FedEx van, or that 18-wheeler with the famous brand name logo on the side. If the camera lingers too long, it could be inferred that you are incorporating that object into your storyline. Legal complications show up when you least expect them!
- *Décor:* Anything and everything on the walls or furniture or exteriors of buildings can be protected by other people's copyrights: posters, paintings, book covers, or other identifiable props like Coke cans, Apple (or any) computers, etc. If you thought you were safe by shooting in your own apartment, hold on. Look around. An object may be in your house, but is it really yours? Louise has American Indian paintings on her wall. However, when a commercial was being filmed in her home, the paintings were removed. Why? Case law has established that a reproduction for sale could not be made of any of the paintings without the artists' permission. If one of the paintings was a permanent background in the shot, it could be construed that the painting was being used for a commercial purpose. Why tempt the litigation gods?
- *Clips:* Stock, excerpts from other works. The producer must get releases for everything seen or heard in the movie. Borrowing a nice scene from your videotape collection is not allowed. What do you do? Spend all your time getting signatures? It is better to be safe than sorry. In *Clearance & Copyright*, Michael Donaldson says that it is always safest to clear. "Fair use" is mentioned in the copyright law;

however, "the law doesn't give a list of uses that are always and under all circumstances permitted under the doctrine of fair use."

Deliverables

Any distributor of short films will require roughly the same delivery of materials (at your expense) as a feature film distributor. These items may include the following:

- One DIGIBETA or BETASP (stereo) videotape master of the picture in the NTSC format (also in PAL format if requested)
- Anywhere from two to five NTSC DVD copies
- Postproduction dialogue list
- Music cue sheet
- Copyright registration for the film and other chain-of-title and insurance information
- Key artwork
- Stills (usually color) in JPEG format
- Release print(s) in available format if requested for theatrical rental(s)
- Current list of festivals and awards
- An authorization to the laboratories and suppliers of, respectively, preprint materials and foreign tracks and accessories to accept orders for materials to permit distributor to service agreements
- Copies of all paperwork giving permission and release for use of actors or statements regarding Screen Actors Guild (SAG) agreement, writers, music, trademarks, and logos; clips or excerpts from other copyrighted material; and locations

Guilds

The SAG offers a variety of contracts that allow a filmmaker to "employ" professional, card-carrying union actors. There are contracts that allow only screening at festivals. Sound good? What if someone comes along and wants to sell the film to television or show it to a paying audience? You must renegotiate the contract with SAG and the actors. New since the previous edition is a Short Film

Agreement, which has replaced the Experimental Film Agreement. It covers productions with a maximum running time of 30 minutes and maximum budget of $50,000. Compensation is deferred unless the project exceeds the budget limitation or has exhibition beyond parameters set in the agreement. These limitations are that the film is *mainly intended for nonpaying environment, such as film festivals, director's reels, visual resumes, and similar venues, that allows the film-maker to display his work and talents. However, if your primary intention is immediate theatrical distribution and/or sale of your project, you are not eligible to use the SAG Student Film Agreement or Short Film Agreement.*

Past experience shows that you cannot convert a short film for revenue-producing markets without each actor's permission. This puts the actor in a bargaining position in terms of money and other demands. In addition, according to the experience of short film producers, SAG does not allow the filmmaker to prenegotiate a "what if" scenario with the actors. From the Guild's point of view, it is protecting the actor from being taken advantage of, because he was willing to be in your ten-minute film. On the other hand, the actors can demand more money than the film will ever make. This happened to one of our filmmakers under the experimental contract. Not expecting the short film to be distributed, he paid his actors because "it was the right thing to do." When the opportunity for distribution arose, he had to get the actors' permission and pay them a second time. Of course, one of the actors then held out for a big payday.

If you have any thoughts of going to a festival, market, or finding distribution in any other way, it is best to go with the low-budget or, perhaps, modified-budget contract. Before deciding, check the current contract information on SAG's indie site (*www .sagindie.com*), find the location of the nearest office, and meet with a representative to discuss all the possible scenarios for your film. There is also a handy "Film Contracts Digest" that SAG can send you. Consider the optimum possibilities for the film and ask the representative what the next step will be, and the next, and the next, etc. Do not assume, as many feature filmmakers do, that SAG won't know. They are very good at knowing if anyone owes money to their members.

The Directors' Guild of America (DGA) also has an experimental contract. It is applicable if the purpose of the film is to provide a DGA member with experience or to serve as a "resume piece," and if the film is equal to or less than 30 minutes in length, is not for commercial release in any medium (this includes the Internet or any other commercial source that may come along), and has a budget less than or equal to $50,000. The film may be entered in festivals and submitted for award consideration to the Academy of Motion Picture Arts and Sciences (Oscars) and/or the Academy of Television Arts and Sciences Awards (Emmys). As with other Guild contracts, the DGA's are constantly updated. Check the DGA's web site and speak with your nearest representative. If you have any thought of commercial uses for the film, it may be best to follow their low-budget contract.

THE FUTURE

Worldwide markets at least doubled from 1996 to 2006. Considering the commercial opportunity at the time, we thought that the markets would double again in the next two years, but they haven't. Undoubtedly, the buyers who were coming on board did not promote other companies to copy them. We still hope to see the market return. When people see that there is money to be made with short films, they will find new ways to create more demand.

Big Film Shorts, while exploring the opportunity for more theatrical screening of short films in the United States, recently made agreements for the viewing of shorts via video-on-demand (VOD). This market has just begun to open and promises to be a profitable opportunity for filmmakers. On different systems—such as Rogers Cable, Cox, Time-Warner, and Comcast—they are using different system labels, but it is all VOD. There are two kinds of VOD: pay-per-view and free-for-view. In the future, the goal is to get sponsors for the free-for-view showings. Although some of the cable systems have technical problems with VOD, the problems are currently being worked out. Because of high-definition broadcasting, the cable companies have more limited space and have been forced to restructure their programming.

Specialty channels may or may not be in existence when you are reading this page. For example, Here! TV and Logo (MTV) are buyers of gay-themed films. Nano (a division of Big Film Shorts) has a VOD channel with cable and satellite agreements for distribution. For these deals, Big Film Shorts shares in the ad revenue. Canal Plus in France has a separate division that buys short films to sell specifically to countries on the continent of Africa. This type of proliferation is important, because the fee a buyer like Canal Plus pays is based on the number of territories they buy for.

China is another expanding market. At this time, the country is due to join two international intellectual properties treaties as part of its World Trade Organization requirements. Analysts forecast major growth in China's digital sections with these agreements in place and the proliferation of new technology.

The burgeoning market of mobile/cellular is in its infancy at this time. Despite CinemaNow and Movielink offering download-to-own movies, studies show that current consumer tastes still lean toward shorter-form video. How this will work out for the filmmaker in terms of remuneration remains to be determined. During the 2006 Sundance Festival, speakers representing both cellular and content providers acknowledged that there was not necessarily crossover from one to the other. For example, one distributor can try to put your film on any screen. However, your cellular provider may use only its own content. Whether or not they have a contract with Google or any other content provider depends on each individual company. Costs could vary widely, again depending on each carrier and the content provider. Nevertheless, one subject on which they all agreed is that this form of download is perfect for short content and perhaps documentaries but not fiction features. Remember that these business models are in constant flux.

From our perspective, the future for shorts is bright. Since everything is still evolving, we can't give the short film market a dollar value. However, as companies see others making money from short films from various outlets, we believe that they will rush to jump on the bandwagon.

New uses for shorts are evolving every day. The number of buyers is increasing, as are the audiences to whom the films are available. As people become used to seeing short films, it is hoped there will be a larger market for DVD collections, Xbox, and other new media.

Index